FIELD HOCKEY

Steps to Success

Elizabeth Anders

with

Sue Myers

Old Dominion University

Human Kinetics

Library of Congress Cataloging-in-Publication Data

Anders, Elizabeth, 1951-
    Field hockey / Elizabeth Anders with Sue Myers.
        p.   cm. -- (Steps to success)
    ISBN 0-88011-673-0
    1. Field hockey.   I. Myers, Sue.   II. Title.   III. Series: Steps
to success activity series.
    GV1017.H7A573   1998
    796.355--dc21   98-27574
                                                          CIP

ISBN-10: 0-88011-673-0
ISBN-13: 978-0-88011-673-2

Developmental Editor: C.E. Petit, JD
Assistant Editors: Cassandra Mitchell, Jennifer Miller, and Sandra Merz Bott
Copyeditor: Allan Gooch
Proofreader: Debra Aglaia
Graphic Designer: Keith Blomberg
Graphic Artist: Francine Hamerski
Cover Designer: Jack Davis
Photographer (cover): Tom Roberts
Illustrators: Paul To, line drawings, and Joe Bellis, Mac art
Printer: Versa Press

Printed in the United States of America   10 9

Human Kinetics
Web site: www.HumanKinetics.com

United States: Human Kinetics, P.O. Box 5076, Champaign, IL 61825-5076
800-747-4457
e-mail: humank@hkusa.com

Canada: Human Kinetics, 475 Devonshire Road Unit 100, Windsor, ON N8Y 2L5
800-465-7301 (in Canada only)
e-mail: orders@hkcanada.com

Europe: Human Kinetics, 107 Bradford Road, Stanningley, Leeds LS28 6AT, United Kingdom
+44 (0) 113 255 5665
e-mail: hk@hkeurope.com

Australia: Human Kinetics, 57A Price Avenue, Lower Mitcham, South Australia 5062
08 8372 0999
e-mail: liaw@hkaustralia.com

New Zealand: Human Kinetics, Division of Sports Distributors NZ Ltd., P.O. Box 300 226 Albany, North Shore City, Auckland
0064 9 448 1207
e-mail: info@humankinetics.co.nz

CONTENTS

PREFACE

Field hockey is an extraordinary team game played by a large number of men and women and boys and girls in more than 80 countries. Whether you are a novice or experienced field hockey player, you will appreciate the game more as your performance improves. This book provides you with a progressive step-by-step plan for developing field hockey skills and game tactics.

To realize the superior fun and enjoyment of playing field hockey, a player should learn and practice the four field hockey components of techniques, tactics, fitness, and motivation. Because field hockey balances all essential physical skills found in a cross section of sports, a field hockey player will encounter numerous mental and emotional challenges in addition to the physical demands. Although physical size is unrelated to success in field hockey, the successful player does need quick and skilled execution of fundamental techniques fueled by intelligence and physical prowess that includes proper body balance, muscular strength, aerobic endurance, flexibility, exceptional hand-eye coordination, and ballistic movement. It is common for the international player who plays on a swift artificial surface to run 2 1/2 to 5 miles during a 70-minute match while encountering individual and team problem-solving situations of coordinated technical skills.

My ideas grew not only from my experiences as a player and coach but also from a constant study of publications on coaching and playing all sports and of leadership information from numerous professions. In addition, I derived a valuable contribution to my teaching ideas from discussing sport and game views with countless players, coaches, and leaders. I also gained a great deal from reading as much as possible on the psychology and development of young people and the various learning and teaching processes that benefit you the player.

I developed the Attack Roles and Defense Roles after much consideration of the need for a system or method of field hockey play in which players could communicate tactical understanding while having a reason to select and execute the proper skills. My goal was to develop a model plan that could simplify the teaching scheme of field hockey to the player and ultimately produce more fun because of the model's clarity in understanding. I organized my teaching model around the individual responsibilities for team play and the emphasis on communicating the organization of these responsibilities. This simple method allows all levels of players and teachers to comprehend and apply technical play, tactical play, physical preparedness, and the psychological aspects that drive the performance. I have attempted to gather a field hockey vocabulary by combining my language with the language used by generations of field hockey players. I am certain the list is incomplete because, as I have discovered, it is an ongoing and challenging process to uncover ways to express what you perceive and then give it meaning.

Very special thanks to Susan Myers, who has provided valuable insight and assisted me in doing this book, and to Dr. Mel Williams, a fellow faculty member and author, for his initial encouragement. Thanks also to Gwen Alexander, Val Cloud, Andi Hoffman, and Vonnie Gros for your contributions to education and to Marge Watson for always being there for me. To Mike Berticelli, a physical educator and outstanding collegiate soccer coach (now at Notre Dame), thanks for spending the many hours with me talking tactics and sport. Libby Williams, my high school coach, and Eleanor Snell, my college coach who has left this world a better place, both hold cherished places in my heart; for these are the people responsible for instilling in me the motivation to play field hockey and to make a difference through the development of a strong team spirit that included consideration for others. And to my parents whom I have given my Olympic medal, I love you.

Elizabeth R. Anders

THE STEPS TO SUCCESS STAIRCASE

Get ready to climb a staircase—one that will lead you to become an accomplished field hockey player. You cannot leap to the top; you get there by climbing one step at a time. Each of the 10 steps you will take is an easy transition from the one before. The first few steps of the staircase provide a solid foundation of basic skills and concepts. As you progress further, you will learn how to pass, receive, control, and dribble the ball, how to shoot, and how to play individual offense and defense based on your attack or defense role at the moment. As you near the top of the staircase, you will become more confident in your ability to play as a team member, both offensively and defensively, and you will learn to communicate effectively with your teammates.

Familiarize yourself with this section as well as "Field Hockey: A Game for Everyone" for an orientation and for help in understanding how to set up your practice sessions around the steps. Follow the same sequence each step (chapter) of the way.

1. Read the explanations of what is covered in the step, why the step is important, and how to execute or perform the step's focus, which may be on basic skills, concepts, or tactics or be a combination of the three.

2. Follow the numbered illustrations showing exactly how to position your body to execute each basic skill successfully. There are three general parts to each skill: preparation (getting into a starting position), execution (performing the skill that is the focus of the step), and follow-through (reaching a finish position or following through to starting position).

3. Look over the common errors that may occur and the recommendations for how to correct them.

4. The drills help you improve your skills through repetition and purposeful practice. Read the directions and the Success Goal for each drill. Practice accordingly and record your scores. Compare your score with the Success Goal for the drill. You need to meet the Success Goal of each drill before moving on to practice the next one because the drills are arranged in an easy-to-difficult progression. This sequence is designed specifically to help you achieve continual success.

5. As soon as you can reach all the Success Goals for one step, you are ready for a qualified observer—such as your teacher, coach, or trained partner—to evaluate your basic skill technique against the Keys to Success Check. This is a qualitative or subjective evaluation of your basic technique or form because using correct form can enhance your performance.

6. Repeat these procedures for each of the 10 Steps to Success. Then rate yourself according to the directions in the "Rating Your Total Progress" section.

Good luck on your step-by-step journey to developing your field hockey skills, building confidence, experiencing success, and having fun!

FIELD HOCKEY: A GAME FOR EVERYONE

Historians have found indications that some structure of the game of field hockey was played by ancient Egyptians, Persians, and Greeks thousands of years before the first Olympic Games in 776 B.C. Later, the Romans influenced the upbringing of the sport during their political and social dominance of present-day Europe. Connections to field hockey include the German game of Kolbe; the Dutch game of Het Kolven, which is an ascendant of ice hockey; and the French game of Hocquet, which many historians believe contributed the name "hockey" to the lexicon of sport. Other historians have connected hockey to the Irish game of hurling, the oldest "organized" game to use a stick and ball. Along with hurling, the Scottish game of shinty and the Welsh game of bandy all used sticks similar in size and shape with limited rules, which led to dangerous and rough games The first Hockey Association was formed in 1875, with governing rules established 11 years later. When members of the Hockey Association established these rules, the door opened for hockey expansion. International field hockey contests were played by men as early as 1895.

Field hockey in the United States is played mostly by girls and women, perhaps because of the game's introduction in 1901 by an English woman, Constance Applebee. Applebee came from England to study at Harvard Summer School. From Harvard, she went to Vassar and then started field hockey at Wellesley, Smith, Radcliffe, Mount Holyoke, and Bryn Mawr Colleges. In 1920, a U.S. women's team traveled to Great Britain to compete internationally for the first time. In 1922, the game had grown so popular with women that the United States Field Hockey Association (USFHA) was founded in Philadelphia. In 1930, the Field Hockey Association of America was formed as the governing body for men. Although men's field hockey in the United States takes a backseat to the women's game in total participants and overall opportunity in the scholastic and collegiate scene, participation by both genders has significantly grown from the influences of foreign players and teachers who have traveled to the United States and helped to sponsor community programs and camps for youth and adults. Numerous amateur leagues and tournaments have become available in many areas of the United States. The Field Hockey Association of America merged with the USFHA in the early 1990s.

Today field hockey has men's and women's Junior (under 21 years of age) World events, club championships, indoor hockey championships, European championships, Asian Games, Pan-American Games, African Games, Champion's Trophies, an Inter-Continental Cup tournament for qualification in the prestigious World Cup, and the pre-Olympic Qualifier tournament for the Olympic Games. Nearly 200,000 girls/boys and women/men have played or currently participate in field hockey in the United States, while millions more participate in nearly 90 countries.

Playing the Game

Field hockey is a swift and skill-based game that gives enjoyment to players of any age level. The game can be modified to satisfy local conditions or different age groups, but throughout this book, the conventional game of outdoor field hockey is described unless stated otherwise.

The aim of hockey is to move the hockey ball up the field and hit or push the ball into the opposing goal cage by using only hockey sticks. Players may hit the ball using only the flat side and edge of the hockey stick, and only the goalkeepers are permitted to use their hands or feet to control or move the hockey ball while protecting their team's goal within the shooting circle, an area with a 16-yard maximum depth from the goalposts. A regulation game has two 35-minute playing periods, and each goal scored counts as one point when the ball has been propelled completely into the goal cage. At halftime intermission, teams change ends of the field. In some tournament events, if the score is a draw after regulation, the teams play two 15-minute overtime periods.

Each team includes a goalkeeper and 10 field players. Every player except the goalkeeper must be proficient at both attacking and defending. Players can move anywhere on the field, whereas each has exact responsibilities within the team's selective system of play.

A coin toss with the team captains and umpires decides which team receives ball possession and field direction to start the game. The winner of the coin toss has the right to choose which field end her team will attack in the first half of play or the right to start the game with ball possession. The game starts with a pass in any direction from the center of the field. The pass that starts the game may not be raised off the ground, and the opposing team must be at least five yards from the ball. Both teams must be positioned on their own half of the field until the ball is in play. Once the game begins, play is continuous, with the clock stopped only after a score, a penalty stroke, or at the umpires' discretion, such as with injury. Play is restarted after a goal by a pass off at the center of the field by the team that had just been scored against.

Learning Field Hockey

A simple way to organize your learning of field hockey is to use a common language to improve the communication of "team" offense and "team" defense. The reference to *Attack Roles* and *Defense Roles* will help field hockey players and coaches on all levels improve and simplify the communication of hockey knowledge in their game development. Through the understanding and execution of role responsibilities, hockey techniques and tactics are communicated and applied to develop a group of individuals who think and play together. For players to make good decisions, they must be exposed to information in order to base or justify their eventual choices. They must know what, why, when, and where to apply a game technique. This knowledge will lead to a better understanding of how to execute skill and, thus, demonstrate quality performance.

The way to learn field hockey is through taking on responsibilities, or **roles**. The giving of "role" assignments to hockey players according to who is in possession of the ball and where the ball is located on the field allows the player to receive more pertinent information in a given situation. The concept of role assignments is centered on (1) the ball and (2) the space on the field. Attack play is the creation of space and the use of space by attack players with and without the ball. Hockey defense is the organization of players to block space and control space.

Learning field hockey techniques and tactics through player roles (responsibilities) will enhance teaching for the coach and reinforce improved performances by players because better decision-making skills are being practiced. Good decisions lead to a higher quality of skill performance, which is always fun!

The Role Players and Their Game Positions

Players participate in three roles both when their teams possess the ball (attack) and when they are without the ball (defense). Each of the three Attack and Defense Roles has player responsibilities. When these responsibilities are understood and exercised, all players on the field, regardless of game position, have to be good at both attacking and defending. It is important to note that field hockey players have possession of the ball only three to five minutes and will be without the ball 65 to 67 minutes. The key to a steady flow of passing options is the intelligent movement of players who are not in possession of the ball. Players must meet the responsibilities of the Attack Roles and Defense Roles and be able to move smoothly and effectively into any given role.

Attack Roles: When a team has a sense of positional play, hockey is a passing game. The Attack Roles are based on team attack in which the ball must move from player to player. It takes two players to complete a pass and at least three players to provide continuity. Attack Role 1 (AR1) is the leader who has a passing role. This is the player who has the ball, and it is her responsibility to pass the ball to achieve penetration, secure an advantage, or merely to maintain ball possession. If the pass is not immediately available, AR1 uses the dribble to achieve a new position to pass. Attack Role 2 (AR2) is the helper who supports his leader in possession of the ball. AR2 moves in a near position to be available for a direct pass from AR1. Attack Role 3 (AR3) is the assistant helper who provides support for AR2 far from the ball. AR3 moves to create space for teammates.

Defense Roles: Team Defense Roles require field hockey players to organize and control and block space together to take the ball away from the opponent. Defense Role 1 (DR1) is the player closest to the ball who has the responsibility to stop forward penetration of the ballcarrier. DR1 is the leader on defense. Defense Role 2 (DR2) is the player who helps DR1 by controlling and closing off the nearest space to the ball. By marking to intercept passes to the nearest opponent, DR2 prepares to help DR1 stop the ballcarrier. Defense Role 3 (DR3) is the assistant helper on defense and is farthest from the ball. DR3's responsibility is to establish a help position for DR2 to provide balance and cover of the penetrating space and the opponent in this space.

Game Positions

When field hockey players learn to retreat to defend and advance to attack, they are ready for game positions discussed in Step 10—"Team Play: Organizing Attack and Defense." Game positions define the overlapping and constant interchanging of the roles of attack and defense. Regardless of the game position, all players take on their Attack Roles when their team is in possession of the ball, and all players perform their Defense Roles when the opponent has the ball.

Rules of the Game

The 15 principal rules for field hockey have been established by the Federation of International Hockey (FIH), the international governing body (see appendix). The rules cover all perspectives, from the organization and conduct of the game through the game procedures. The FIH rules are standard throughout the world and pertain to all competition. Variances in some rules may occur in youth and school organizations and, in the United States, in college-sponsored programs.

Field of Play: Dimensions and Markings

Before each game, it is the umpire's duty to check for proper field lines and markings (see illustration 1). The field of play is rectangular—100 yards long and 60 yards wide. All lines and shooting circles on the field are 3 inches wide. Players are not permitted to add marks or lines to the field of play. The back line, the goal line (part of the back line between the goalposts), and the sidelines are part of the field of play. This means that the ball must travel wholly over the line(s) to be considered out of play. The centerline is 50 yards from the back lines, and two 25-yard lines are marked across the field. At each of the four corners of the field, a 4- to 5-foot flag post is placed off the field or near the outer edge of the field corners. Also, one flag post is placed at each 25-yard line, 1 yard outside the sidelines. This post serves as a marker to assist the umpire in awarding a penalty corner when the defensive team commits an intentional foul within their 25-yard area.

A line 2 yards long is marked across the centerline and the 25-yard lines to assist in the control of the sideline hit from a ball that travels out of play. These six short lines are marked 5 yards parallel and away from the outer edge of the sidelines.

A "16-yard mark" is placed inside the field of play on each sideline, parallel to the back line and 16 yards from the back line's inside border. The 16-yard mark must be 12 inches in length. Other 12-inch lines include the penalty-corner hit marks. These marks are lined inside the field of play on the back lines at 5-yard and 10-yard intervals that are measured from the outer edge of both sides of the goalposts. Also on the back line and sideline are long-corner hit marks that

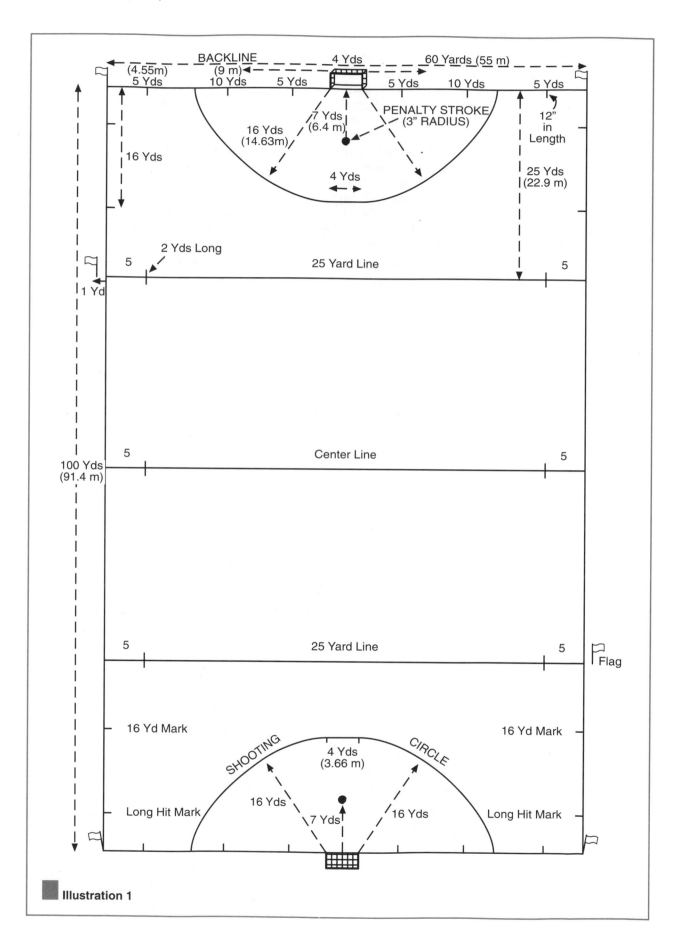

BACKLINE 4 Yds 60 Yards (55 m)
(4.55m) (9 m)
5 Yds 10 Yds 5 Yds 5 Yds 10 Yds 5 Yds

7 Yds
(6.4 m)

PENALTY STROKE
(3" RADIUS)

16 Yds
(14.63m)

16 Yds

4 Yds

12"
in
Length

25 Yds
(22.9 m)

5 2 Yds Long 25 Yard Line 5

1 Yd

100 Yds
(91.4 m)

5 Center Line 5

5 25 Yard Line 5 Flag

16 Yd Mark 16 Yd Mark

SHOOTING 4 Yds CIRCLE
(3.66 m)

16 Yds

Long Hit Mark 7 Yds 16 Yds Long Hit Mark

Illustration 1

are marked inside the field of play 5 yards from the corner of the field where the back line and sideline meet.

The penalty spot is a 6-inch diameter spot placed 7 yards in from the center of the inner edge of the goal line. This spot marks the area where the ball is placed to take a penalty stroke.

Shooting Circle

The shooting circle is a semicircle (see illustration 2) drawn from the back lines 16 yards from each outer edge of the goalposts. The shooting circle extends 16 yards onto the field of play and includes a 4-yard straight line that runs parallel to the goal line. The line that marks the shooting circle is 3 inches wide and is part of the space enclosed by the semicircle. A ball that is wholly on the shooting circle or partly on the inside of the circle is considered a ball that is inside the circle.

Goals: Posts, Crossbar, Net, Backboard, Sideboards

A field hockey goal is rectangular, consisting of two goalposts, a horizontal crossbar, a net to cover the sides, back, and top of the goal cage, a backboard, and two sideboards. The goalposts are positioned perpendicular to the ground 4 yards apart and are connected by a horizontal crossbar 7 feet from the ground. The goalposts may not extend beyond the crossbar nor may the crossbar extend beyond the goalposts. The 2-inch-wide posts and crossbar are painted white and consist of a depth of not more than 3 inches. The 1 1/2-inch diameter mesh net is attached to the back of the posts and crossbar at 6-inch notches and secured solidly behind the goal and on the outside of the backboard and sideboards. All goals have a dark-painted backboard on the inside consisting of a height of 18 inches from the ground and a length of 4 yards. The two sideboards are also 18 inches in height but not less than 4 feet in length and are also painted a dark color on the inside. During a penalty corner, a direct shot that uses a backswing must hit the backboard or sideboard to count as a score. The goal cage is positioned at each end of the field on the center of the goal line so that the front base of each goalpost touches the back outer edge of the goal line or back line with the center of the goal 30 yards from the sideline.

The Ball

The hockey ball is similar in size to an American baseball, with a circumference from 8 13/16 inches to 9 1/4 inches. The spherical ball is made of hard natural or artificial materials with a hollow or solid interior. The weight may be between 5 1/2 ounces and 5 3/4 ounces. Younger players are permitted to use a lighter ball weighing 4 ounces. The outer hard surface of the ball can

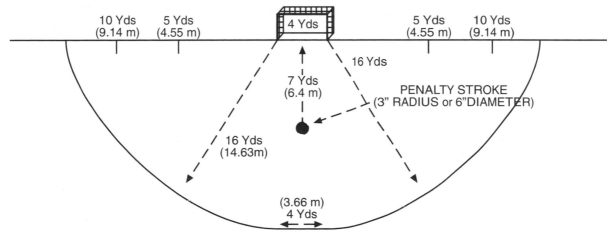

All lines are 3 inches wide. All short line marks must be inside the field and are 12 inches in length. The penalty stroke spot is marked 7 yards in front of the center of each goal.

Illustration 2

be smooth, be made of plastic or leather, have seams or be seamless, or be dimpled as a golf ball. The seamless ball is preferred for the artificial playing surface. For international games where the artificial surfaces are watered before the start of the match and at halftime intermission, the type of ball that performs best has a plastic cover that does not absorb moisture and is well balanced to withstand friction and bounce. The ball color is white for international games, but the captains in other games may agree on any color hockey ball as long as it contrasts with the field color.

The Stick

Most adult hockey players use 36- to 38-inch sticks that weigh 18 to 20 ounces. The maximum stick weight is 28 ounces and minimum stick weight is 12 ounces (see illustration 3). Selection of the proper stick length and weight will enhance development of correct skills. A common but unscientific method used to select the appropriate hockey stick length is to place the head of the stick on the ground alongside the leg. The top of the handle should reach the player's hip.

The curved head of the stick is made of wood void of sharp edges or metal fittings and cannot exceed 4 inches. The edges must be rounded. The stick shaft and handle may be made of wood or a combination of glues, fiberglass, rubber, plastics, and aluminum. The international stick certified by the FIH commonly consists of mulberry wood for the head and Tahiti and Manau cane in the handle areas. Sections of the stick are laminated with fiberglass, carbon fiber, Kevlar. For youth play, the entire stick, including the head, can be made of plastic or fiberglass materials. High school levels permit fiberglass, wood, and aluminum (handle only) sticks.

All field hockey sticks must pass through a 2-inch ring from the head of the stick to the top of the handle. The playing surface of the stick is the flat side, sometimes referred to as the *left face* of the stick. It is permissible to use the edge of the stick to strike the ball, but players are not permitted to use the *right face*, or the rounded side, of the stick. All players, whether left-handed or right-handed, must always use the flat side of the stick and edges to play the ball. A recently developed goalkeeper stick provides a "S"-shaped shaft to increase the stopping surface area.

Player Attire and Equipment

Players on the same team must wear similar uniforms, including socks of color and style that are approved by the local hockey organization. Adult men wear shorts and numbered shirts. Female players wear short tennis skirts or kilts with numbered shirts. Boys' and girls' youth teams wear shorts with some girls' teams starting in skirts. No matter what age level, players may not wear anything that could injure other players.

Protective gear for the lower legs include shin and ankle guards. Special hockey shin guards are made from lightweight plastic or foam and help reduce injury from the ball or from other players' sticks. Soccer shin guards are sometimes used by beginning players. Although hockey is a safe sport, it is strongly recommended that players wear mouth guards to protect the teeth and mouth. Mouth guards can be made by a dentist so that comfort and clear verbal communication are possible.

Depending on the playing surface, footwear varies but is very similar to what a soccer player will choose on similar playing surfaces. For grass fields, players wear leather or nylon shoes that have rubber or molded cleats on the sole. For the wet synthetic or artificial turf field, players wear a shoe that has smaller multistuds on the sole. If playing indoors or on a dry artificial surface, a flat-soled tennis shoe or cross-trainer shoe is recommended. Players should choose shoes wisely. Field hockey is an aggressive game of stops, starts, pivots, changes of direction, and hard sprinting. Feet need durable support and protection.

Goalkeeping Attire and Equipment

A goalkeeper is required to wear shorts and a differently colored shirt from that of her own team and that of the opponent. Goalkeeper is a specialized position needing special protective equipment providing mobility and armor to play the position confidently and safely. Goalkeepers should never take shortcuts with protective equipment because a hockey ball can be hit very hard at the goal. Today's field hockey game demands that the goalkeeper wear the following protection (see illustration 4): fully protective headgear such as an ice hockey-style goalkeeping helmet with a full

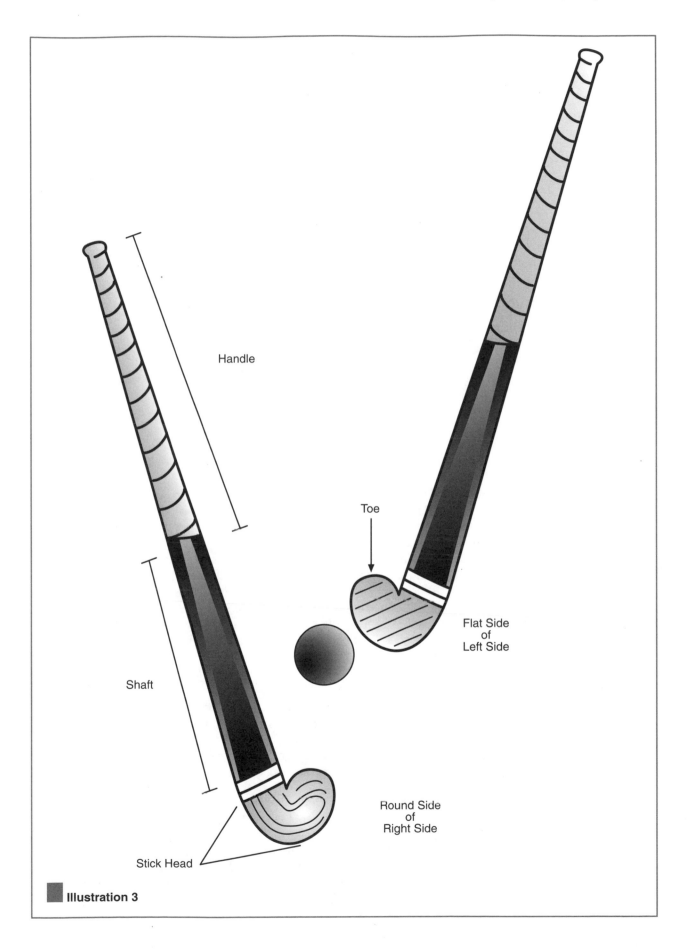

Handle

Toe

Flat Side
of
Left Side

Shaft

Round Side
of
Right Side

Stick Head

Illustration 3

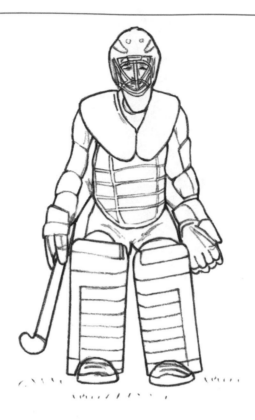

Illustration 4

face mask and cover for all the head including the back; a throat protector; upper body protectors such as a chest pad, shoulder pads, elbow pads, and abdominal protector; padded goalkeeping pants or overalls to include a pelvic protector; leg guards or pads having a width of no more than 12 inches void of rough edges or protrusions; kickers (boots) for the feet and ankles that are light and comfortable so that the ball can be cleared from inside the shooting circle by kicking it like a soccer ball; a lightweight field hockey stick; and gloves with well-padded knuckles or gauntlets that are a maximum of 8 inches in width and 13 inches in length when placed flat and faced upward. Goalkeeping gloves have maximum 6-inch-long fingers measured from their base, with the left glove being extra padded in the palm area for blocking shots. The right glove must be flexible enough to grip the stick at all times because throughout the game the stick is held in the right hand only.

The Teams

Field hockey is played between two teams of not more than 11 players from each team. Of these 11, one must be a goalkeeper. If the goalkeeper is suspended or incapacitated, she must be replaced immediately by another goalkeeper. If another goalkeeper is not available, the field player replacing the goalkeeper must wear protective headgear and a differently colored shirt from her teammates and opponents. When a goalkeeper is suspended, the team must have one fewer player on the field.

   Player substitution in field hockey is very similar to ice hockey. The player(s) being replaced have unlimited reentry, and the number of players being substituted is limited to two at a time. The player(s) being substituted must run completely off the side of the field near the centerline before the substitute may enter the field of play. The game clock continues during the "rolling" substitution procedure unless the umpire has suspended play because of injury or the issuing of a card reprimand. Suspended player(s) may not be permitted a substitute as their team must continue the game with fewer field players than their opponents.

Captains

Every team has a captain on the field who wears a differentiating armband. A team captain has four main responsibilities during the course of a game: (1) meet with the umpires to participate in the coin toss for the choice of ends or possession of the ball at the opening pass; (2) ensure proper execution of substitution and identify the goalkeepers or, if necessary, players who substitute for the goalkeepers; (3) in the event the captain is either replaced or suspended, ensure that another captain is designated instantly and that the new captain wears the captain's armband; and (4) ensure that team players show proper behavior.

Umpires and Timekeepers

A field hockey game is controlled by two umpires who administer the rules and ensure fast and fair play. Umpires position along the sidelines, venturing onto the field only when necessary. They maintain sole accountability for decisions on the ball that goes out of play for the full length of their nearer sideline (see illustration 5) and back line. Umpires' responsibilities include decisions on corners, penalty strokes, and goals in their own field half and free hits in their own circle. They also have the responsibility to make certain that the full time or agreed time is played, and they are responsible for keeping a written record of goals scored and warnings or suspensions issued. One or two timekeepers may be positioned at the score table to keep the game time.

Umpires blow a whistle to (1) start and end each half of the game; (2) signal fouls and enforce penalties or suspend the game for any other reason; (3) start and end a penalty stroke; (4) signal a goal and to restart after a goal is scored or after suspension of play; (5) sometimes indicate that the ball is entirely out-of-bounds when it is not obvious to the players; and (6) restart the game after an unsuccessful shot from a penalty stroke.

Advantage Rule

The advantage rule allows the game to flow even though a foul may have occurred. A good umpire applies the advantage rule often and wisely by anticipating what will happen in the next few

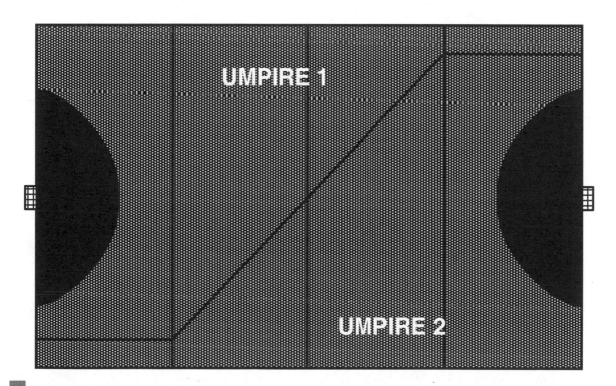

Illustration 5

seconds. When using the advantage rule, the umpires delay enforcing a penalty in situations in which an advantage would be given to the offending team.

Player Conduct Fouls

The major field hockey fouls include the following:

1. Play the ball with the rounded side of the stick.
2. Take part in or intrude in the game without their own sticks in their hands.
3. Play the ball above the shoulder with any part of the stick.
4. Lift sticks over the heads of players or raise sticks in a manner that is dangerous, intimidating, or restraining to other players.
5. Play the ball wildly in a way that is dangerous or is likely to lead to dangerous play.
6. Hit, charge or shove, kick, trip, hold, hook, strike at, or handle another player's stick or clothing.
7. Throw any object or piece of playing equipment onto the field, at the ball, at a player, or at an umpire.
8. Stop the ball with the hand or catch it; intentionally stop, kick, propel, pick up, throw, or carry the ball in any manner other than with their sticks.
9. Use the foot or leg to support the stick in a tackle.
10. Intentionally raise the ball from a free hit or at another player.
11. Intentionally raise the ball so that it lands directly in the shooting circle.
12. Approach within 5 yards of a player receiving a falling aerial ball before the ball is played to the ground.
13. Obstruct an opponent from playing the ball by interposing or shielding the body or stick between the ball and the opponent.
14. Delay the game by wasting time.

When the ball is inside the shooting circle, the goalkeeper has special privileges to safely use his stick, pads, or kickers to propel the ball. The ball may be stopped, but not propelled, using the goalkeeper's hands or body. The goalkeeper is not permitted to lie on the ball (obstruction foul). In addition, the goalie can stop or deflect the ball with the stick above her shoulder unless deemed dangerous by the umpire.

Penalties

Hockey players who break the rules are penalized with a free hit, a penalty corner, or a penalty stroke.

Free Hits

A free hit is awarded for a foul by an attacker and for an unintentional foul by the defensive players outside their circle. A free hit is taken from the area or close to the area where the foul occurred, except when a foul occurs by the attacker inside the 16-yard area to the back line. In this case, the free hit by the defending team may be taken on the spot of the foul or from a spot up to 16 yards from the back line exactly in line with the foul. A free hit is given for a foul by the defender occurring within 5 yards of the circle; all players of both teams must be at least 5 yards from the ball. Opposing teams must be 5 or more yards from the ball for all free hits between the 25-yard lines. The ball must be stationary, and the player taking the free hit may push or hit the ball but may not raise the ball into the air. In all cases, the ball must move at least 1 yard, and after playing the ball, the striker may not play the ball again or approach within the playing distance of it until the ball has been played by another player. If another foul occurs by the same team before the free hit has been taken, the umpire may progress the free hit spot 10 more yards but not into the shooting circle.

Penalty Corners

Penalty corners are special situations of hockey that are awarded against the defending team for deliberate fouls within the 25-yard area or for accidental fouls within the shooting circle. A penalty corner is also given when the defending team intentionally plays the ball over the back line.

The setup procedure for the penalty corner requires that not more than five defenders, including the goalkeeper, start with their sticks, hands, and feet behind the back line. The remaining defenders position beyond the centerline. The penalty corner is taken by an attacker hitting or pushing the ball from a spot on the back line in the circle 10 yards from the goalpost on whichever side the attacking team chooses. The player serving the ball must have at least one foot behind the back line with the remaining attackers on the field with their sticks, hands, and feet outside the shooting circle. No player from either team shall be within 5 yards of the ball, nor may they cross the back line or the centerline or enter the shooting circle until the ball is played by the attacker starting the penalty corner.

To score from the penalty corner, the ball must be stopped motionless outside the circle on the ground and played into the circle before a shot on goal. If the first shot is a hit, the ball must cross the goal line at a height of not more than 18 inches (the height of the backboard) for a goal to be scored, unless it touches the stick of another player or body of a defender while traveling toward goal. On second and subsequent hits or flicks at goal, the shot may be raised to any height. The player serving the corner from the back line cannot score a goal directly from the push or hit, even if the ball is deflected into the goal by a defender.

If the ball travels more than 5 yards from outside the circle, the penalty corner rules no longer apply. For any violation of the rules by the attacking team, a free hit is awarded to the defending team. If the defending team violates the penalty corner rules, the attacking team retakes the penalty corner or may be awarded a penalty stroke if the defending team persistently fouls after a previous warning or penalty has been given. A game cannot end on an awarded penalty corner. The penalty corner is played out until the defending team clears the ball 5 yards beyond the shooting circle or until the attack team fouls.

Penalty Strokes

A penalty stroke is awarded to the attacking team for a deliberate foul within the shooting circle by the defender or an unintentional foul by the defender in the circle that prevents the probable scoring of a goal. Persistent breaking over the back line at penalty corners will also merit a penalty stroke.

The game clock is stopped for a penalty stroke. The setup procedure for the penalty stroke places all players, other than the defending goalkeeper and the attacker who is taking the stroke, on the field beyond the nearer 25-yard line. The attacker may not take the stroke until the controlling umpire confirms that both the stroker and the goalkeeper are ready and the whistle has blown.

The stroke is taken from a spot 7 yards in front of the center of the goal line. Without faking or using a backswing, the attacker is allowed to push or flick the ball at any height at goal. The attacker may take one forward step, but the rear foot may not pass the front one until the ball has been played. The defending goalkeeper stands with both feet on the goal line. The goalkeeper may not move either foot until the ball is played. If the goalkeeper commits a foul to prevent a goal from being scored during the penalty stroke, a penalty goal may be awarded.

If a goal was not scored or awarded from the penalty stroke, a 16-yard free hit is given to the defending team at the top of the circle, 16 yards from the center of the back line.

Cards for Reprimands

Umpires carry three differently colored and differently shaped cards to warn players of bad behavior and unwarranted dangerous fouls. Cards are used by umpires to reprimand players for misconduct; rough and dangerous play; hitting a dead ball away; delay-of-game tactics; and attitude and verbal misbehavior. The green card is a triangular-shaped card used to caution or warn a player. The square yellow card means a player is temporarily suspended from the game. Five minutes is the usual time duration of suspension. The round red card means the player is sent off the field for the rest of the game. A suspended or ejected player may not be replaced by another player.

Game Start and Restart

A field hockey game is started and restarted (after a goal is scored or to start the second half) with a pass off from the center of the field. The pass off may be hit or pushed along the ground. All players other than the player making the initial pass must be in their half of the field and opponents must be at least 5 yards from the ball. As in all free-hit situations, the ball must move at least 1 yard, and the player playing the ball may not touch it again until it has been played by someone else.

Push-Ins/Hit-Ins

When the ball goes outside the field of play completely over the sideline, a free hit or push pass is taken on the sideline where the ball went out of play by a player of the opposing team. The ball must be stationary and may not be raised. The player playing the ball may be on or off the playing field. Players from the opposing side must be at least 5 yards from the ball.

16-Yard Hits

Similar to soccer's "goal kicks," 16-yard hits, or defense hits, are taken by the defense when the attacking team plays the ball over the back line. The hit is taken from a spot exactly opposite from where the ball crossed the back line and not more than 16 yards from the back line.

Long Corners

If the defending team unintentionally plays the ball over the back line, the attack team takes a free hit from a spot on the sideline 5 yards from the corner flag. A penalty corner is awarded to the attack team when the defense intentionally hits the ball over the back line.

Bully

A bully is used to restart the game when the ball has to be replaced, when there is a simultaneous foul by both teams, when the ball is lodged in player's or umpire's equipment or uniform, or when time has been stopped for any reason other than a goal or a foul. The bully is taken on a spot chosen by the umpire but not closer than 16 yards to the back line. A player from each team faces each other with their back lines to their right and the ball on the ground between them. All other players must be 5 yards away as the two players tap the ground and each other's stick alternately three times before playing the ball.

Scoring

Each goal counts as one point and can be scored only when the ball is fairly played in the shooting circle by an attacker. The ball has to pass completely over the goal line (see illustration 6) between the goalposts and under the crossbar to be a goal. A goal is still scored if the ball touches one or more defenders before penetrating the goal.

Accidents/Injuries

If a player is injured, the umpire stops the game temporarily and ensures that the injury is treated off the field as soon as it is safe to do so.

Field Hockey Today

The modern game of hockey is characterized by players with skill, stamina, strength, and tactical knowledge. Field hockey requires that players develop into complete players, those who can defend as well as attack. A good hockey player always attempts to play the game hard by placing skill and fair play as her most important motives.

Because field hockey is an international game with global appeal (see Appendix), its future appears to be very promising. In the United States, thousands of youth are participating in hockey-related programs. The number of school-sponsored programs for girls is increasing. At the collegiate level, more than 200 member institutions of the National Collegiate Athletic Association

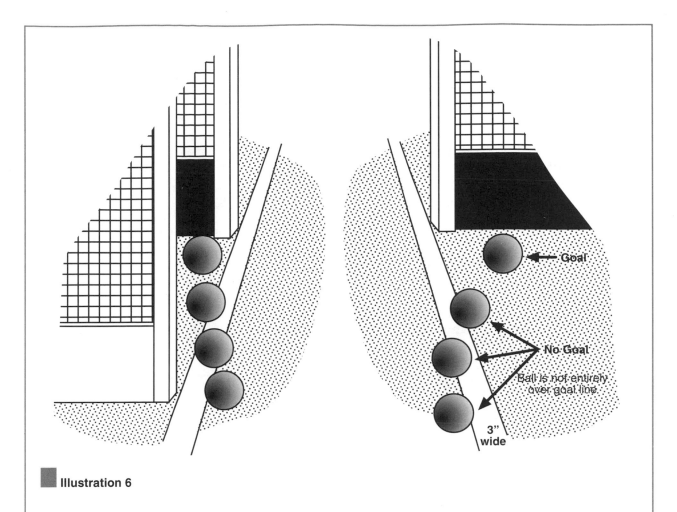

■ **Illustration 6**

(NCAA) sponsor varsity women's programs with field hockey scholarships available in more than 75 Division I universities. Many schools belonging to the National Association of Intercollegiate Athletics (NAIA) also field varsity teams. Adults have numerous opportunities to play field hockey on organized club teams and association- and section-sponsored teams. The first American hockey milestone was at the 1984 Olympic Games in Los Angeles. The U.S. women's team, in its first Olympic appearance, earned a bronze medal. This was a tremendous feat after qualifying for the 1980 Olympic Games with a third-place finish in the 1979 World Cup. The U.S. boycott of the 1980 Olympic Games in Moscow prevented the United States and many other nations from showcasing women's field hockey for the first time in the Olympic Games.

Warming Up for Success

Modern-day field hockey requires players to realize the importance of warming up for the physical demands of field hockey components. Hockey requires a player to play 70 minutes of sharp changes of direction, walking, jogging, sprinting, running forward and backward, and shuffling the feet for various distances and speeds. A field player may be required to run up to five miles in a typical game. Before, every practice or game, you should perform a series of warm-up activities to prepare your body for effective performance. Warm-up exercises are designed to stimulate increased blood flow and elevate muscle temperatures that in turn will help to prevent muscle and joint injuries during the actual practice session or game. Warm-up exercises will also improve your muscular contraction, response time, and flexibility and will help to reduce next-day soreness.

The length of the warm-up period will vary for each individual, but generally 15 to 20 minutes is sufficient time to elevate your muscle temperature. A good indication that the muscle temperature has been elevated is when you start to sweat. It is important to elevate your heart rate (increasing blood flow to muscles) from the resting rate before performing flexibility exercises.

Choose one or more exercises such as dribbling with a ball or passing with a teammate while jogging to increase the blood flow to the muscles and raise the overall body temperature. Next, perform a series of stretching exercises that work all the major muscle groups used in field hockey.

Field hockey players need flexibility to reach out and stop the ball or tackle at full stretch. An increased level of muscular flexibility will improve the range of motion around joints, which enhances the performance of hockey skills. Stretching exercises continue to promote circulation and are beneficial in many ways. Through stretching exercises, muscle tension is reduced and coordination is enhanced. A limited range of motion can be a restricting element of performance and can lead to injury such as muscle strains. Static stretching that avoids bouncing and jerking movement will increase your flexibility. Do a gradual extension of the muscle or group of muscles to the point in which you feel a mild tension, then relax and hold that position for 30 to 60 seconds. Stretch each muscle group twice, and be sure to include the hamstrings, quadriceps, lower back and hips, groin, calves and Achilles tendons, and shoulders and arms.

Your objective is to improve your range of motion in a safe, injury-free style, not to compete by outstretching your teammates. After performing static stretches, you are ready for the final phase of the warm-up. Ballistic activity and sprint running comprise the last step to preparing the body for success during the hockey practice or game. Ballistic exercises consist of dynamic stretching and sport-specific movements that are quick and forceful. Along with sprinting, ballistics improve explosiveness of initial movement and the speed of hockey skill. Because field hockey demands intense explosive and reactive movement to perform the skills of hitting, dribbling, and tackling, it is important to do ballistic exercises and accelerated sprints that promote the development and maintenance of muscular strength in the following muscle groups: abdominals, legs and hips, shoulders and chest, arms, and hands.

The warm-up is complete and your body is now prepared for the hockey practice or game. At the end of each practice session or after a game, do a warm-down. A warm-down time consists of exercises that allow your body functions and heart rate to return to their resting levels. Perform jogging, walking, and stretching exercises for each of the major muscle groups. Stretching after a game or strenuous practice session will help prevent muscular soreness. Stretch each major muscle group for 30 seconds and repeat once if necessary.

In summary, because field hockey requires a good endurance capacity and strength base, a player must warm up to prevent or delay fatigue. Fatigue will affect a player's performance by reducing skill and decision making. Hence it is important for the hockey player to remember that successful performance is built on physical preparation and technical perfection. On the technical and skill side, field hockey is comparable to playing golf while running. Whenever possible, include a ball and stick in your warm-up exercises to incorporate skill training. It is important to remember that inadequate physical warm-up and warm-down care will remain a limiting factor in acquiring hockey skill. Take care of your body.

STEP

1

MOVING WITH THE STICK: IMPROVING YOUR QUICKNESS

To play near your potential is the mark of a successful field hockey player and, ultimately, a successful hockey team. Individual players who develop the proper and quick execution of fundamental hockey skills exemplify the beauty of team play. Because field hockey is a team game, individual execution of skills is critical before you can experience playing well within a team. Passing, receiving, dribbling, tackling, shooting, moving with and without the ball, and defending are the fundamental hockey skills to learn to effectively play the Attack and Defense Roles. No matter your present player level, correct balance and footwork are the foundation for all hockey success.

Success in field hockey is often associated with speed, but balance and quick feet or agility are the most important physical attributes you can possess. Little can be done to improve your innate sprint speed, but balance and foot agility for executing hockey skills can be improved significantly through practice. Proper body balance is controlled by the extremities of the head, feet, and hands with the stick. When these extremities are in balance, your body is ready to move quickly and skillfully. It is essential to place a priority on executing physical control of the body, feet, and stick before attempting to perform skills too rapidly. Rushing your execution of hockey techniques will only promote mistakes and bad habits, which reflect lack of emotional balance as well as body balance. Quickness is specific to the hockey skill being performed. The successful hockey player must seek an absolute point of balance in relationship to the ball with every offensive and defensive technique.

Why Balance and Footwork Are Important

Like the golfer who spends a great deal of time perfecting her body posture before swinging the club, the field hockey player must also prepare the body for skill. Unlike the golfer who has much more time to position the feet, head, and hands before striking the ball, the hockey player often is moving or running when performing a skill. Whether you are passing, receiving, dribbling, or tackling, the body must be momentarily in control before any degree of skill can be performed successfully. Of course, how quickly you can perform each technique correctly with balance will be a primary factor in your progress. The hockey athlete must first strive to perform the technique correctly and practice to the point that training becomes habitual. Once you have reached this level, then you can emphasize doing the skill more quickly.

Balance is closely related to footwork, which is basic to all fundamental hockey skills. Effective footwork allows you to be ready to start and stop and change direction with quickness and balance. Footwork also prepares the body for skill performance. Good footwork is important to all the Attack Roles and Defense Roles. As an attack player with or without the ball, you have the advantage over your defender in knowing what moves you are going to make and when you will make them. Attack footwork is used in shooting, to fake your opponent off balance, to dribble around the reach of an opponent's stick, to cut to receive a pass, to avoid collision with the opponent, and to maneuver in congested space to get to the goalkeeper's rebound.

Developing good footwork is particularly important when playing hockey defense. Much of your defensive success will depend on your ability to react instantly in any direction to the moves of your opponent and the speed of the ball. With hard work, you can improve your footwork to the level in which you can force your opponent to react to you. Good footwork can enable you to disrupt the attack plan of your opponent by forcing errors in ballhandling and forcing bad passing decisions that could result in an interception for your team.

By thoroughly understanding the basic mechanics of body balance and footwork, you can improve your agility and stickhandling hockey skills.

A Balanced Attack Stance

Hockey players must seek an absolute point of balance in relationship to the ball. With a well-balanced position (see figure 1.1), essential in learning how to play Attack Role 1, you are prepared to dribble quickly in any direction, to stop under control keeping the ball "hugged" to your stick, to pass or shoot the ball in any direction, and to receive the ball from any direction. Relax your body in a position behind the ball. Keep your head over your waist, leading the upper body as it bends forward toward the ball. Stagger your feet shoulder-width apart with your weight centered on the balls of the feet. Knees are flexed and hips are lowered in a semicrouch position ready to move. Your arms are kept away from the body and both hands remain separated on the stick in a "shake hands" position. Keep the head of the stick on the ground, and if you are in possession of the ball, have your stick hug the ball.

Figure 1.1 Balanced stance.

Hands on the Stick

No matter whether you are left-handed or right-handed, the "shake hands" grip (see figure 1.2) is the basic hockey grip and the starting point for other grips. Shake hands with the hockey stick by holding it in both hands on the handle. Point the head of the stick forward with the toe of the stick pointing up. The reverse grip for playing the ball's left side uses the "shake hands" grip with the toe of the stick pointing down. Place the top of the handle in your left palm and grip it firmly. Pay extra attention to your left hand's position, because your left hand's fingers will turn the flat side of the stick to the ball to dribble, receive, pass, and tackle. Place your right hand, somewhat more relaxed than the left, a comfortable distance (5 1/2 to 7 inches) down the handle. Adjust this distance based on what skill you are performing and the distance to the ball. Each hand's forefinger and thumb form a "V," centered on a line from the toe up the middle of the handle. Keep your arms and the stick away from your body.

Control Box: The Distance of the Ball From the Feet

For each player, there is a correct distance separating the ball and the feet. It will vary a little according to height, body build, and point of balance. The ball is controlled in an imaginary control box area consisting of the space in front of the feet, within bounds of the width of the feet. The control box is created for you to realize your proper point of balance in relationship to the ball. Maintaining the head of the stick and the ball position within the control box will promote proper body posture and balance. This in turn will enhance every hockey attack technique you attempt to perform, such as dribbling, passing, and receiving.

To determine your control box, grip a hockey ball in your left hand and your hockey stick with your right hand. Squat down and extend the ball out in front of

a

b

Figure 1.2 Hands on the stick: *(a)* shake hands grip; *(b)* reverse shake hands grip.

your feet as far as you can reach without losing balance (see figure 1.3). Place the ball on the ground and stand up, keeping the feet the same distance from the stationary ball. Position your head, feet, and hands (stick) in a balanced attack stance, an alert yet relaxed semicrouch position that is coiled for quick movement. Address the ball with the stick next to the ball's right side. Keep the ball within bounds of the width of the feet to prevent loss of ball control.

Your body must be trained to become a master of correct posture with precise "ball-to-feet" judgment so your stick can complete the connection for proper skill execution. Establishing an imaginary control box is an integral component for successful hockey skills.

FIGURE 1.3 **KEYS TO SUCCESS**

CONTROL BOX

Preparation

1. Ball in left hand and stick in right hand ____
2. Squat down ____
3. Reach and place ball in front of feet, centered ____
4. Measure distance from ball to toes ____
5. Visualize control-box area ____

a

Execution

1. Shake hands grip using both hands ____
2. Place stick head along the right side of ball ____
3. Contact lower half of ball with stick ____
4. Maintain measured distance of ball from feet ____
5. Balanced attack stance ____
6. Head over ball ____
7. Focus on ball ____

b

Follow-Through

1. Move ball in control box ____
2. Stick remains hugged to lower half of ball ____
3. Maintain body balance ____
4. Maintain precise distance of ball from feet ____
5. Head up and see field ____

c

MOVING WITH THE STICK SUCCESS STOPPERS

Moving efficiently with your stick is crucial for your preparation for hockey skills. Even slight body balance and stick grip errors may result in poor skill execution or failure to choose the most appropriate movement for a particular situation. It is important to develop correct positioning of the body in relation to the ball and stick. Common movement and stick handling errors are discussed here along with suggestions for correcting them.

Error	Correction
Attack Stance	
1. Your balance is off in a forward direction.	1. Flex your knees to get low, rather than bending at the waist, so you are ready to move backward as quickly as you can move forward.
2. Your balance is off in a backward direction.	2. Keep your heels off the ground and stagger your feet shoulder-width apart. Knees must remain bent so you can lean your head forward and maintain balance.
3. You easily lose balance to either side.	3. Spread your feet shoulder-width apart and flex the knees so you are balanced and ready to move in any direction.
Hands on the Stick	
1. Loss of stickhandling speed.	1. The hands are too far apart on the stick. Split the hands only 5 1/2 to 7 inches and relax the right hand grip. Remember to use the shake hands grip with "V" alignment and turn the stick with the left hand.
2. You frequently lose control of the ball.	2. The hands are too close together. Split your hands between 5 1/2 to 7 inches and bend your knees to establish your control box.
Control Box	
1. Stick contact is being made on the top half of the ball, resulting in a loose, uncontrolled ball outside the control box.	1. The ball is too far from the feet, which impairs the ability to reach the lower half of the ball. Decrease the distance the ball is from the feet and bend your knees.
2. Eyes strain to find the ball, and you frequently advance the ball with your feet.	2. Move the ball away from the feet and into your control box area where you can see it.
3. Balance is distorted, and you experience a loss of speed with the ball.	3. Gravity too low, and the ball is too far from feet. Move feet and head closer to the ball so the head leads the upper body toward the ball.
4. Overreaching for the ball and difficulty in controlling the ball.	4. The ball is too far from your feet, which hinders the ability to get your stick on the lower half of the ball for control. Move the feet closer to the ball and keep knees flexed for good body balance.

A Balanced Defense Stance

As a hockey defender whose main objective is to take the ball from the opponent, you must be able to instantly move in any direction and change direction while sustaining body balance. Before you attempt to tackle the ball, you must get control of the space and position to block the forward space to the goal. This requires a well-balanced stance fundamental in learning how to play Defense Role 1. Your defense stance (see figure 1.4) resembles your basic attack stance with additional emphasis on effectively positioning the feet and body to force the opponent in a direction you want her to go. You must establish a lead foot and refuse to allow the ball to go past your lead foot. When you use the right foot as your lead foot, your defensive plan is to force the opponent with the ball to your left side. You execute forcing in the left direction from a balanced defense stance by placing your left foot directly opposite and in line of the opponent's left foot. To force the ballcarrier to your right side, establish your left foot as your lead foot and place your right foot opposite the attacker's right foot.

Your head leads the upper body, with your feet staggered and shoulder-width or wider apart. Keep one foot in front of the other at all times, hips facing forward, and evenly distribute your weight on the power points (balls) of your feet. Flex your knees so your body is low and coiled, ready to move or react in any direction. Grip your stick in both hands using the basic shake hands grip. It is important to keep the head of your stick on the ground in front of your feet and legs to prevent the opponent from pushing the ball into your feet. A well-balanced defense stance and a low stick are important because they allow you to use excellent judgment of distance, which means you will know when to tackle and when not to tackle.

Figure 1.4   Defense stance.

Protect the Lead Foot

In the basic defense stance, your feet are staggered with one foot in front of the other. The front foot is called the *lead foot*. Establishing a lead foot enables you to move back in the direction of the back foot with ease. Moving or pushing back requires only a short step with the back foot as you begin to move. To move back in the direction of the lead foot requires footwork that incorporates the *drop step*, a more difficult skill than protecting the lead foot.

You must protect your lead foot as you establish your balanced defense stance. It is vital that you have a purposeful plan to force the opponent to a side direction so that a lead foot is immediately established and then protected.

DEFENSE STANCE SUCCESS STOPPERS

You won't get a chance to use your shooting or dribbling skills unless you first gain possession of the ball. Most errors in challenging for the ball result from lack of body control, poor timing of the challenge, and improper stick handling. Here is a list of common errors and suggested methods of correcting them.

Error	Correction
1. You easily lose balance.	1. Keep your heels off the ground and stagger your feet (establish a lead foot) shoulder-width apart. Keep your knees bent and maintain proper body balance with head, feet, and hands (stick position).
2. You fail to protect the lead foot because you overreact to the ball movement.	2. Know what direction you want to force the dribbler and establish a lead foot early.
3. You are easily faked by your opponent's stick and ball movement.	3. Keep your eyes focused on the ball. Maintain a controlled playing distance from the ball and remain in balance when tackling the ball.
4. You become off balance in the direction of your stick reach.	4. Keep your weight centered and remain on the power points of your feet. Flex your knees and hold your stick near the ground away from the body and in front to protect your feet from the ball.

Executing Attack Footwork

Movement with and without the ball is important to all three Attack Roles play. As an attack player, you have a slight advantage over the defender in knowing what move you will make and when you will make it. The effective attack player moves swiftly with balance. Once you have developed the skills, your footwork and fakes will allow you to maintain your balance as you attempt to escape your opponent. Moving continuously with and without the ball also demands superior fitness. Successful hockey players develop their physical condition as they master the necessary skills to excel in the three Attack Roles.

When you are near the ball, both hands must remain on your stick in a shake hands grip. When you are 30 or more yards from the ball, you can grip your stick with only the right hand (see figure 1.5) so you can freely pump your arms for greater pace and distance. But both hands must immediately grip the stick in preparation to play the ball.

You should master three basic attack footwork movements so that you can perform the Attack Roles: (1) breakdown steps, (2) change of pace, and (3) change of direction.

Figure 1.5 Stick grip when running.

Breakdown Steps

Breakdown steps are used both in attack and defense footwork and are the most fundamental skill for balance and foot movement. The attack hockey player uses breakdown steps to prepare the moving body for receiving and passing skills (see figure 1.6). When sprinting, you must quickly bring your body under control into your basic attack stance.

To execute breakdown steps, shorten your running strides into quick, choppy steps, without crossing your feet. Feet are staggered with one foot up and one back as you keep your weight evenly distributed on the balls of the feet. Lower your hips by bending the knees. As your momentum slows from the shorter strides, push off the power point of your back foot and step with the lead foot to briefly move into your attack stance. The head must be up to see the field and the ball, with both hands on the stick prepared to play the ball.

FIGURE 1.6 | **KEYS TO SUCCESS**

ATTACK FOOTWORK—BREAKDOWN STEPS

a b c

Preparation

1. Hold stick with shake hands grip ____
2. Burst into a short run ____
3. Head leads a relaxed upper body ____

Execution

1. Square shoulders and toes to ball ____
2. Shorten strides to choppy steps and keep feet shoulder-width apart ____
3. Flex knees in semicrouch with heels off ground ____
4. Stick and arms away from body ____
5. Stick head touches ground ____
6. Focus on ball ____

Follow-Through

1. Maintain balance on power points of feet ____
2. Head up to see field ____
3. Ready to play the ball ____

Change of Pace—Stutter Step/Hesitate

The change of pace is a style of movement that varies your running speed to fool and break away from your defender. Without changing your basic running form and balance, change from a fast running speed to a slower pace and then quickly back to a fast run. The most frequently used change-of-pace footwork in field hockey is the *stutter step*, also called the *hesitation step* (see figure 1.7).

As you run, keep your head up so you can see the field and the ball. Take your first step with your back foot, crossing it in front of your lead foot. Run on the power points of your feet with your toes pointing in the direction you are going. Lean your upper body slightly forward and pump your arms forward in opposition to your legs, keeping your elbows flexed. Your stick grip will vary from a right-hand-only grip for open field runs to a shake hands grip to prepare your stick to play the ball. Completely extend your support leg. Get your knee up and thigh parallel to the ground as you bring the leg forward.

The deception of the change of pace comes from illusion and quickness in changing speed. To slow your speed, shorten your stride or decrease your stride frequency. Use less force to push off from your back foot and avoid leaning your head and shoulders back as you slow your pace. To increase your speed, increase your stride frequency or lengthen your stride. To accelerate quickly to a faster speed, push forcefully off the back foot. With the change-of-pace footwork in attack movement, you will be at least a step faster than your defender, which will enable you to win the

space or get to the ball first. The *stutter step*, or hesitation attack footwork, will allow you to fool your opponent into slowing down or stopping, which grants you an immediate advantage to change direction or accelerate to break away from the defender. To execute the stutter step, move lightly on the forward parts of your feet using short, choppy steps. Lead the upper body with your head and maintain body balance, slightly crouched with every joint flexed and relaxed. Both hands remain on your stick as you pump your feet in place. Push off the rear foot to accelerate forward. The left foot pushes from the ground to go to your right; to go to your left, push off the power points of your right foot.

FIGURE 1.7   **KEYS TO SUCCESS**

ATTACK FOOTWORK—STUTTER STEP

a

b

c

Preparation

1. Hold stick with shake hands grip ____
2. Burst into a short run ____
3. Head leads a relaxed upper body ____

Execution

1. Square shoulders and toes to ball ____
2. Shorten strides ____
3. Keep feet shoulder-width apart ____
4. Flex knees in semicrouch and pump feet ____
5. Burst into another short run ____

Follow-Through

1. Maintain balance on power points of feet ____
2. Head up to see field ____
3. Ready to play ball ____

Change of Direction—Stop and Turn

Change-of-direction footwork is specifically important for getting open to receive a pass or for taking your opponent's defensive stance off balance. An effective change of direction such as the *stop and turn* depends on sharp cutting from one direction to another. The change of direction can be a simple attack move if you concentrate on a two-count move: right-left cadence or left-right cadence. To execute a basic change-of-direction move, begin with a three-quarter-length step with one foot, rather than a full step. On your first step, flex your knee as you plant your foot firmly to stop your momentum, turn on the ball of your foot, and push off in the direction you want to go. Shift your weight and take a long step with your other foot, pointing your toes in the new direction. Keep your head up to see the field, and keep both hands on your stick if you are near the ball.

The *stop and turn* allows you to change direction to create space between you and the opponent (see figure 1.8). The increased space will give you more time to successfully receive a pass from a teammate or, if you have the ball, successfully dribble into the free space behind you. Before any turn or pivot can be made, you must learn to make a good stop from a short burst of speed. The quick burst of speed is to fake your opponent into thinking that you are going to run by her.

It is important to get your hips in a low balanced position, with the knees bent and the head up to see the field. The head should remain above the midpoint of the two feet. Stop your run by shortening your strides into a staggered hop and lean in the opposite direction. Your rear foot is flexed at the knee to lower your body to a "sitting" position. The rear foot becomes the pivot foot, which turns the body with the other foot following. After completing the turn, you should be facing the direction from which you want to receive the ball, with your feet spread shoulder-width apart, the body in good balance on the balls of your feet, and the ball away from the reach of the defender.

FIGURE 1.8

KEYS TO SUCCESS

ATTACK FOOTWORK—STOP AND TURN

a   b   c

Preparation

1. Head up to see the field and ball ____
2. Shake hands grip ____
3. Burst into a short run ____

Execution

1. Hop before stop ____
2. Back foot lands first; lead foot lands second ____
3. Feet staggered shoulder-width apart and knees flexed ____
4. Turn on balls of feet ____
5. Push off in new direction and shift weight ____
6. Long second step ____

Follow-Through

1. Maintain balance ____
2. Eyes on ball ____
3. Stick head low ready to receive ____
4. Head up to see field ____

ATTACK FOOTWORK SUCCESS STOPPERS

Effective attack movement with or without the ball must be performed swiftly with balance. Breakdown steps, a change of speed, and a change of direction are essential attack footwork you will need to master.

Most attack footwork errors cause poor preparation for receiving and a loss of ball possession. Here is a list of common errors and suggested methods of correcting them.

Error	Correction
Breakdown Steps	
1. You overrun the ball, and your stick is too close to your feet.	1. Begin shortening your strides sooner to get your body and feet balanced before the ball arrives.
2. Your stick is too far from the ground, and you are not in balance.	2. Keep your heels off the ground and bend your knees to prepare the stick to play the ball.
Change of Pace—Stutter Step/Hesitation	
1. Change from slow to fast is not quick.	1. Push forcefully off your back foot to quickly accelerate.
2. Change from fast to slow is not deceptive.	2. Keep your head and upper body leaning forward to prevent defenders from quickly spotting the change of pace.
3. Change of speed does not evade your defender.	3. Pump your feet in place to get your defender to stop his feet, then lower your hips and push off into a burst of speed.
Change of Direction—Stop and Turn	
1. Turns are rounded rather than sharp.	1. Use a three-quarter-length first step and flex your knee so you can pivot sharply. Shift your weight and push off in the direction you want to go. The second step is a long explosive step.
2. You are not deceptive because you have a tendency to slow your speed too much on your approach to change direction.	2. Stay in your normal running form and concentrate on a two-count directional move such as right-left or left-right or stop-turn.
3. You run too great a distance, making your stops slow.	3. Use quick, brief breakdown steps or a short hop to stop.
4. The turn is slow and labored.	4. Feet are too wide. Keep your feet shoulder-width apart so you can execute a long second step with the back foot while pushing from the lead foot.

Executing Defense Footwork

If you stop your feet, you're beat! To perform successful defensive footwork needed in the three Defense Roles, you must possess lots of desire, discipline, anticipation, and superb fitness—so you can keep your feet moving! The key is to move your feet with balance so you can react to your opponent's attack moves and block the forward space to the goal.

Defensive footwork requires short, quick steps with your weight evenly distributed on the power points of the feet. Avoid crossing your feet. Push off the foot farther from where you are going and keep adjusting with the lead foot. The only time you change your closer foot or lead foot is when your opponent moves by your lead foot. Always execute a *drop step* to recover your defensive position.

Your feet are staggered shoulder-width apart so that you can make instant lateral, forward, or backward movement. Keep your hips low as your upper body is directed forward by your steady head. Keep your eyes on the ball so that you can become a better judge of the distance between your probing stick and the ball. Hold your stick in both hands out in front of your feet. Your defensive footwork calls for an active stick that starts the stick head from the ground and inches closer to the ball as you time when to tackle.

The four basic defensive footwork movements are (1) engaging distance and give, (2) slide or shuffle, (3) drop step, and (4) backward run.

Engaging Distance and Give

Engaging distance is also referred to as the approach distance needed to move up on or close up on your opponent to apply defensive pressure. *Give* refers to the movement of pushing back away from the ball or opponent to avoid getting too close before you can reestablish your defense stance to pressure the ball (see figure 1.9). As a Defense Role 1 player, you ultimately want to take the ball from your opponent by blocking and controlling the forward space to the goal. This is not an easy skill; it requires agile footwork combined with good judgment and body balance. The most important aspect of successful defensive footwork is judging the distance to get close enough to the ball or opponent. You must be close enough to be a defensive threat without being eliminated by the opponent. Your engaging distance measures approximately 1 or 1 1/2 stick lengths, depending on the speed of your opponent, where you can reach the ball with your stick by taking one short, quick step. Approach the ball at a speed that will enable you to maintain your balance and change direction backward.

To execute your engaging-distance and give footwork, use short, quick approach steps without crossing your feet, and protect your lead foot by positioning it slightly outside the opponent's body. If your opponent makes a move toward the goal on the side of your back foot, you must "give," or push back, without losing balance. As with your "engaging," or approach, steps, use short, quick *give* steps without crossing the feet and losing balance.

Engaging-distance and give footwork techniques basically require the same footwork but in different directions. They both use short, quick steps, with one foot up and the other foot back. Keep your weight evenly distributed on the power points of the feet. Push off the back foot and step with your lead foot to approach; push off your front foot and step with your back foot to give. While engaging, never cross your back foot in front of your lead foot, and while giving, never cross your lead foot in front of your back foot.

FIGURE 1.9 **KEYS TO SUCCESS**

ENGAGING DISTANCE AND GIVE

a

b

c

Preparation

1. Position between ball and goal ____
2. Shoulders and feet face ball ____
3. Run or move toward ball; evaluate ball distance ____
4. Eyes on lower half of ball ____
5. Use two-handed shake hands grip ____

Execution

1. Engage by pushing off back foot; give by pushing off lead foot ____
2. Use short, quick steps on power points ____
3. Lead foot outside of opponent's body ____
4. Align back foot with forcing direction ____
5. Feet shoulder-width apart ____
6. Flex knees in semicrouch posture ____
7. Head steady over waist; eyes on lower half of ball ____
8. Stick head on ground in front of feet ____
9. Pressure ball with quick tracking stick ____

Follow-Through

1. Maintain balanced defense footwork ____
2. Judge distance with patience ____
3. Decide when to tackle ____

Slide/Shuffle

Maintain a balanced defensive stance between your opponent and the goal you are defending by using slide or shuffle footwork. If the opponent moves to the side, quickly move your feet by sliding or shuffling to the side. Your feet remain staggered with an established lead foot (see figure 1.10). Use short, quick steps with your weight evenly distributed on the balls of your feet.

To slide in a forward, or north, direction, push off the far or back foot and step closer to where you are going with the lead foot. To slide in a back, or south, direction, push off the lead foot and step with the back foot. To execute the lateral, or east/west, directions, push with the lead foot to slide. Keep your stick head down on the ground and judge your distance from the opponent and the ball.

FIGURE 1.10   **KEYS TO SUCCESS**

SLIDE/SHUFFLE

a   b   c

Preparation

1. Shoulders and feet face ball ____
2. Both hands in shake hands grip ____
3. Lead foot outside of opponent's body ____
4. Align back foot with forcing direction ____
5. Feet shoulder-width apart with knees flexed ____
6. Head steady over waist ____

Execution

1. Push off far foot from desired lateral direction ____
2. Step with foot closest to desired lateral direction ____
3. Use short, quick steps along the ground ____
4. Stick head on ground in front of feet ____
5. Keep arms away from body ____
6. Pressure ball with quick stick probes ____

Follow-Through

1. Maintain balanced defense stance ____
2. Judge distance with patience ____
3. Head up to see field ____

Drop Step

The *drop step* is defensive footwork used when you fail to protect the lead foot. The opponent has forced you to move back in the direction of your lead foot, which is a more difficult skill than moving in the direction of your back foot (see figure 1.11).

To execute the drop step, you drop step or reverse the lead foot back while pivoting on your back foot as you start to move. After making the drop step in the direction of the opponent's move, use quick slide steps to re-establish your defensive stance with a lead foot forward. Keep your head up to see the field and your eyes on the ball. Avoid turning your back to the ball or to your opponent. Aggressively push off your back foot in the direction of your drop step. Your drop step is straight back, moving your foot low along the ground.

FIGURE 1.11 **KEYS TO SUCCESS**

DROP STEP

a

b

c

Preparation

1. Shoulders and feet face ball ____
2. Both hands in shake hands grip ____
3. Opponent dribbles by lead foot ____

Execution

1. Reverse pivot on back foot ____
2. Drop step with lead foot straight back ____
3. Protect space between the feet with stick ____
4. Eyes on ball and distance from ball ____
5. Reestablish defensive position by giving (or running) ____
6. Hips face ball to reestablish lead foot ____

Follow-Through

1. Protect lead foot ____
2. Maintain balanced defense stance ____
3. Prepare to change direction and judge distance ____

Backward Run

A somewhat common movement pattern, the backward run footwork is challenging but very useful for the hockey player in the three Defense Roles. The ability to backpedal or run backward for a short distance allows you to see the field in front of you. You can be a better judge of your distance from the ball, the opponent's speed of attack, and movement from your teammates.

To execute the backward run, drive back off the power points of the feet, keeping your head slightly forward to maintain balance. Your knees should remain flexed, with one hand or both hands on your stick ready to reposition into your balanced defensive stance. Your feet stay low to the ground during the quick, short, backward running strides. Concentrate on alternately "swinging" your lower legs back to always land and push off the balls of your feet. You should only backpedal a short distance, preparing to position into your balanced defense stance at any moment.

DEFENSE FOOTWORK SUCCESS STOPPERS

Balanced defense footwork is vital for your positioning to effectively control and block space. Defensive footwork must be practiced often to successfully move in a position to regain possession of the ball. Most defensive footwork errors result from poor judgment of the distance from your stick and the ball, a lack of body control, and a lack of desire to keep your feet moving. Here is a list of common errors and suggested methods of correcting them.

Error	Correction
Engaging Distance and Give	
1. You move up too fast when engaging, losing your balance in a forward direction and preventing a quick change of direction in the backward or lateral direction.	1. Close up with control using short, quick steps. Keep your feet shoulder-width apart and weight evenly distributed on the balls of your feet.
2. In your approach to the ball, you cross your back foot in front of your lead foot, preventing a quick change of direction.	2. To approach, push off the back foot and step with your lead foot. Keep your feet shoulder-width apart and do not cross your feet.
3. In your "give" footwork, you cross your lead foot in front of your back foot, preventing a quick change of direction.	3. To give, push off the lead foot and step with your back foot. Keep your feet shoulder-width apart and do not cross your feet.
Slide/-Shuffle	
1. You cross your feet, preventing a quick change of direction.	1. Always keep your feet shoulder-width apart.
2. You lean or reach too far with your stick, losing your balance.	2. Keep your head steady and slightly forward, basic grip on your stick, and keep your stick out in front of your feet on the ground.
Drop Step	
1. Your drop step lacks explosiveness and is too slow.	1. Execute your drop step straight back and low to the ground. Avoid circling your lead foot or lifting the lead foot.
2. When your opponent moves, you turn your back, losing temporary sight of opponent and ball.	2. Drop step in the direction of the opponent's move, keeping your eyes on the ball and the opponent.
3. After the drop step, you use "give steps" rather than reestablishing your defensive position of distance and balance. The opponent runs by and in behind you.	3. Reestablish your defensive position by judging whether to use slide steps or instead run and turn into position with your lead foot forward. The speed of the opponent and distance to move will help you make a good judgment.
Backward Run	
1. You lose your balance and fall backward.	1. Stay on the power points of your feet and keep the head slightly forward throughout your backpedaling footwork.

BALANCE AND FOOTWORK DRILLS

1. Two-Cone/Two-Tennis-Ball Drill

Place two tennis balls at one of the two cones positioned 5 yards apart. Start at the cone that is away from the tennis balls, with your feet facing forward. Run and pick up both tennis balls and sprint back to the start cone. Place the balls down at the start cone and jog back to the other cone. Repeat the exercise immediately, using an explosive sprint to pick up and return the tennis balls to the original cone. Turn and sprint back to the start cone to complete the repetition.

Success Goal = Do 3 sets of 10 repetitions _____

Success Check
- Balance _____
- Move on balls of feet _____
- Use breakdown footwork _____

To Increase Difficulty
- Place cones 10 yards apart.
- Increase speed of repetition.
- Run backward after the ball pickup.
- Increase to 12 repetitions.

To Decrease Difficulty
- Place cones 3 yards apart.
- Decrease repetitions.

2. Slide Feet

Place two cones 6 or 7 yards apart. Hold your hockey stick using the shake hands grip. Start with both feet behind and on the outside of first cone to prepare to slide in a lateral direction to the left or right. Slide feet sideways to the outside of the other cone. Complete as many lateral slides as you can in 30 seconds.

Success Goal = Number of slides to cone(s) in 30 seconds _____

Success Check
- Balance _____
- Move on balls of feet _____
- Feet shoulder-width apart _____
- Feet and shoulders face forward _____
- Feet stay close to ground _____

To Increase Difficulty
- Place cones 10 yards apart.
- Increase speed of repetition.
- Run 5 yards and slide the remaining 5 yards.
- Increase time to 40 seconds.

To Decrease Difficulty
- Place cones 4 yards apart.
- Decrease to 20 seconds.

3. Five-Run Dice

Place five cones 7 yards apart in the shape of dots on the sides of dice. Using a shake hands grip, carry your hockey stick in your right hand midway down the handle. Start at the center cone and sprint to touch the top right cone. Sprint back to the center cone and then sprint to touch the bottom right cone. Return to the center cone and continue to sprint to touch the upper left cone and sprint back to center. Go touch the bottom left cone and back to the center cone. Repeat the sequence to see how many touches you can do in 30 seconds.

Success Goal = Number of cone touches in 30 seconds _____

✔ Success Check
- Balance _____
- Move on balls of feet _____
- Use breakdown footwork _____

To Increase Difficulty
- Place cones 10 yards apart.
- Increase speed of repetition.
- Run backward to center cone.
- Increase time to 40 seconds. .

To Decrease Difficulty
- Place cones 3 yards apart.
- Decrease to 20 seconds.

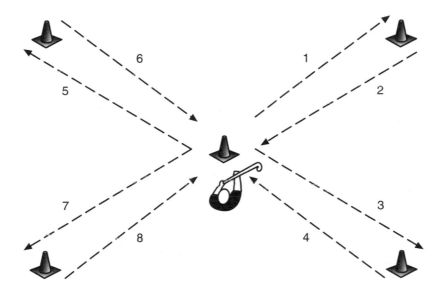

4. Slide and Reach

Place two cones or markers 7 yards apart. Put down an object (tennis ball) on the outside of each of the two cones. Hold your hockey stick using the shake hands grip. Stand between the two cones and slide in a east or west direction and reach from a low defense position to pick up the object. Stay balanced with weight evenly distributed between your feet. Slide back to center into your defense stance and then slide in the other east-west direction to reach for the object. Repeat the slide and reach to place the objects back in their original positions. Count the number of slide and reaches you can do in 30 seconds.

Success Goal = Number of slide and reaches in 30 seconds _____

Success Check
- Balance _____
- Move on balls of feet _____
- Feet shoulder-width apart _____
- Feet and shoulders face forward _____
- Feet stay close to ground _____

To Increase Difficulty
- Place cones 15 yards apart.
- Increase speed of repetition.
- Run, use breakdown steps into a defensive slide and reach.
- Increase time to 60 seconds.

To Decrease Difficulty
- Place cones 5 yards apart.
- Decrease to 20 seconds.

5. Slide and Move Forward

Use four cones to create a U-shape area 7 yards long and 4 yards wide. Center a cone in between the 4-yard cones. Carry your hockey stick using a two-handed shake hands grip. Position your feet behind the center cone at the base of the U and slide to the right outside of the end cone. Sprint forward to the top cone 7 yards away, break down your footwork, and establish your right foot as your lead foot. Slide back to center start cone and repeat the slide going to the left outside of the end cone. Sprint forward, break down, and establish your left foot as your lead foot, then slide back to the center start cone. Keep your shoulders and hips facing forward throughout all slides and sprints. Count the number of times you return to the center cone in 30 seconds.

Success Goal = Number of times you returned to center cone in 30 seconds _____

Success Check
- Balance _____
- Move on balls of feet _____
- Feet shoulder-width apart _____
- Feet and shoulders face forward _____
- Feet stay close to ground _____

To Increase Difficulty
- Place lateral cones 2 yards apart and horizontal cones 10 yards away.
- Increase speed of repetition.
- Backward run to return to center cone.
- Increase time to 60 seconds.

To Decrease Difficulty
- Use only 1 cone in place of the 3 cones in the lateral row.
- Decrease to 20 seconds.

6. W Runs

Place five cones 7 yards apart in a "W" formation. Use your right hand only to carry your hockey stick. Start at an end cone and sprint in a diagonal forward direction to the outside of the second cone, break down your footwork, and immediately backpedal around the third cone. Sprint to the fourth cone of the "W" formation, break down, and backpedal back and around fifth cone. Sprint to start cone and repeat as many trips as you can in 30 seconds.

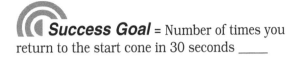

Success Goal = Number of times you return to the start cone in 30 seconds ____

Success Check
- Balance ____
- Move on balls of feet ____
- Breakdown footwork ____
- Feet and shoulders face forward ____

To Increase Difficulty
- Place cones 10 yards apart in "W" formation.
- Increase speed of repetition.
- Increase time to 60 seconds.

To Decrease Difficulty
- To Decrease Difficulty
- Place cones only 5 yards apart in "W" formation.
- Decrease to 20 seconds.
- Eliminate the backpedal and use only the forward sprint and breakdown.

7. Drop Step

Mark with cones or use two parallel lines that are 36 inches apart. Carry your hockey stick using the shake hands grip. With your back to both lines, start with heels in front of the nearest start line. Drop one foot back, followed by the other foot, into the area between the two lines. Keep your feet and shoulders facing forward and repeat the drop step into the next area outside the parallel line. Sprint back to the area in front of the start line by using breakdown footwork, touching the ground in front of you with both hands. Count the number of hand touches in 30 seconds.

Success Goal = Number of times you touch the ground at start area in 30 seconds ____

Success Check
- Balance ____
- Move on balls of feet ____
- Drop step footwork ____
- Breakdown footwork ____
- Feet and shoulders face forward ____

To Increase Difficulty
- Place cones or use lines that are 48 inches apart.
- Increase speed of repetition.
- Increase time to 60 seconds.
- Specify which foot to use for the drop step.

To Decrease Difficulty
- Use 24 inches between lines or cones.
- Decrease to 20 seconds.

8. Cha Cha Cha Breakdown Footwork

Use four cones to set up a 10-yard-by-10-yard grid. In the center of the grid, mark a 24-inch-by-36-inch rectangle using markers (for example, hockey sticks, T-shirts). Hold your hockey stick and position to start along the right side of a grid cone. Run as fast as possible in a diagonal direction to the left and use at least three breakdown running strides in the middle of the rectangular area. Bring your body into control from the sprint with breakdown footwork of a rhythmic count of one-two-three, or cha cha cha. Continue to sprint diagonal forward around the outside of the second cone in the top left of the grid. Run to the third cone in the upper right side of the grid and go around it. Sprint to the rectangle and use your "cha cha cha" footwork inside the center. From the breakdown footwork, run to the fourth cone in the lower left side of the grid. Go around the fourth and run to the start cone to complete one trip. Complete as many trips as you can in 30 seconds.

Success Goal = Number of times you return to the start cone in 30 seconds ____

Success Check
- Balance ____
- Move on balls of feet ____
- Breakdown footwork ____
- Feet and shoulders face forward ____

To Increase Difficulty
- Place cones for a 15-yard-by-15-yard grid.
- Carry your hockey stick.
- Increase speed of repetition.
- Increase time to 60 seconds.

To Decrease Difficulty
- Use a 5-yard-by-5-yard grid.
- Decrease to 20 seconds.

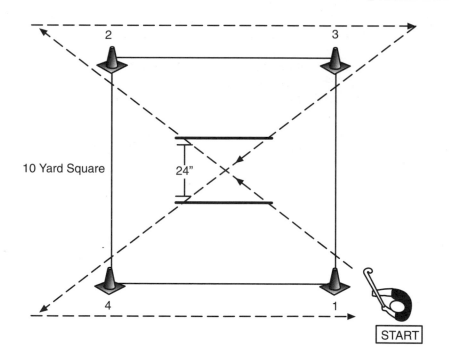

10 Yard Square

24"

START

9. Breakdown and Give Run

Use any field line on the hockey field and start 7 yards away, facing the line. Run to the line gripping your hockey stick with both hands. As you arrive closer to your "line" destination, break down your footwork into smaller strides, which will bring your body under control on the line. Remain on the power points of your feet and immediately give or push back away from the line at least 3 yards. Do the exercise 10 times, counting the number of repetitions that balance was maintained.

Success Goal = 8 of 10 repetitions completed with balanced footwork _____

Success Check
- Balance _____
- Hold hockey stick _____
- Move on balls of feet _____
- Breakdown footwork _____
- Feet and shoulders face forward _____
- Give/push back away _____

To Increase Difficulty
- Start run 10 yards from designated line.
- Increase speed of repetition.
- Make a 10-yard-by-10-yard grid with a back line and add a partner who tries to score by running over your back line. Establish control of your partner's movement by establishing balance and keeping your partner in front by breaking down and giving.

To Decrease Difficulty
- Start run only 5 yards from field line.
- Decrease to 8 repetitions.

10. Lateral Slide

Set up an area of four markers or four parallel lines 24 inches apart. Start with your feet shoulder-width apart on the left side of the first marker or line. Slide to your right into the 24-inch space between the first line and the second line. Both feet must touch in each space. Continue sliding to the next space and so forth until you slide over the last line. Return to the start position by sliding in the opposite direction, touching both feet in all the 24-inch spaces. A completed trip is counted when you return to the start position. Slide for 20 seconds and count the completed trips.

Success Goal = Number of sliding trips completed in 20 seconds _____

Success Check
- Balance _____
- Move on balls of feet _____
- Lateral slide footwork _____
- Feet and shoulders face forward _____

To Increase Difficulty
- Place an additional marker or line.
- Increase speed of repetition.
- Increase time to 30 seconds.
- Hop, jump, or run in place of sliding.

To Decrease Difficulty
- Use 3 markers or lines.
- Decrease to 15 seconds.

11. Box Exercise

Use cones to mark a 3-yard-by-3-yard square. Hold your hockey stick in both hands. Begin with both feet on the outside of the box and slide the near foot inside the square followed by the other foot. Slide both feet to the outside of the box, always exiting on a new side from the entry side. Continue sliding in and out of the box for 30 seconds. Count each time you slide both feet over a new side of the box as one time.

Success Goal = Number of times you slide over a new box side in 30 seconds _____

Success Check
• Balance _____
• Move on balls of feet _____
• Feet shoulder-width apart _____
• Feet and shoulders face forward _____
• Stick held in both hands out in front of feet _____

To Increase Difficulty
• Place cones for a 5-yard-by-5-yard square.
• Increase speed of repetition.
• Increase time to 60 seconds.
• Hop on 1 foot only or on both feet.

To Decrease Difficulty
• Use a 2-yard-by-2-yard grid.
• Decrease to 20 seconds.

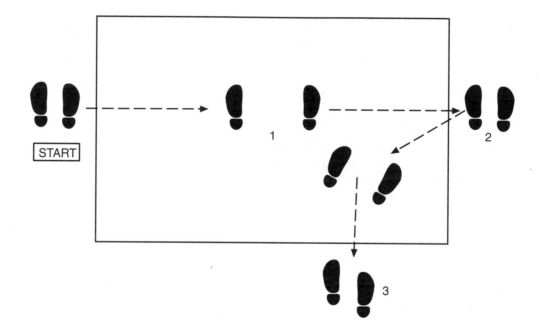

MOVING WITH THE STICK SUCCESS SUMMARY

To execute fluid individual hockey skills and successfully blend these skills with teammates are the ultimate goals of every hockey team. Without proper training in footwork and body balance while handling your hockey stick, effective performance of hockey skills will only be a wishful dream. To learn and advance in the techniques of field hockey, players of all levels must focus on the correct body balance and footwork movement while carrying the hockey stick.

STEP 2

PASSING AND RECEIVING: DEVELOPING YOUR TECHNIQUE (ATTACK ROLE 1)

The true elegance of field hockey is the team passing game. Unfortunately, many players are remembered for their dribbling skills instead of their passing skills because dribbling appears to be more spectacular. Bad passing will destroy any team's chances of success, no matter how much stickwork and dribbling ability the players possess. Hence, it is the passing and receiving skills that are most important. To master passing and receiving, you must develop the Attack Role 1 techniques of pushing, hitting, and occasional lifting.

All team sports demand interaction among members, so passing becomes a priority in all basic skills. Passing and receiving the hockey ball require that players work the ball in combination. The key to a steady flow of passing options is the intelligent movement of players who are not in possession of the ball. Depending on the game situation, you may choose to pass the ball along the ground or lift it through the air. As a general rule, the pass along the ground is easier to receive and control than the ball dropping from the sky. Skillful teams will keep the ball on the ground.

Passing and Receiving in Field Hockey

Winning team play depends on effective passing combinations and solid receiving skills. Failing to accurately pass the ball and receive and control it will cause loss of ball possession. The critical elements for passing include a sense of correct timing, correct pace or speed, and the ability to read the play and judge the distance for accuracy. Every player and team can improve if adequate attention is given to timing, accuracy, and power.

You will improve your level of hockey by passing the ball on the ground whenever possible. In the information that follows, you will first learn about the various Attack Role 1 techniques used to pass the ball along the ground and then learn how to practice the proper methods to receive and control passes on the ground.

Passing Ground Balls

Always have a target. The two requirements of a good pass to your selected target are *accuracy* and *timing*.

Accuracy: The factors that govern an accurate pass include the accuracy of direction and the speed of the pass. The position of the target (receiver's stick or free space to enable receiver to run to the pass) and the width of the passing lane determine the direction that you pass the ball. The passing lane must allow the ball to clear the opponent's stick. The shorter the pass, the more precise it must be. The short, direct passes must be firm and fast, eluding a successful ball trap. A longer pass permits the receiver more time to move into position if the direction of the pass is in error.

The speed of the pass is determined by the distance between the passer and receiver, the width of the passing lane, the ground or surface conditions, and the distance from the passer to the point where the receiver runs to the ball. Every pass has a correct speed. A firmly hit ball is easier to stop than one that is poking along the ground. A common error is to under-hit a short pass.

Timing: The major factor in determining **when** to give a pass is that the receiver must be free or prepared to receive the ball. Hence, the passer must hold the ball and look before passing. The pass should arrive when the receiver wants the ball.

Push Passing

The push pass is the most common field hockey pass. Mastery of the push technique, which is primarily used to play the ball over distances of 5 to 15 yards, will give accuracy, quicker release time when needed, and complete control over the pace of the ball. Although the push pass does not generate the same ball speed as the hit, it is very effective and accurate. A good push passer can predict when and where the ball will stop rolling. The first essentials of the push technique are accuracy and a quick release. The next essential of the push stroke is variation of pace. Accuracy depends upon correct position of the feet, which balance the body.

To execute the push pass on the forehand side (figure 2.1), point your left shoulder at your target and use the shake hands grip. Placing your body sideways to the line of the pass enables you to transfer your body weight through the front leg. Your center of gravity is lowered during the pass, with your feet a little more than shoulder-width apart. Your head is down and your hands are split on the stick in the shake hands grip. There is no backswing, so your stick must start next to the ball. Keeping the stick next to the ball helps disguise direction and time of release. The face of the stick is closed slightly to keep the ball on the ground. The ball is positioned under your eyes with your weight evenly distributed. Push the ball using the head of the stick as you transfer your body weight to the left or front leg. You should feel as if you were pushing through the ball while controlling the stick with mainly your right hand. The left hand starts the push and the right hand provides direction only. With your hands and stick away from your body, it is very important to follow through with your stick in line with your target.

The push pass on the backhand side (figure 2.2) is used to pass the ball over short distances when there is neither time nor space for moving into a forehand position. To execute the reverse stick push pass, point your right shoulder at your target and grip the stick in a reverse grip position. The ball should be near the front foot so that the stick will be at a 45- to 60-degree angle to the ground when it comes in contact with the ball. The power of the reverse stick push comes from the firm pulling of the right hand. Your head should remain over the ball as you make the pass.

FIGURE 2.1

KEYS TO SUCCESS

FOREHAND PUSH PASSING

a   b   c

Preparation

1. See receiver(s) and opponent(s) ____
2. Quick footwork ____
3. Left foot and shoulder point to target ____
4. Shake hands grip ____
5. Weight balanced over balls of feet; head steady over ball ____
6. Stick next to lower half of ball; face of stick closed slightly ____
7. Ball in control box; focus on ball ____

Execution

1. Transfer weight forward ____
2. Maintain stick next to ball ____
3. Left hand pulls stick forward ____
4. Push through lower half of the ball ____
5. Right hand exerts pressure and direction ____
6. Head steady over path of ball ____
7. Extend arms as left hand goes past left foot ____

Follow-Through

1. Generate momentum through the ball ____
2. Transfer weight through front leg ____
3. Finish with stick/arms extended to target ____
4. Return to ready position ____

FIGURE
2.2   KEYS TO SUCCESS

REVERSE PUSH PASSING

a   b   c

Preparation

1. See receiver(s) and opponent(s) ____
2. Quick footwork ____
3. Right foot and shoulder point to target ____
4. Reverse grip ____
5. Weight balanced over balls of feet; head steady over ball ____
6. Stick next to lower half of ball; face of stick closed slightly ____
7. Ball in control box ____

Execution

1. Transfer weight forward ____
2. Maintain stick next to ball ____
3. Left hand pulls stick forward ____
4. Push through lower half of the ball ____
5. Right hand exerts pressure and direction ____
6. Head steady over path of ball ____
7. Extend arms as right hand goes past right foot ____

Follow-Through

1. Generate momentum through the ball ____
2. Transfer weight through front leg ____
3. Finish with stick/arms extended to target ____
4. Return to ready position ____

Hitting

Players use the hit to move the ball quickly over longer distances and to score simply because of the ball speed this technique generates. The hit, or drive as it sometimes is named, is a striking pattern that is most significant to hockey because (1) the hit beats more opponents with one-ball touch in an instant, (2) the hit uses more hockey real estate when changing the point of attack from sideline to sideline and back line to back line, (3) the hit provides the power to direct the pace and speed of play, which is vital in transitional demands, (4) the hit extends the opportunity to share the ball among your other teammates, which is essential for team play, and (5) the hit is used to score more often than any other hockey passing technique. The

hockey player, of course, must be able to perform all kinds of hits while running with an active ball and when in a free hit situation. The most important aspect of the hit is to pass the ball accurately with the proper speed. The hitter must pass to a selected target and not be afraid to hit short passes firmly. Every hit should have a planned destination and particular target. Therefore, the mechanics of the hit become as important to the player who receives the ball as to the player who hits it.

Hitting a hockey ball requires the hips to move slightly laterally and not rotationally as in the golf swing. It also requires correct foot spacing from the ball, with the left shoulder pointing in the direction of the hit. It is crucial that the hitter obtain the footwork speed and balance to change direction and move into position for hitting. If you are able to consistently perform the proper "foot-to-ball" distance before striking the ball, you will be well on your way to executing the hit that will outperform your opponent. After you prepare your feet in relation to the ball, you are ready to perform a fluid swing using the four action phases of the hit: (1) grip, (2) take back swing, (3) weight transfer and contact, (4) follow-through. Remember that the hit requires you to look before passing!

The position for hitting (figure 2.3) starts with a controlled ball about nine inches in front of and in line with the front foot. The first phase of the hit is the grip, which is the same as the receiving grip (shake hands grip) except the hands are brought together to act in unison to strike the ball. With the hitting grip, make certain your forefinger of the left hand is in contact with your little finger of the right hand. There are three methods to bring the hands together for the hit: (1) The left hand remains near the top of the stick and the right hand is moved up to join. This method is the most commonly used and provides the most leverage for the swing. (2) The right hand remains in its original receiving grip and the left hand moves down to join the right. This method restricts leverage and requires wrist action during the swing. (3) The left hand is moved down and the right hand is moved up to meet each other on the handle in the middle of the shake hands grip. This method combines power and control.

The second action phase of the hit is the take away swing, or the backswing. Your body weight shifts slightly to the back foot/leg/hip as you take your stick back and away from the ball. Keep your head down in line to the ball and your eyes on the bottom half of the ball. Your body remains low with your knees bent and feet shoulder-width apart. The left arm is nearly straight but not rigid on the take away swing, with the right elbow slightly bent close to 90 degrees. The arms swing freely away from your body, coordinating the shoulders and legs for the third phase of the hit.

During the third phase of the hit, your body weight is first transferred to the front leg as your stick sweeps down and through the lower half of the ball. Pulling your left hip and pushing from the rear (right) foot to the front foot initiates the transfer of body weight. This hip pull, or weight transfer, will fluidly bring the straight left arm forward, directing the stick downward into the ball. Your right hand and arm ride on the momentum of the pull from the hips and the relatively straight left arm. Eyes and head stay down to see the base of your stick strike the lower half of the ball. The knees are relaxed and bent while your arms swing freely through the ball. On contact with the ball, the flat face of your stick is at a right angle to the ground and your hands are aligned with your wrists. Inches before contact, the right hand, working in unison with the left, snaps at the ball, with the flat part of the stick making solid contact behind and on the lower half of the ball. The speed of your hands is most significant during this action. Although the lower body—hips and legs—moves first and initiates speed, the arms and hands freely follow and convey that speed through the hit, which gives force to the ball.

In the follow-through phase of the hit, your weight is now relocated to the front leg, with the hands extended out toward the target. After the stick-to-ball contact, continue to give direction to the hit during those few inches after the ball leaves the stick. The ball will surely follow the line or path your stick head enters after those few critical inches from the ball. Continue to finish the follow-through by transporting the stick's momentum until the stick and hands are out in front of the left leg.

**FIGURE
2.3**   **KEYS TO SUCCESS**

HITTING

a   b   c

Preparation

1. Look up and select target ____
2. Short steps, quick footwork ____
3. Left shoulder points toward target; head down and over ball ____
4. Prepare a controlled ball ____
5. Feet 12 inches apart ____
6. Ball in line of left foot ____
7. Weight evenly distributed on balls of feet ____

Execution

1. Bring hands together in shake hands grip ____
2. Transfer weight to back leg ____
3. Keep head down and over ball; knees bent and shoulder-width apart ____
4. Arms: left nearly straight and right elbow tucked ____
5. Weight transfer to front leg/hip on downswing ____
6. Align hands with wrists before contact ____
7. Flat stick head contacts lower half of ball ____

Follow-Through

1. Fluid transfer of weight through front leg ____
2. Knees remain relaxed and bent ____
3. Keep head down and see ball leave stick ____
4. Arms/stick finish in line to target ____
5. Return to ready position ____

Receiving Ground Balls

Receiving the hockey ball means fielding the ball on the stick so that it is instantly brought under control without a rebound. Good receiving mechanics will place the receiver in a multiple-threat position to hold the ball, elude an opponent, pass to a teammate, dribble to free space, or shoot. It is impossible to overemphasize the importance of sound receiving techniques because they are the prelude to ball possession, stickwork, good passing, shooting, and attack tactics.

The essence of receiving (figure 2.4) is to allow the ball to come to the stick, even if you are running to meet the ball/pass. Any forward movement of the stick will promote a rebound. A receiver wants a ball passed accurately to the stick so that it can be trapped and used immediately. Requirements for a quality pass include a smooth rolling ball along the ground and a direct pass with a minimum amount of rolling time. The best position for receiving a ball along the ground is facing parallel to the line of the ball. Receiving ground balls requires that you learn and perform receiving techniques on the right side of the body (referred to as *forehand* receiving) and the left side of your body (*reverse*, or *backhand*, receiving). Because 90 percent of your passing techniques originate from the right side of the body, it is important after reverse receiving to control the ball to the right side of the body to establish a multiple-threat position with the ball.

Good forehand and backhand receiving techniques are the basic tools to help you put together a winning team effort. Use the following list of forehand and reverse receiving principles to receive ground balls.

Forehand Receiving

- Point your left shoulder along the ball's line of direction.
- Always keep both hands on the stick and use the shake hands grip or receiving grip. Lunge with only one hand when time and distance prevent using two hands.
- Body must be balanced with knees bent and your weight evenly distributed on the balls of the feet.
- Keep your head steady and eyes on the ball.
- Bottom of your stick head is still along the ground in your control box.
- Left hand in front of right and in line with the left knee.
- Stick angle is inclined forward 70 degrees to the ground so that a wedge is made between the ground and stick where the ball is allowed to come to the stick. The rebound will be downward from the flat surface of the stick if the stick is inclined forward—the ball moves toward the ground. Grass surfaces or heavier grounds have greater capacity to absorb a rebound, so a more upright stick will suffice. On hard, fast ground or artificial surfaces, a more acute angle of the stick to the ground will be necessary.

- On contact, the hands act as a pillow because skillful receiving requires great sensitivity of touch. Underspin occurs if the ball comes to the stick, and, if you move your stick forward to the ball, topspin occurs away from your stick.
- Keep your stick still and stop the lower half of the rolling ball in your control box. Always receive the ball on the part of the stick where the straight blade of wood meets the ground as if you are using a straight stick without a toe.

Reverse (Backhand) Receiving

Receiving ground balls with the backhand follows forehand receiving principles except for the following techniques:

- Point right shoulder along the ball's line of direction.
- Both hands grasp your stick in a reverse position in which the stick toe faces your feet and the flat side of the stick faces the ball. Lunge with only the left hand gripping the stick when time and distance prevent using the two-handed receiving grip.
- Body balance is the same as forehand receiving.
- Place left hand in front of right and in line with the right knee.
- Once you receive the ball on your left side or reverse, move the ball immediately to your right side in a multiple-threat position.

FIGURE 2.4 **KEYS TO SUCCESS**

RECEIVING GROUND BALLS ON FOREHAND AND REVERSE (BACKHAND)

a

b

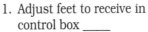

c

Preparation

1. Left shoulder points to oncoming ball (for receiving on reverse, right shoulder points to oncoming ball) ____
2. Move toward ball with short, quick steps ____
3. Shake hands grip (for receiving on reverse, use reverse shake hands grip) ____
4. Weight evenly distributed on balls of feet ____
5. Bottom of stick head on ground; stick wedge 70 degrees forward to ground ____
6. Keep receiving stick still ____
7. Head steady and focus on ball ____

Execution

1. Adjust feet to receive in control box ____
2. Allow ball to come to stick ____
3. Receive on left side of stick and contact lower half of ball on stick blade ____
4. Head steady over and in line of ball ____
5. Control the ball into space away from nearby opponent ____

Follow-Through

1. Maintain body balance ____
2. Head up and watch the field ____
3. Ball next to stick (for receiving on reverse, take ball to right side of body) ____
4. Ready to pass, shoot, or dribble ____

GROUND BALL SUCCESS STOPPERS

Error	Correction
Push Passing	
1. Your push pass comes off the ground.	1. Slightly close the face of your stick where the top of stick blade is ahead of underside of hook. Finish your follow-through with the head of the stick low along the ground.
2. Your pass is inaccurate.	2. Feet must be shoulder-width apart to establish body balance with left shoulder pointing to target. Using a shake hands grip, keep the stick next to the ball, and push the ball using the head of the stick as you transfer your body weight to the left or front leg.
3. You slap at the ball.	3. Start with ball next to stick.
Hitting	
1. You mishit the ball.	1. Keep your head down with eyes on ball instead of target. Maintain bent knees.
2. You undercut or slice the ball.	2. Keep your feet shoulder-width apart and position the ball 9 inches in line with your front foot. Face of stick must be flat at moment of impact. Keep your knees bent.
3. You top the ball or it bounces.	3. Bend your knees and position the ball farther from your feet. Strike the lower half of the ball with the blade square.
4. Your hit is choppy.	4. Position the ball in your control box of the front foot instead of near the back foot and follow through after impact.
5. Your hit has little power or accuracy.	5. Make sure hands are together. Coordinate left hand/arm on downswing and in the transfer of weight through the front leg.
Receiving Ground Balls	
1. Ball goes under your stick.	1. Keep your head down, stick head on the ground, and watch the ball come to your stick. Trap the lower half of the ball.
2. The ball rebounds off your stick.	2. Keep stick still and angle stick forward to create a 70-degree wedge to the ground.
3. Ball hits your feet.	3. Move the stick and hands away from your body.
4. Ball pops up in air off your stick.	4. Relax your shake hands grip and keep knees bent. Distribute weight on balls of feet.

Aerial Balls

Although the best field hockey is played on the ground, an aerial ball is effective in some situations. For example, an opponent may be blocking the passing lane between you and your teammates who are away from the ball (Attack Role 2 or 3). Or you may decide to lift a ball to drop into open space behind the opposing defender. You may even use a lifted pass to score a goal when the opposing goalkeeper drifts too far forward from her goal line or in a penalty stroke situation. On artificial surfaces, a low aerial below the knee is used more often to beat an opponent who plays with his stick low in a horizontal blocking manner. Also, the lofted ball can be useful on heavy, waterlogged grass fields. To take advantage of any situation in which the aerial ball is used, you must become skilled at accurately passing and receiving various heights and speeds of one basic aerial technique, the *flick*. Do not confuse the flick with the nearly obsolete *scoop* pass, which was used years ago on slow, rarely mowed grass fields and before the proliferation of artificial playing surfaces. In the mid-1980s, FIH outlawed lifting a free hit.

Passing Aerial Balls

Skillful players rarely use the aerial pass as a means of attack because the hang time of an aerial assault allows more time for the opponent to reposition and defend. Aerial balls can be used only during open play. A player using the aerial pass will be penalized if she lifts the ball in a manner that causes danger (for example, an aerial ball into the shooting circle). When the aerial ball is passed to an occupied area in which possession is contested by the defender and attacker, the umpire will penalize the passer of the lifted ball as "dangerous" and will award the free hit to the opponent. To avoid the free hit penalty on a high lifted ball, the aerial passing team must remain at least 5 yards from the opponent receiving the aerial ball.

The aerial flick uses the stick to shovel the ball into the air, and if enough coordinated strength is injected into the lifting moment, the ball may be hurled 50 or more yards. Remember, aerial passing is not a substitute for stickwork or passing ability.

Flicking

The flick is a push pass lifted into the air. The flick technique is used to lift the ball at various heights into the air for long or short distances and at a greater speed. Use this technique to play the ball to a teammate over an opponent who is blocking the passing lane. Or, use the flick as an air pass through a narrow gap to surprise an opponent who is expecting to intercept a ground pass. The high flick can be used to lift the ball into the air to make play for tightly marked attack wings. The high flick pass can be dropped into the space behind the opponent where the attack wing can use her speed to run to collect the ball. The most important use of the flick is in penalty strokes or in shooting powerfully at goal.

In executing the flick (figure 2.5), the differences from the push pass are that the face of the stick is open, that your right shoulder is lower, that the ball is slightly ahead of the left foot, and that your stick follow-through varies with the height of the aerial. Your grip is the shake hands grip and your body position can be in front of or parallel to the line of the ball. The parallel position is better for weight transfer. While keeping your head over the ball, drop your right shoulder and insert the lower part of your stick face under the lower half of the ball and prepare to throw the ball into the air. Your right arm exerts power as you transfer body weight from your right leg to your left leg.

Keep your body down low until the ball leaves your stick. The right hand controls direction and speed of the flick by throwing or whipping the ball with the face of the stick from an open stick blade to left stick blade rotation. This whiplike action imparts rapid side topspin onto the ball. Follow through with your hands and stick forward and upward, directing height, distance, and speed to the target. If you want the ball to go knee height, follow through with the right hand in a knee height position. If an overhead height is desired, transfer your weight and follow through higher.

FIGURE
2.5
KEYS TO SUCCESS

FLICKING

a   b   c

Preparation

1. See receiver(s) and opponent(s) ____
2. Short steps, quick footwork ____
3. Left foot and shoulder point to target ____
4. Shake hands grip ____
5. Weight balanced over balls of feet ____
6. Ball positioned in control box slightly ahead of left foot; head steady over ball ____
7. Open stick next to bottom half of ball; focus on ball ____

Execution

1. Drop right shoulder and transfer weight forward ____
2. Maintain open stick next to ball ____
3. Left hand pulls stick forward ____
4. Lift through lower half of the ball ____
5. Right hand exerts pressure and direction ____
6. Head steady over ball ____
7. Extend arms as left hand goes past left foot ____
8. Open to left stick rotation ____

Follow-Through

1. Generate momentum through the ball ____
2. Transfer weight through front leg ____
3. Finish stick toe up and arms extended to target ____
4. Return to ready position ____

Receiving Aerial Balls

You must be able to receive and control balls dropping from the air both while facing the ball and while running forward. Field hockey rules require that the ball be below shoulder height when it is played with the stick. Keep your eyes on the ball and your stick below shoulder level as you use short, quick steps to move into line with ball. If facing an approaching aerial ball to your right or left side, receive in a position similar to a baseball outfielder who readies to catch a fly ball (figure 2.6). When running forward away from the origination of the lifted pass, look over your shoulder on the side the ball is approaching, catch the ball on your fore-

hand or reverse, play it down, and go! Play the ball downward so that it lands close to the right foot, thus generating a multiple-attack threat. Use your shake hands or receiving grip with all aerial receiving.

With a lifted pass approaching your right side, position your left elbow up to keep the blade of the stick horizontally straight and position your right elbow pointing backward, not tucked. Knees are bent with most of your body weight on your right foot. Your right shoulder is in line to the approaching ball. The shaft and facing of your stick are inclined forward so the rebound is directed vertically to the ground. Always position behind the dropping aerial so you can let the ball hit your stick on the shaft below the right hand, knee height or lower. The greater the pace, the more inclined the stick will be with a relaxed grip. The ball is immediately brought under control near your right foot.

For an aerial ball approaching your left side, the stick is held vertically. Your body weight is shifted to the left foot, and your stick is taken across the front of the body with the left elbow well up. Your right elbow points across the body to the right. If a ball is lifted far to your left, a reverse stick is used as in a horizontal position. Once the aerial ball is directed downward, use your stick to check/control the ball before making your next move.

FIGURE 2.6 **KEYS TO SUCCESS**

RECEIVING AERIAL PASSES

a

b

c

Preparation

1. Position behind descending ball ____
2. Shake hands grip ____
3. Raise receiving stick below shoulder level ____
4. Balanced stance with knees bent ____
5. Determine aerial line and prepare horizontal/vertical stick ____
6. Stick wedge 70 degrees forward to ground; steady receiving stick ____
7. Left foot in front of right; head steady and focus on ball ____

Execution

1. Transfer weight to side of approaching aerial ____
2. Receive ball on stick shaft at knee level ____
3. Direct rebound downward ____
4. Place stick behind the ball ____
5. Control ball to right side of body ____

Follow-Through

1. Control the ball into space away from nearby opponent ____
2. Look up to pass, shoot, or dribble ____

AERIAL SUCCESS STOPPERS

It takes time to master the passing and receiving techniques of aerial balls. Successful execution requires confidence, proper technique, and a great deal of practice. Most errors that occur when passing and receiving aerial balls can be attributed to improper stick position and foot distance from the ball, poor balance, or both. The following is a review of performance errors that occur when passing and receiving aerial balls and suggestions of how to correct them.

Error	Correction
Aerial Passing	
1. Height of pass is too low.	1. Contact the lower half of the ball with face of open stick and lift the ball upward. Stick follow-through is high.
2. Poor accuracy.	2. Left shoulder and foot point to the target, and your stick follows line of ball toward the target.
3. Your pass is too short.	3. Keep your head over the ball as you generate the lifting action. Extend your arms/ stick forward and upward and use a complete follow-through motion toward your target.
Aerial Receiving	
1. The ball bounces forward off your stick and out of your range of control.	1. Keep your stick still and incline shaft of stick forward to rebound the ball down to the ground at your feet. Ball-to-stick contact is above the stick's head and below the right hand at knee height.
2. The ball pops up and over your body or hits your body or stick handle.	2. Prepare your feet using quick, short adjustment steps. Transfer weight to side of approaching aerial ball. Watch the ball drop below waist and onto the shaft-to-head portion of the stick.
3. Body too close to ball and ball bounces out of control upon contact.	3. Break down your run into short, quick steps to balance your attack stance. Ready a horizontal or vertical stick using a shake hands grip.

PASSING AND RECEIVING DRILLS

1. Rebound Board Passing

Position yourself with a ball approximately 5 yards from a rebound board or goal cage with an 18-inch board. Use the forehand push to pass the ball off the board so it rebounds back to you. Receive and control each rebound on either the forehand or reverse side; then immediately pass it off the board again. This is commonly referred to as "two-touch" passing—control the ball with your first touch and pass it with the second touch.

Success Goal = 30 of 40 two-touch passes off the board without error _____

Success Check
- Short, quick steps _____
- Left shoulder pointing to target _____
- Stick still to allow ball to come to stick _____
- Push the lower half of the ball _____

To Increase Difficulty
- Move 10 yards from board.
- Increase speed of repetition.
- Receive all passes on the reverse side.
- Hit every pass.

To Decrease Difficulty
- Move closer to the board.
- Allow three touches to receive and pass the ball.
- Receive all passes on your forehand side.

2. Rapid Partner Pass

Stand with your left shoulder side pointing to a partner 7 yards away. Position two cones to represent a goal 2 yards wide. Attempt to pass a ball back and forth as rapidly as possible through the cones using the forehand push pass. Receive and control each pass on the forehand side. Award one team point for each ball passed between the cones using only two touches. Play for 30 seconds. Compare your point total against other pairs of teammates. Repeat for five rounds.

Success Goal = Score the most points _____

Success Check
- Use short, quick steps _____
- Ball played in control box _____
- Stick remains still _____
- Contact lower half of the ball _____
- First touch to receive, second touch to pass _____

To Increase Difficulty
- Increase distance to 10 yards.
- Increase time to 60 seconds per round.
- Reduce goal width to 1 yard.
- Receive on the reverse and pass on the forehand.

To Decrease Difficulty
- Decrease passing distance to 5 yards.
- Allow three touches to receive and pass the ball.
- Increase goal width to 3 yards.

3. Lift to Partner

Face a teammate at a distance of 10 yards. Flick a stationary ball chest high or lower to your partner. Partner receives the ball and then returns the ball to you with a forehand push pass. Execute 15 flicks to partner's right side and 15 flicks to partner's left side. Change roles with your partner.

Success Goal for Aerial Pass =
10 of 15 flicks to partner's right side _____
10 of 15 flicks to partner's left side _____

Success Goal for Receiving = 20 of
30 balls to the proper sides controlled and dropped to feet within range of control _____

Success Check
• Short, quick steps _____
• Open stick next to ball _____
• Left shoulder and hip to target _____
• Push and lift stick from underneath ball _____
• Follow through with height of stick _____

To Increase Difficulty
• Decrease flick distance to 5 yards to lower pass to knee height.
• Lift a rolling ball to partner's left side only.

To Decrease Difficulty
• Allow partner to catch the flick pass in hands using a tennis ball.
• Allow partner to hand toss the aerial ball.

4. Partner Hit Passing

Position yourself 15 yards from a teammate. Use the forehand hit technique to pass a ball back and forth along the ground to your partner. Use only two touches to receive and pass the ball. Receive the ball with either forehand or reverse. Perform 20 passes. The player receiving the pass should not have to move more than 2 yards in any direction to collect the ball.

Success Goal =
16 of 20 passes accurately passed within 2 yards of your partner _____
17 of 20 balls received and returned to partner using only two touches _____

Success Check
• Short, quick steps _____
• Point left shoulder to target _____
• Keep stick still on receiving _____
• Hands together on hit _____

To Increase Difficulty
• Use two cones to place a goal 2 yards wide in the center of the passing line.
• Increase passing distance.
• Receive with reverse only.

To Decrease Difficulty
• Reduce passing distance.
• Allow three-touch passing.
• Hit and receive only on the forehand side.

5. Hit at Various Targets

Set up five goals at various angles 15 yards away from two stacks of 10 balls. Position two cones to represent each of the five goals 2 yards wide. Stand between the two ball stacks located 3 yards on your right and left sides. Run to a stack of balls and prepare to hit one ball to any of the five targets. After hit passing a ball, run to the other ball stack and control the ball and again hit to any of the targets. Continue for 15 seconds. Award point for each accurate pass through a target. Compare your point total against other teammates. Repeat for five rounds.

Success Goal = Score the most points ____

Success Check
- Short, quick steps ____
- Prepare ball in control box in front of left foot ____
- Left shoulder to target ____
- Hands together for hitting ____
- Contact lower half of ball ____

To Increase Difficulty
- Increase passing distance.
- Increase time to 30, 45, or 60 seconds per round.
- Have partners pass the ball from ball stacks.
- Reduce goal width to 1 yard.

To Decrease Difficulty
- Decrease hit-passing distance to 10 yards.
- Push pass to targets.
- Increase goal width to 3 yards.

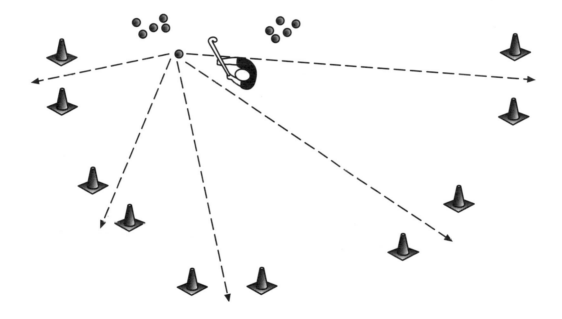

6. Partner Reverse Receiving and Passing

Set up a 2-yard-by-7-yard square using four cones. Stand with your right shoulder pointing to a partner 7 yards away on the outside of the opposite side of the square. Attempt to receive on your reverse or backhand side a forehand push pass from your partner. After reverse receiving, pull and control the ball to your forehand side by moving 2 yards to your right, and forehand pass the ball back to your partner on the outside of the cones. Always pass the ball on the outside of the square. Award one team point for each ball received on reverse and passed on forehand outside the square to partner. Play for 30 seconds. Compare your point total against other pairs of teammates. Repeat for five rounds.

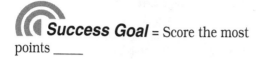**Success Goal** = Score the most points _____

Success Check

- Short, quick steps _____
- Receive with still, inclined stick _____
- Right shoulder to partner's pass _____
- Hands split on stick _____
- Stick next to lower half of ball _____

To Increase Difficulty

- Increase passing distance.
- Hit pass instead of push.
- Increase time to 45 or 60 seconds.
- Receive on forehand and move to left direction to pass from the forehand.

To Decrease Difficulty

- Decrease push passing distance.
- Decrease time.
- Receive and pass on the forehand side only.

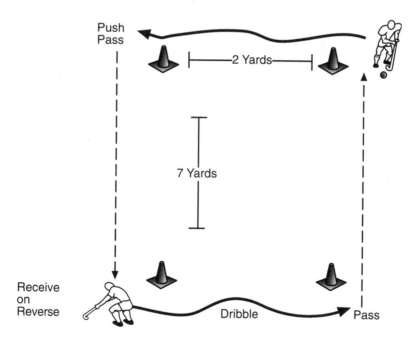

Push Pass

2 Yards

7 Yards

Receive on Reverse

Dribble

Pass

7. Receiving Box With Pressure

Outline an area of approximately 20 yards square and play with at least three teammates. Set up a "receiving" square using four cones or spot markers centered at the back of the playing area. Use cones to represent two goals each 2 yards wide, randomly 10 yards on each side of the receiving square. You start 5 yards on the outside of the receiving square with a defender starting 5 more yards behind you. A teammate positioned 10 yards in front of the square has six balls and passes you a ball as you run into the receiving square. Score a point for each pass that is received and passed accurately through the 2-yard target before the defender tags you. If you are tagged before you have passed the ball, your pass through the target is not counted. The defender is permitted to pursue when the receiver initially moves in any direction. Try to use only two touches to receive and pass the ball. Execute five rounds of six balls, alternating Attack and Defense Roles after each round. Compare your score with those of your teammates. Use any of the ground-pass techniques discussed in Step 2.

Success Goal = Score the most points or 4 out of 6 during each round _____

Success Check
- Short, quick steps _____
- Receive the ball without a rebound on your first touch _____
- Control ball into space away from defender _____
- Pass the ball quickly and accurately while balanced _____

To Increase Difficulty
- Decrease distance defender starts from receiver.
- Increase passing distance from square to targets.
- Decrease width size of targets.
- All passes have to be hit.
- Receive all passes on reverse.
- Increase number of balls per round.

To Decrease Difficulty
- Reduce passing distance.
- Increase width size of targets.
- Passers only use push passes.
- Increase distance defender starts from receiver.
- Eliminate defender.

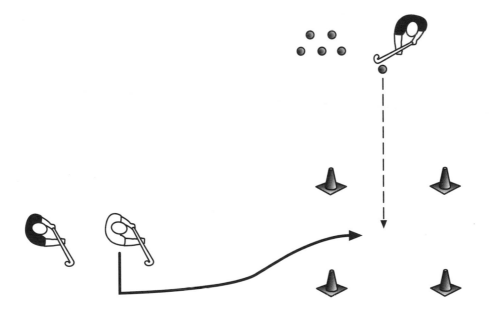

8. Tennis Hockey

Play in an area 15 yards wide and 20 yards long. Mark the area with cones at the corners and centerline. Divide into teams of two and position on opposite halves of playing area. Flip a coin to determine which team gets to serve first. To serve, you must hit or push pass the ball over the centerline from behind the back line. To score a point, the serving team or receiving team must successfully hit or push the ball out of the reach of the opponent(s) and over their back line. The receiving team attempts to receive the serve, and using only two touches, passes the ball back to the server's side of playing area. Use tennis scoring; the first team to score four points wins the game and the first team to win six games wins the set. Play one set and challenge another pair.

A point is awarded when

■ the serve or return goes out-of-bounds over the sideline;

■ the receiving team uses more than two touches when playing the ball; or

■ a player uses her body to stop or control the ball.

Success Goal = Win 6 games in the set before the opponent ____

Success Check
- Short, quick breakdown steps ____
- Look up before passing ____
- Control lower half of ball ____
- Prepare receiving technique early ____
- Prepare passing technique early ____

To Increase Difficulty
- Increase playing area.
- Allow aerial lifts.
- Play the best of 3 sets.

To Decrease Difficulty
- Increase number of players per team.
- Allow three touches to return the ball.

PASSING AND RECEIVING SUCCESS SUMMARY

The ultimate goal of every field hockey team is to play together as a unit. To achieve this goal, each team member must possess solid passing and receiving skills. Beginners should start by practicing passing and receiving without the pressure of time, opponents, and the restriction of space. This will permit a higher concentration on the correct skill. As your technical skills improve, progress to more game-related training by adding limited pressure of time and opponent(s) and begin to restrict space for passing and receiving. Eventually you will be able to execute in the full-sided game the Attack Role 1 techniques of passing and receiving.

STEP 3

BALL CONTROL AND DRIBBLING: EXPANDING YOUR TECHNIQUE (ATTACK ROLE 1)

After receiving the ball from a teammate or intercepting an opponent's pass, you must execute good individual ball-possession skills that will give your team more time and space to be successful. The next Attack Role 1 techniques to learn are the vital individual skills of ball control and dribbling. To be a successful field hockey player, you must build up speed in moving the ball with your stick because stickwork is the essence of these skills.

Ball control must not be confused with receiving and passing. Ball control consists of the skilled movement(s) of the ball that accompany your footwork, your changes of direction, and your body swerve and balance. Most importantly, ball control means the ability to keep the ball close to your stick. The loss of ball control adversely affects the decision and the execution of your next move. Your next move may be a pass, a dribble, or a shot on goal depending on the situation and, of course, your ability to get the ball under your control.

There are two basic ball-control techniques—the ball check and the drop step. The *ball check* brings the ball under control when it scampers outside your control box. It is used to slow or stop the ball from running away or to change directions during dribbling. The *drop step* moves the ball back and away from the opponent while keeping the ball next to your stick. A successfully executed drop step provides more space between the Attack Role 1 player and the opposing defender, which provides more valuable time for your next attack move.

Dribbling is virtually stickwork on the run. Running with the ball, or dribbling, serves the same purpose as dribbling in soccer or basketball—it allows you to keep possession of the ball by moving play into open areas of the field away from opponents, it creates space for teammates to use, and it leads to goal-scoring opportunities. Use the dribble to beat an opponent in the attacking zone near the opponent's goal. Penetrating this area of the field while maintaining ball possession will provide goal-scoring chances. Keep in mind that excessive dribbling does not promote team play. Resist dribbling to take on opponents in the defending zone

nearest your own goal. Loss of possession in this area can lead to a scoring opportunity for the opponent!

Four dribbling techniques are important in game situations—the power dribble, the speed dribble, the Indian dribble, and the spin dribble. The *power dribble* is used to maintain possession of the ball in tight crowded spaces. The *speed dribble* is used to advance the ball into open spaces on a straight or diagonal line. The most emphasized and effective element in speed dribbling is to "cut" the ball on a diagonal line to the open space, which moves the opponent laterally. The most advanced dribbling skill is the *Indian dribble*, which is used to disguise the dribbler's next move. When executed correctly with control and speed, the Indian dribble misfoots the opponent with its back and forth forehand-to-reverse stick movement. The *spin dribble* is used to protect the ball while moving away from the nearest opponent who is blocking your desired forward space.

Why Are Ball-Control and Dribbling Skills Important?

The best means of attack is to possess the ball! Without possession of the ball, your team cannot score goals. The ability to control the ball to execute a multiple-attack threat and to beat opponents in one-on-one situations, particularly in the attacking half of the field, and the ability to prevent defenders from gaining ball possession are crucial to individual and team success.

The aim of ball control is to sidestep and sway with the ball from a stationary or running position. To get under control by getting the ball in position for your next move in the shortest amount of time requires a consistent relationship with the ball, your feet, and the stick. The criterion for strong ball control is that the ball must be next to your stick and in a push position. This position will enable you to look up to pass or dribble or elude the advancing opponent. In field hockey, it is difficult to isolate the relationship that exists between your footwork, your body balance, your running speed, and your ball control. Handling your stick with a ball establishes the necessary stickwork for ball-control and dribbling skills and, subsequently, demands daily attention. There is no shortcut to acquiring efficient stickwork for ball-control and dribbling skills that demand coordination of footwork and balance, concentration, and a light touch of your stick to the ball.

How to Execute Ball-Control/Stickwork Skills

The basis of ball control/stickwork is moving the ball from left to right by means of a reverse stick. This requires that the stick be turned over the top of the ball. You must learn to turn the stick because field hockey rules prevent the use of the rounded side—right side—to control or pass the ball. The two ball-control techniques—the ball check and the drop step—use a split grip with a changeable "V" of the left hand. The left hand turns and controls the stick. The right hand's function is to allow the stick to be turned by the left hand and occasionally add power. Before learning dribbling, hockey players should practice sidestepping to the left and right, diagonally forward to the right, and diagonally back to the right and left—the *drop step*. When your ball-control techniques improve, practice against the pressure of an opponent. The greater the speed of an approaching opponent, the smaller the sidestep. If the opponent is more cautious, your stickwork and sidestep distance must increase.

The Ball Check

Never move the ball into such a position that it becomes more readily available to your opponent than to you.

The ball check, or sudden stop, is a ball-control technique that prevents the ball from running away from your control box and into the opponent's reach (figure 3.1). It is also useful for the Attack Role 1 (AR1) player to control a through ball and to "stop and go" with all dribbling techniques.

Whether you are stationary or running, the ball check can be executed from various directional ball movements. The "left-to-right" and "right-to-left" ball movements are coordinated with sidesteps, body swerves, weaving, and hesitations, constantly integrated with the ball-check technique. The ball check also accompanies the drop step ball-control movement in which the ball and stick follow a diagonal line backward.

To execute the ball check, the ball is positioned in your control box where it can be momentarily halted so that your control, balance, and coordination are unified. Keep your stick near the lower half of the ball, and prepare to change your left hand from the shake hands grip to the back of the stick. With the shake hands grip with toe of stick pointing upward, the forefinger and the thumb of both hands form a "V" shape that points downward along the edge of the stick. To execute ball-control and dribbling techniques, the changeable "V" of the left hand adjusts a quarter turn to the right and runs down the back side of the stick. To momentarily halt the roll of the ball, you must place the facing of the stick on the lower half of the ball while maintaining the 12-inch to 18-inch ball-to-feet distance. A ball check on the reverse side should be immediately followed by a ball-control movement to the right side of your body so that you are ready to pass, dribble, or shoot.

FIGURE
3.1
KEYS TO SUCCESS

THE BALL CHECK

a

b

c

Preparation

1. Receive with short steps, quick footwork ____
2. Split grip with left hand adjusted ____
3. Ball in control box ____
4. Feet shoulder-width apart ____
5. Knees flexed, body slightly crouched ____
6. Head down, eyes see ball ____

Execution

1. Quick glances at opponent ____
2. Left hand turns stick ____
3. Allow stick to rotate in right hand ____
4. Ball 12 inches from left or right foot ____
5. Check ball movement ____

Follow-Through

1. Move ball to right side of body ____
2. Change "Vs" to shake hands grip ____
3. Ready to pass, dribble, or shoot ____

The Drop Step

The drop step is an individual ball-control technique that coordinates ball movement in a forward-to-back direction away from the opposing defender. It is used to make space for the ballcarrier—AR1. The more space you have between you and the opponent, the more time you have to execute the skill of passing.

To execute the drop step, you must time your drop step move with a hip turn to the left or right to coincide with the defender's forward commitment (figure 3.2). If the opponent has time to change direction and tackle the ball, you executed the drop step too soon. The key to the successful performance of any ball-control skill that involves a change of direction and change of pace is moving the ball along with the foot and maintaining consistent ball-from-feet distance. As in the ball check, you must change the "V" of your left hand grip so that the left hand turns your stick. Keep your knees bent and feet shoulder-width apart for body balance. Your head stays over the ball positioned in your control box in line with the right or left foot, and your stick remains next to the lower half of the ball. If drop stepping to your right, your right foot and ball are simultaneously moved diagonally back by transferring your body weight from your left to right foot. The left drop step transfers your weight from your right foot to your left. The drop step should be followed by a ball check to prevent the ball from going beyond the foot. When executing a left drop step, immediately move the ball to the right side of your body to prepare for a multiple-attack threat.

FIGURE 3.2 **KEYS TO SUCCESS**

THE DROP STEP

 a

 b

 c

Preparation

1. Receive with short steps, quick footwork ____
2. Split grip with left hand adjusted ____
3. Ball in control box ____
4. Feet shoulder-width apart ____
5. Knees flexed, body slightly crouched ____
6. Head down, eyes see ball ____
7. Stick next to lower half of ball ____

Execution

1. Quick glances at approaching opponent ____
2. Simultaneously push ball and transfer weight to back foot ____
3. Left hand turns stick; allow stick to rotate in right hand ____
4. Ball kept 12 inches from left/right foot ____
5. Stick on lower half of ball ____
6. Check ball movement ____

Follow-Through

1. Move ball to the right side of body ____
2. Keep stick on lower half of ball ____
3. Shake hands grip ____
4. Ready to pass, dribble, or shoot ____

BALL-CONTROL SUCCESS STOPPERS

Slight errors in judgment or technique can result in loss of ball possession when in a restricted space. Most ball-control errors are due to incorrect stickhandling in changing grips, poor body balance, inadequate footwork, the inconsistent relationship of the ball to the feet, and the poor judgment of opponent's positioning. It is important to maintain as much space as possible between the ball and your nearest opponent. To do so you must constantly readjust your position in response to the challenger's movements. Common ball-control errors are discussed here, along with suggested corrections.

Error	Correction
The Ball Check	
1. You lose control of the ball.	1. Split your hands farther apart and bend your knees more. Position the ball away from your feet about 12 to 18 inches so you can see it in your control box. Your left hand controls and turns your stick. Keep your head steady over the ball and eyes on the ball.
2. You are snatching at the ball on the upper half of ball.	2. Move the ball away from your feet and keep the ball in your control box, in line with and in front of your feet.
3. You lose the ball on your reverse stick side.	3. The ball must be within your control box and not be allowed to pass your left foot. Keep your stick near the lower half of the ball, and use your left hand to turn the stick counterclockwise.
The Drop Step	
1. Your stick is slower than the ball.	1. Control is primary, and speed is secondary. Keep your stick close (less than 1 inch) from the lower half of the ball. Use your left hand to turn the stick; the right hand allows stick to turn.
2. Approaching opponent has time to change direction and tackle you.	2. Your foot and ball must move at the same time to coincide with defender's forward commitment to tackle.
3. The ball gets too close to your feet or outside your control box.	3. Keep the ball in your control box in line with your feet and about 12 inches to 18 inches from your feet. Move your foot first to start ball movement.

How to Execute Dribbling

Although passing is the best and most effective way of beating an opponent, it is necessary to use individual Attack Role 1 technique of dribbling to set up attack play. Even if dribbling is easier to learn and to coach than passing, close ball-control and efficient stickwork abilities will enhance the field hockey player's dribbling.

All dribbling techniques contain several common elements found in ball-control movements. In addition to the close control of the ball, these include sudden change of direction and speed, body swerves and fakes, and deceptive sidesteps. Inside attack players need closer stickwork and dribbling techniques because of the frequently encountered tight spaces. The outside attack players have more open space, so dribbling speed with the ball check must be developed.

The most effective way to acquire dribbling skills is through practice. Repeated practice will get you familiar with the ball at the base of the stick and will develop awareness of control. You will need strong back and leg muscles because the body is crouched while running. Your weight is on the power points of your feet so that there is a lightness in movement. You must keep your head down and eyes on the ball but be able to take quick glances at the opponent to evaluate her distance, the state of balance, and position. To keep the ball close to your stick in the control box, you must run with a low enough center of gravity. To coordinate the stickwork with changing direction while running with the ball requires you to improve your footwork. Remember, your speed of execution of dribbling techniques will only develop as your ball control increases.

There are two basic levels of dribbling—the fundamental level and the advanced level. The fundamental level consists of one dribbling technique called the speed dribble, which is used for open field runs with the ball. The advanced level consists of three dribbling techniques, which use both the forehand and the reverse stick positions—the power dribble, the Indian dribble, and the spin dribble.

The Speed Dribble

The speed dribble is sometimes named the open field, or forehand dribble. The object of the speed dribble is to run with the ball into open field space to gain ground and move the opponent. The speed dribble can be a straight-line run, or more effectively, it can be "cut" on a diagonal line (see figure 3.3) forward. Cutting the ball or dribbling on a diagonal laterally moves the opponent, freeing the forward penetration through spaces closer to goal.

To execute the speed dribble, the ball is restricted to the forehand side or right side of the body three to four inches outside of the right foot so that your running action is not impeded. Use the shake hands grip and keep the stick head close behind or next to the ball. When dribbling on an artificial surface, always keep the blade of the stick beneath and in constant contact to the ball, which requires a lower running posture. On rough grass surfaces, your stick must be more vertical, with your left hand slightly inclined in front of the right. From this stick position, tap or push the ball forward as you run. It is very important to maintain a low running position to avoid losing contact with the ball. Running at maximum speed naturally places your body in a more upright position, which may force your stick too far from the ball, resulting in diminished ball control.

To pass to the left from the speed dribble, move the ball to the front of the left foot. When you pass from the speed dribble, the speed of the dribble must be reduced to execute a quality pass. Always practice using various speeds, but remember, skill is primary and speed is secondary as you practice to unify both. If speed is emphasized as most important, your level of skill will be reduced.

FIGURE 3.3 | **KEYS TO SUCCESS**

THE SPEED DRIBBLE

Preparation

1. Receive ball ____
2. Body slightly crouched ____
3. Use shake hands grip ____
4. Ball to right of body ____
5. Stick behind and close to ball ____
6. Glance up to see field ____

a

Execution

1. Focus on ball ____
2. Contact lower half of ball ____
3. Push/tap ball ahead outside of right foot ____

b

Follow-Through

1. Head up for good field vision ____
2. Accelerate with ball on right side ____
3. Push ball ahead ____

c

The Power Dribble

When opponent(s) crowd the area of the field where AR1 has the ball or when a one-on-one move is needed to beat a Defense Role 1 player, use the power dribble to create additional space. The power dribble uses forehand and reverse stick positions and allows development of the change of direction. When you develop into a talented power dribbler, you will resemble a coordinated bundle of ball, stick, and person efficient in changing direction and speed while the ball remains glued to your stick.

To execute the power dribble, push or silently tap the lower half of the ball in unison with your directional footwork. The ball never loses contact with the blade of the stick (figure 3.4). Compared to the speed dribble, a lower body posture is necessary for proper footwork to coordinate the power dribble. The position of the left hand is vital as it must be changed drastically from receiving, pushing, hitting, and speed dribbling. The left hand holds the stick near the top handle and does all the work in turning the stick from a right to left (counterclockwise) and back to right movement. The right hand does not firmly grip the stick, only the fingers and thumb of the right hand encircle and hold the stick in a relaxed position about 5 1/2 to 7 inches below the left hand. The right hand grips the stick only to support the left hand when moving the ball on backhand and forehand sides. Relax your right hand grip when the left hand rotates the stick over the top of the ball. The "V" formed by the left thumb and forefinger must be moved toward the back of the handle so changes of direction and speed can be successfully developed.

FIGURE 3.4 **KEYS TO SUCCESS**

THE POWER DRIBBLE

a

b

c

Preparation

1. Receive ball next to stick ____
2. Knees flexed ____
3. Crouched position with low center of gravity ____
4. Lead with head over ball ____
5. Glance eyes up to see field ____

Execution

1. Change grip of left hand ____
2. Stick next to lower half of ball ____
3. Deceptive sidesteps, body swerves with taps of ball ____
4. Control ball with stick turn over top of ball ____
5. Allow stick to rotate in right hand ____
6. Ball in control box ____
7. Change speed, direction, or both ____

Follow-Through

1. Maintain stick close to ball ____
2. Accelerate away from opponent ____
3. Look up ready to pass or shoot ____

The Indian Dribble

The basis for all advanced skills in field hockey are initiated by the stick in the reverse position. The Indian dribble, or zigzag, is a more advanced development of the reverse stick. The object of the Indian dribble is to wrong-foot the opponent by sweeping or zigzagging the ball across in front of your feet in both directions. Moving the ball from side to side—forehand to backhand and vice versa—combines the elements of successful ball control and stickwork.

To execute the Indian dribble, use the split grip with the "V" of left hand near the back of the stick handle (figure 3.5). The feet remain shoulder-width apart with bent knees; the body is crouched slightly. The ball position is 18 to 24 inches from your feet when running with the ball. If slowed or stationary, the ball distance from the feet is 12 inches. Keep the ball out in front of you where you can see it. The head remains still and leads the upper body forward to the ball. The stick must move faster than the ball when it is turned over the top of the ball because it must reach a position to check the ball's zig or zag movement *before* the ball arrives. The zigzag ball movement involves total coordination of stick, ball, and feet. When the ball is in front of the right foot, your weight is on your right leg. The ball is dragged to your left foot and your left foot now bears your body weight.

Your stick contacts the lower half of the ball, which improves the speed of the Indian-dribbling skill. Your stick must embrace the ball no more than 1/2 inch from the ball. It is important to concentrate on the left foot as your left side boundary when keeping the ball within the bounds of your control box or limits of your advancing feet. However, there are moments in which you take the ball beyond your feet, such as a change of direction or to evade an opponent.

In a stationary position, top players perform the zigzag move more than 90 times in 60 seconds. Using lots of concentration and correct technique, you can perform more than 50 zigzags in one minute. If you are inspired and determined to work hard, the Indian dribble can be a very dangerous and glamorous attack technique for you.

FIGURE 3.5 **KEYS TO SUCCESS**

THE INDIAN DRIBBLE

a   b   c

Preparation

1. Receive ball ____
2. Feet shoulder-width apart ____
3. Knees bent, body crouched ____
4. Head leading ____
5. Ball in control box lane ____
6. Split grip ____

Execution

1. Change "V" position of left hand ____
2. Glance eyes up ____
3. Quick, short forward strides or sidesteps ____
4. Stick on lower half of the ball ____
5. Work ball with silent embracing tap movement ____
6. Ball checked within bounds of advancing feet ____
7. Keep correct angle of zigzags ____

Follow-Through

1. Dribble within limits of own advancing feet ____
2. Keep ball in front ____
3. Follow ball with ease ____

The Spin Dribble

The spin dribble is used to protect the ball while pivoting or turning away from a defender who is blocking the forward space. As with all dribbling techniques, proper positioning of your body in relation to the ball and the opponent is very important. Establish a pivot foot and position sideways, assume a slightly crouched posture, and spin dribble or drag the ball in the direction—forehand or reverse—farthest from the opponent (figure 3.6). In the crouched position, you have a wide support base and can create greater distance between the opponent and the ball. In field hockey, the Attack Role 1 player—the player with the ball—may not stand still and shield the ball, which is an obstruction foul. To avoid the penalty, you must pivot and move with the ball immediately away from the Defense Role 1 player.

FIGURE 3.6 **KEYS TO SUCCESS**

THE SPIN DRIBBLE

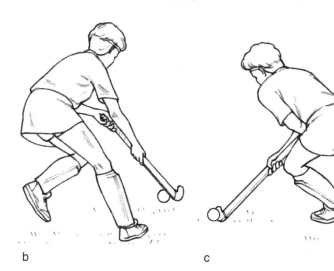

a   b   c

Preparation

1. Close control of ball ____
2. Position to pivot or turn ____
3. Crouched posture, knees flexed ____
4. Head down ____
5. Eyes glance up to see opponent ____

Execution

1. Use body fakes and deceptive sidesteps ____
2. Control ball in directional pivot/turn ____
3. Maintain ball control with reverse/forehand stickhandling ____
4. Maintain base of support during pivot ____
5. Alternate vision from ball to opponent ____
6. Maintain correct ball-from-feet distance ____

Follow-Through

1. Readjust body position in response to opponent ____
2. Accelerate away from opponent ____
3. Maintain close control ____
4. Prepare to pass or shoot ____

DRIBBLING SUCCESS STOPPERS

Slight errors in judgment or technique may result in loss of possession when dribbling the ball in open or crowded spaces. Most dribbling errors are due to incorrect handling of the stick, poor body balance, inadequate footwork, erratic relationship of the feet to the ball, and poor judgment of the opponent's positioning.

It is important to achieve penetration while maintaining possession of the ball. To do so you must constantly change direction and speed with your dribble in response to the challenger's movements and available free spaces. Common dribbling errors are discussed here, along with suggested corrections.

Error	Correction
Speed Dribble	
1. You kick the ball with your feet.	1. The ball must be ahead on the right side of your body 3 to 4 inches outside of the right foot, not restricting your run.
2. You are chasing after your uncontrolled, rolling dribble.	2. Lower your body posture so that you can keep your stick close to the lower half of the ball.
Power Dribble	
1. Loss of ball control.	1. Your hands are too close together and body too upright. Position the ball away from your feet so you can see the ball.
2. Pushing or tapping ball on the upper half of the ball.	2. Ball should be positioned 12 to 24 inches from your feet in your control box; concentrate on touching the lower half of the ball.
3. Stick is slow and clumsily handled.	3. Allow the stick to rotate in your right hand while your left hand turns the stick.
Indian Dribble	
1. Weak left-to-right movement.	1. On the reverse stick side, check the ball and keep ball from passing outside the left foot.
2. Your zigzag dribble escapes on your backhand side.	2. Turn your stick counterclockwise so it is in position to touch the lower half of ball before the ball arrives.
3. Loss of dribbling speed and overreaching for ball.	3. The ball is too far from your feet and outside your control box. Place your stick on the lower half of the ball and keep it embracing ball.
4. You are dribbling the top half of the ball.	4. Do not lift your stick over the ball higher than 1/2 inch.
Spin Dribble	
1. You run into the defender.	1. Begin your sideways position to pivot/turn away from the defender a few yards sooner.
2. The umpire calls you for obstruction.	2. Keep moving with the ball *away* from the nearest defender.
3. Ball hits your feet.	3. Stick and hands too close to your body.

BALL-CONTROL AND DRIBBLING DRILLS

1. 15-Yard Repeat Dribble

Set up two cones 15 yards apart. Using the speed dribble and ball check, start at one cone and dribble as fast as you can past the other cone. Stop your dribble with a ball check and turn to return using the speed dribble to the start cone. Count each 15-yard dribble without error as one point. An error occurs if the ball rolls out of your control as you dribble or ball check. Do as many as you can in 20 seconds. Repeat five times.

**Success Goal** = Score the most points _____

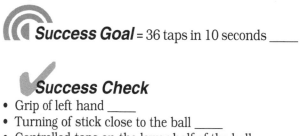**Success Check**
• Use short, quick steps _____
• Stick next to lower half of ball _____
• Ball on right side of body _____
• Slow down with ball check and turn _____

To Increase Difficulty
• Increase dribbling distance.
• Increase time to 30 seconds.
• Set up obstacles between cones and use power dribble through obstacles.
• Spin dribble before reaching each cone.

To Decrease Difficulty
• Decrease dribbling distance.
• Decrease trips to 15 seconds.

2. Stationary Right-to-Left and Left-to-Right Stickwork

Start in a stationary position with feet shoulder-width apart. Place a ball 12 inches in front of your feet and in line with the right foot. Grip your stick with your left hand using the reverse grip where the "V" is on the back of the stick. Add your relaxed right hand. Place your stick on the right side of the ball and begin to tap the lower half of the ball to the left and back to the right, keeping the ball in the boundary lane in front of your feet—your control box. Tap or push the ball, then turn your stick counterclockwise over the top of the ball to tap it back to the right. Your stick distance from the ball should only be one to two inches. Your aim is to increase the speed of your stick as control develops. Count the number of taps you perform without error in 10 seconds. Errors consist of the ball being tapped outside your left or right foot or when your stick is greater than two inches from the ball. Do 10 rounds of 10 seconds.

Success Goal = 36 taps in 10 seconds _____

Success Check
• Grip of left hand _____
• Turning of stick close to the ball _____
• Controlled taps on the lower half of the ball _____
• Ball remains in control box _____

To Increase Difficulty
• Increase time.
• Walk, jog, or run while tapping.

To Decrease Difficulty
• Decrease time.
• Decrease number of repetitions.

3. Box Exercise for Stickwork

Using four cones, set up a 3-yard-by-3-yard box or square. Start with a ball on the outside of the box. Keep your stick on the ball as you move your feet with the ball. The object is to move the ball and both feet to the inside of the box and back out on a different side from which you enter. Do 20 sides and score one point for each successful ball-control movement through the sides of the box without error. An error occurs when you lose control of the ball outside your range of control.

 **Success Goal** = 16 of 20 ____

✔ **Success Check**
• Short, quick steps ____
• Maintain balance and ball control ____

 To Increase Difficulty
• Add a defender who pressures on the outside or inside of the box.
• Decrease box size.
• Do timed executions.

To Decrease Difficulty
• Increase box size.
• Reduce number of attempts.

4. Faking With Ball Control

Set up two cones 5 yards apart along a line on the hockey field or in a gymnasium. Stand with a ball on one side of the line midway between the cones while a teammate (defender) faces you without a ball on the opposite side of the line. Your objective is to dribble the ball laterally to one cone or the other before the defender can get there. The defender tries to react instantly to your every move so that you cannot beat her to a cone with the ball. Use body fakes, deceptive sidesteps, and quick change of speed and direction to unbalance the defender. Neither player is allowed to cross the center line between the cones at any time during the exercise. You score a point each time you dribble and stop the ball at a cone before the defender can establish position there. Play for two minutes; switch roles and play again. Play a total of six games, three as the dribbler and three as the defender.

 **Success Goal** = Most total points in three games as the dribbler ____

✔ **Success Check**
• Keep stick next to ball ____
• Sudden changes of speed and direction ____
• Deceptive body and sidestep moves ____
• Body control and balance ____
• Distance ball from feet ____
• Ball check ____

 To Increase Difficulty
• Increase distance between cones to 8 to 10 yards.
• Increase number of games.

To Decrease Difficulty
• Decrease distance between cones.

5. Ball Check and Drop Step

Set up one row of three cones 2 yards apart. Start 2 yards from first cone with a ball next to your stick. Take the ball forward to the first cone and check the ball; move ball to the second cone and check the ball and immediately move the ball to the third cone and check the ball. Drop step with the ball to your right back to the second cone and check the ball. Repeat another drop step with the ball back to the first cone and check the ball. Finish the set by executing a right-side drop step with the ball back to the start line. Complete as many sets as you can in 30 seconds.

Success Goal = Most completed sets

____

Success Check
• Balance and body control ____
• Stick grip ____
• Ball distance from feet ____
• Ball control ____

To Increase Difficulty
• Increase time.
• Decrease cone distance to 1 yard.
• Drop step with ball to left side.
• Increase number of cones.

To Decrease Difficulty
• Do untimed sets.
• Decrease time.
• Walk through drill.

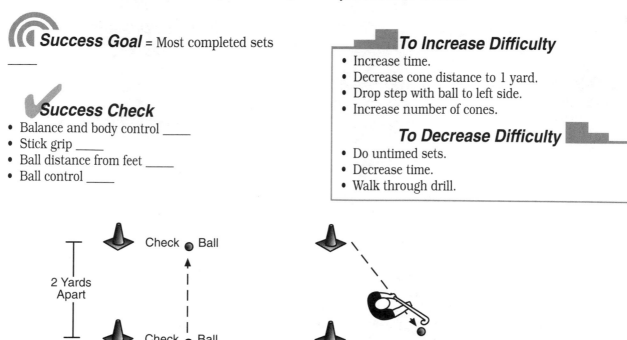

6. One-Versus-Two Stickwork

Set up a 20-yard-by-20-yard grid area. Start three players inside the grid to include one AR1 player and two opposing defenders. The objective is for the attack player to possess the ball as long as possible, avoiding the defenders' attempts to steal the ball. Time the amount of ball possession the attacker accrues before loss of possession. When the attacker loses possession, he is finished, and a new teammate becomes the attacker and attempts to possess the ball inside the grid area. Switch roles and continue to play until each player has had three chances to play AR1.

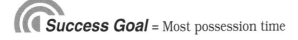

Success Goal = Most possession time

_____

Success Check
• Keep ball in close contact to stick ____
• Sudden changes of speed and direction with ball ____
• Deceptive body and foot movements ____
• Dribble into open space ____
• Protect ball without obstructing ____

To Increase Difficulty
• Decrease grid size.
• Increase number of defenders.

To Decrease Difficulty
• Increase grid size.
• Reduce number of defenders.

BALL CONTROL AND DRIBBLING SUCCESS SUMMARY

Dribbling is a skill you can practice by yourself. A good hockey player will build up speed in moving the ball with her stick. You will greatly improve your team's ability to attack and score goals if you practice your stickwork—the essence of ball control and dribbling. Handling the ball with your stick is fun to practice. All you need is a ball, a level spot, and an eagerness to improve. Always concentrate on your synchronization of stick, ball, and feet so that you are effective in changing direction and speed, deceptive with your body and foot movements, and able to keep your stick on the lower half of the ball.

STEP 4

TACKLING: ENGAGING DISTANCE AND GIVE (DEFENSE ROLE 1)

C hampionships are won by defense! The ability to stop the opponent with the ball game after game will put your team in a position to win. The heart of the defense is the player nearest to the ballcarrier. This Defense Role 1 player (DR1) leads the effort to regain ball possession for her team. How you perform the DR1 skills is the start of "team" defense.

To win the ball back from a talented Attack Role 1 dribbler requires more than average defense skills. It requires footwork, body balance, self-discipline, and a very determined attitude. In field hockey, the term tackling is used to describe the techniques applied by the Defense Role 1 player to the ball, not the dribbler of the ball. A good DR1 player possesses a sense of very good timing—she knows when to tackle and when not to tackle. During the transition from Defense Roles 2 and 3 (Step 9), the DR1 player can avoid the risks of having to tackle by intercepting the pass on its way in. Three basic defensive techniques—*engaging distance*, the *jab tackle*, and the *block tackle*—are used in direct encounter and in pursuit, both on the forehand and backhand sides of the body. Engaging distance and give is the most crucial technique to learn because defense requires excellent distance judgment, much like the skill of passing. The successful execution of the jab tackle and the block tackle to gain back the ball only become possible if you learn to properly engage your distance from the ball.

Why Are Ball-Tackling Techniques Important?

The best means of defense is to possess the ball! Without the ball, your team cannot score goals to win. In addition to pass interceptions, tackling to win ball possession is critical in individual as well as team success. All field players and even the goalkeeper—although techniques differ—must learn to execute tackling techniques because when your team loses possession, all players fall back on defense and must be in position to regain possession of the ball. Do not settle for merely spoiling

the opponent's attack by poking the ball out of play. Gain possession of the ball by executing proper tackling techniques.

Tackling has two objectives: (1) to obtain possession of the ball by taking it purely and fairly and (2) to stop the forward progress and control by AR1 by blocking space with a tackling threat. Of course, a clever dribbler will not be tackled and will choose to pass to another area of the field. A battle of cleverness develops between the tackler and the dribbler, each attempting to outmaneuver or force the other into an error. A common fault of the DR1 player is to charge the ballcarrier who is in full control of the ball or to charge after a loose ball that is closer to the opponent. In addition to these mistakes of committing the body and feet to the ball, another error to avoid is swinging or flailing your stick at the ball. Understanding the correct approach, or the *engaging distance and give*, will prevent you from performing these faults and will eventually prepare you to execute successful jab and block tackles to win the ball back.

How to Execute Tackling Techniques

Whether the ballcarrier is coming forward toward you or whether you are in pursuit of the dribbler to your left or right side, there are basic requirements for all tackling techniques. The ball must be within the reach of your stick. To determine your reach, your body must be in a low-crouch position with your knees and back bent. Your balance is essential to quick movement to adjust to the dribbler. Your body weight must be downward on the power points of your feet and not forward because a commitment of your weight forward will reduce the time of recovery. Remember the cliche—if you stop your feet, you're beat! It is vital to have a balanced defensive stance (figure 1.4) that establishes a lead foot for ready agile footwork.

For the most part, your stick is initially held in both hands to balance and prepare your reach distance. The jab tackle is a one-handed tackle executed with the left hand. However, the right hand is immediately placed on the stick in the shake hands grip once you are ready to steal the ball. The head of the stick is sliding on the ground because the ball is on the ground and is controlled by the dribbler. From here, the stick tracks the ball and tries to hasten the dribbler's stick movement, perhaps causing errors such as a loss of ball control or taking the stick too far from the ball. When you use the stick to tackle, it must be done with decisive contact to the lower half of the ball as the ball-check skill promotes. Your eyes must remain on the ball and not on any deceptive body, stick, and foot movements that the AR1 dribbler is trained to perform.

A patient and calm DR1 player will avoid committing the body, feet, or stick in a hasty forward or lateral direction. As a patient DR1 player, you will better judge the distance the ball is from your own stick and from your opponent's stick. You will also be alert to any sudden change of pace or change of direction from the dribbler, both of which are the basis for determining when to apply the jab and block tackles. If AR1 beats you, your immediate priority is to deny further penetration. Channel AR1 into areas of the hockey field where space is limited (for example, into a nearby teammate or toward the nearest sideline), or force AR1 to pass the ball square that doesn't penetrate or back toward his own goal. If you can delay penetration via the pass or dribble, your teammates will have time to recover to goal-side positions and support you in defense.

Engaging Distance and Give

Although the engaging distance and give technique (see figure 1.9) was introduced in Step 1 with the explanation of defensive footwork, it is impossible to isolate the importance it has in your preparation and actual execution of tackling. The concept of engaging distance to the ball and giving ground is so significant to the Defense Roles and especially to one-on-one defense that an adjunct review is necessary. As the Defense Role 1 player (DR1), your responsibility is to block the dangerous space to the goal with your positioning and halt the ballcarrier's forward progress. The key in all one-on-one situations is to keep the ball in front of you and maintain your playing or reaching distance to the ball. Execute *engaging distance and give* technique by applying the following suggestions:

■ *Keep the ball in front of you.* Position yourself between the dribbler and the goal you are defending. This *goal-side positioning* (see Step 9) is important to shut off the opponent's direct route to the goal.

■ *Engage or approach AR1.* Move up to deny time and space to the ballcarrier. As a general rule, the closer AR1 is to your goal, the closer DR1 should be. AR1,

who is within the shooting circle, must be denied the opportunity to shoot the ball.

■ *Give back by pushing off the lead foot.* To cover penetrating passing options, quickly initiate body balance. Evenly distribute your weight on the power points of your feet and maintain a low center of gravity. Move in a balanced position if the dribbler suddenly sidesteps or swerves laterally.

■ *Evaluate.* The less space you allow for the opponent to maintain control of the ball, the less time AR1 will have to make decisions and handle the ball. Evaluate the distance the ball is from the dribbler's stick and from your stick. Give AR1 a bit more space if she has great speed or quickness with the ball. This will prevent AR1 from simply pushing the ball forward and outracing you. If AR1 relies on a high degree of skill rather than quickness, close up quickly within your stick reach distance. Deny AR1 reasonable time and space to exercise those skills to beat you.

■ *Maintain a lead foot.* A lead foot will help you to hold or *give* ground with AR1's speed and ball-control ability. Force the dribbler to make a decision by keeping your stick on the ground to track the ball. Be patient and calm. Keep your eyes on the lower half of the ball, looking for tackling moments or, depending on the situation, giving more ground, delaying for help from a teammate, or forcing the ball in a direction. Be ready to "check" the ball with your stick—avoiding the overcommitment with a reckless stick swing.

■ *Tackle the lower half of the ball.* When the time is best for you and the team, tackle hard and gain possession of the ball. This decision of when to tackle is based on judgment from your eyesight that you are within your effective stick reach and that your stick is closer than the AR1's to the ball.

The Jab Tackle

The one-handed jab tackle is more popular on artificial surfaces and can be used in a variety of one-on-one defensive situations. Usually the jab tackle, sometimes called the "poke," is not as strong a tackle as the block tackle and is used to actually fake or bluff a dribbler, not win the ball outright with this poking action. A successful jab typically forces the dribbler to part with the ball, and the pressure defender goes in to cleanly steal the ball. You can also use the jab to delay the opponent's attack until more of your teammates are in defensive help positions. Forwards use this tackle often for tackling back in retreat. Generally, you will use this tackle from a front position with a lead foot to the dribbler as you are running alongside. The secret of the jab tackle is the greater reach of the left hand and the easy shift into other tackles. The quick poking action of your stick gives an element of a sneak attack as the objective remains to force the ball beyond the dribbler's stick for the steal. In the shooting circle where fouls result in penalty corners and penalty strokes, you should use a two-handed jab or block tackle to better protect from the ball hitting your feet. To execute the jab tackle (figure 4.1), use the following suggestions:

■ *Stick position.* Initially both hands are on your stick to prepare to jab tackle. Your left hand grips the top of the stick and the face of the stick is turned slightly to the right so the flat side of the stick is facing upwards, placing the "V" of your left hand on the front of the handle. The head of the stick is on the ground or as close to it as possible throughout the entire tracking and poking action of the stick.

■ *Balanced body and lead foot.* Knees are bent with a slightly crouched, balanced body. To jab tackle a dribbler who is in front of you and moving to your right side, place your left foot forward as your lead foot. Your right foot is forward to tackle a player moving to your

left side. Running along the dribbler's right side, lunge to jab at the ball by thrusting the head of the stick at the lower half of the ball. Running along AR1's left side requires that you overtake the dribbler's run to avoid fouls of body contact and obstruction. Because the dribbler will be carrying the ball on her forehand side, you must outrun the dribbler's run before reaching for the ball with the left-handed jab.

To jab tackle while running along the sides of the ballcarrier, much of your weight is transferred through to the left leg at the moment the stick is jabbed. Whether you are jab tackling alongside or from a front position, avoid transferring all your weight on the lead foot because this commitment makes it difficult to recover on missed attempts.

■ *Time jab or poke under the ball.* Always time your jab downward in a stabbing motion under the ball. Recoil your jab to hold your stick in both hands ready to rejab, block tackle, or pass the ball.

FIGURE 4.1 **KEYS TO SUCCESS**

THE JAB TACKLE

a

b

c

Preparation

1. Engage/give distance with breakdown footwork ____
2. Establish lead foot ____
3. Both hands split on stick ____
4. Feet shoulder-width apart ____
5. Low center of gravity on power points ____
6. Head of stick on ground ____
7. Eyes on lower half of ball ____

Execution

1. Change left-hand "V" grip to right ____
2. Sense moment to jab ____
3. Weight transfer with downward stick jab ____
4. Contact lower half of ball ____
5. Recoil stick to both hands ____
6. Keep stick head on ground ____

Follow-Through

1. Shake hands grip ____
2. Control ball ____
3. Keep stick next to lower half of ball ____
4. Prepare to pass, dribble, or shoot ____

The Forehand Block Tackle

Use the block tackle when an opponent is power dribbling directly at you or after a speed dribbler has been forced into you. Your stick is used as a vertical or horizontal barrier in front of your feet or wide to your right or left side. The horizontal stick position with knuckles of the hands on the ground is used more frequently on artificial surfaces. But on grass surfaces the vertical stick is more successful. Generally the block tackle is used when you have successfully forced or channeled the AR1 dribbler into a one-on-one situation in which the dribbler has no other choice but to try to beat you with the forward dribble. Although it is the most common method of tackling, block tackling requires good body balance to position the feet and a sense of very good timing. To execute the forehand block tackle (figure 4.2), use these following suggestions:

■ *Position goal side.* Move between AR1 and the goal you are defending in a controlled and balanced approach. Your left foot and left shoulder leads as you persuade the AR1 dribbler into a position for the forehand tackle. When forcing the dribbler to your right side and to the outside of the field near the sideline, use a wide forehand block tackle. Always position to play goal side and on the inside to deny the dribbler escape routes to the shooting circle in the center.

■ *Line your right foot and hip to the ball.* Ignore the dribbler's stick and foot fakes as you line your right foot and right side with the ball. Your knees must be bent and your body crouched to provide a lower center of gravity.

■ *Low stick head using shake hands grip.* Keep your eyes on the lower half of the ball with both hands split on your stick in a shake hands grip. Improved timing and strength will allow you to grip the stick and tackle with only a left hand grip. Sometimes the forehand block tackle is preceded by fake jabs or a show of a block on your left side. In any event, the head of your stick always remains close to the ground, ready to block the ball as the dribbler takes her stick away from the ball.

■ *Timing is a key ingredient for the block tackle.* Time your tackle for the spot where the ball is farthest from the opponent's stick and allow the ball to come to your stick as you give backward with your feet. Your stick must align in a two-o'clock position from your feet. It is important not to move your stick forward or swing at the ball as you will certainly give the ball back to the dribbler. Use the strength of your legs and forearms to trap the ball and immediately control the ball away from the dribbler.

FIGURE 4.2

KEYS TO SUCCESS

THE FOREHAND BLOCK TACKLE

Preparation

1. Position goal side ____
2. Engage/give distance with breakdown steps ____
3. Establish left lead foot and shoulder; line right foot to ball ____
4. Shake hands grip ____
5. Low center of gravity on power points ____
6. Head of stick on the ground ____
7. Eyes on lower half of ball ____

a

Execution

1. Time block and give back with feet ____
2. Keep body and feet balanced ____
3. Trap and contact lower half of ball ____

b

Follow-Through

1. Control ball away from dribbler ____
2. Keep stick on ball ____
3. Look up to pass ____

c

The Reverse Block Tackle

The reverse tackle is a more difficult tackle to master and almost impossible to cleanly execute if the dribbler has won the goal-side position on you. However, when the sideline is an ally, left-side defenders must be familiar with this tackle. The principles of the reverse block are the same as the forehand block. The only difference is the stick position, which is outside the line of your body on your left side but still in front. Good dribblers who cleverly get the ball to their forehand side nearly always attempt to beat left-side defenders on their backhand side. Let the one-on-one battle begin because as a good Defense Role 1 player, you have learned to use quick footwork and a balanced body to force or channel the ball to your forehand.

To execute the reverse block tackle (figure 4.3), hold your stick in your left hand using a reverse grip. Your body must be in a low position on goal side with your right shoulder and foot leading. Lock your left elbow and point the toe of your stick on the ground. Time your block tackle to trap the ball using a vertical or horizontal stick (knuckles of left hand on ground) so that AR1 overruns the ball.

FIGURE 4.3 **KEYS TO SUCCESS**

THE REVERSE BLOCK TACKLE

a b c

Preparation

1. Position goal side ____
2. Engage/give distance with breakdown footwork ____
3. Establish right lead foot and shoulder; line left foot to ball ____
4. Reverse "V" grip of left hand ____
5. Low center of gravity on power points ____
6. Toe of stick on the ground ____
7. Eyes on lower half of ball ____

Execution

1. Time block by lowering handle of steady stick ____
2. Keep body and feet balanced ____
3. Trap and contact lower half of ball ____

Follow-Through

1. Control ball away from dribbler ____
2. Keep stick on ball ____
3. Look up to pass ____

Recovery Tackling

Every player will be required to tackle while retreating or recovering because the ball will sometimes get into the space behind you. Tackling while in a recovery run does not differ from the principles of direct-approach tackling. You still must concentrate on applying your performance checklist from your engaging-distance and jab-and-block techniques—body balance and footwork; stick position and grip; stick tracking with timing to tackle; and patience. The only variation in recovery tackling is that the execution requires the DR1 to run at maximum speed.

To execute recovery tackling, your objective must be to keep the ball to one side by running parallel—like a railroad track—alongside the dribbler. Always sprint using your maximum speed to overtake the dribbler on the goal-line side. You surely will be beaten once again if you insist on overcommitting and running toward the ballcarrier or directly at the ball.

The qualifications for recovery tackling from the dribbler's forehand side are speed and body posture. You must run faster than the dribbler to overtake her, and when you are ahead of the dribbler, concentrate on timing of when or when not to tackle. Never tackle while still trailing behind the opponent, which is dangerous to the dribbler and will certainly be penalized. Attempting to tackle before you are in position usually results in pushing, tripping, and stick obstruction fouls by DR1. When running at your maximum speed, your body will be in a more upright position. You must lower your center of gravity while running when you are ready to tackle. Lunge your stick toward the lower half of the ball and control the ball away from the attacker.

The requisites for recovery tackling from the dribbler's backhand side are speed and patience as this tackle is the most difficult of all defensive efforts. Again you must run to overtake and pass the dribbler on the goal side so that your body is even with the ball. Your stick is in your left hand only, using the reverse "V" grip. As soon as you run even with the ball, lower your body posture for a possible tackle. If the dribbler keeps the ball next to his stick, keep tracking your stick and time your jab or block to the lower half of the ball when the ball is no longer on AR1's stick. In addition to your goal-side positioning and speed of recovery, a high level of patience will help you decide when or when not to tackle.

TACKLING SUCCESS STOPPERS

Defense Role 1 tackling techniques must be practiced as often as Attack Role 1 techniques. Although dribbling or shooting skills may be more fun to practice, you will not get a chance to use those skills in game situations unless you first gain possession of the ball. Most tackling errors result from poor judgment of distance, timing of the tackle, lack of body control, or improper technique. You must maintain a low center of gravity, get close enough to the ball, and then time your tackle with proper technique and determination. The following is a list of common errors and suggested methods of correcting them.

Error	Correction
Engaging Distance and Give	
1. AR1 has a lot of dribbling space.	1. Engage your distance closer for an effective reach and better tackling threat.
2. You run toward an opponent who has close control of the dribble and get eliminated.	2. Establish a lead foot and give back to keep dribbler in front.
3. AR1 fakes and swerves around you.	3. Eyes must only concentrate on the lower half of the ball to maintain your reach distance.

Error	Correction
The Jab Tackle	
1. Your reach is restricted.	1. Crouch your body in a low position with your left foot and shoulder leading. Hold your stick in your left hand for jab.
2. Your jab misses the ball and the ball goes under your stick.	2. Concentrate on poking under the lower half of the ball.
3. Stick is slow and clumsily handled.	3. Change your left hand "V" to the front of the stick and jab down under the lower half of the ball.
4. Unable to recover or retreat in time from a missed jab tackle.	4. Do not overly commit in a forward direction by placing all your body weight on the lead foot; recoil your stick quickly and maintain body balance.
The Block Tackle	
1. Slow to move with AR1's sidestep.	1. Stay on the power points of your feet and keep one foot in advance of the other.
2. You block tackle the ball but you lose it immediately.	2. Keep your stick still in a two-o'clock position and let the ball come to it. Apply your stick to the lower half of the ball and exert control with your right hand on stick. Control the ball away from the dribbler.
3. You hasten your approach and tackle before your teammates are in position to cover inside passing options.	3. Delay your approach by holding and giving.
4. AR1 pushes the ball between your feet and in behind you.	4. Keep the head of your stick on the ground in front of your feet. Keep moving your feet to block the space in behind.
Recovery Tackling	
1. You are guilty of slow footwork during the recovery run.	1. Run at your maximum speed to overtake or position along the goal side of the dribbler. Run parallel like a railroad track.
2. The dribbler beats you again after you have caught up to her.	2. Avoid stepping to the ball. Maintain a parallel running position with patience.

TACKLING DRILLS

1. Pull the Flag Game

Use four cones to set up a 10-yard-by-10-yard grid. Attack players wear flag football belts with only one flag positioned on the right hip. If belts and flags are not available, use a scrimmage vest to tuck in the side of the attack player's shorts. Inside the grid area, one attack player goes against one defender. The attack player attempts to maneuver in behind the defender and across the goal line without losing his flag. The object of the DR1 player is to keep the attacker in front and pull the attacker's flag. DR1 scores one point each time she pulls the attacker's flag. DR1 stays in the grid and repeats one-on-one defense five times before switching roles. The player scoring the most points wins.

Success Goal = Score the most points _____

Success Check
- Maintain body balance and control _____
- Keep attacker in front _____
- Don't overcommit _____
- Focus on position of flag _____

To Increase Difficulty
- Increase grid width.
- Place a 2-yard goal on goal line.
- Increase repetitions.

To Decrease Difficulty
- Reduce grid width.
- Decrease repetitions.

2. Blocking Space

Set up a goal line using two cones 5 yards apart. Position Defense Role 1 player between the cones to protect the goal line and the spaces in behind the goal line. A dribbler who starts 7 yards in front of the goal line dribbles or pushes ball to penetrate the ball through the cones and behind the DR1. DR1's objective is to protect and block the space between the cones by using tackling techniques of engaging/give distance for reach, jabs, and blocks. Award yourself one point for each successful steal in three minutes of play. Rest, then switch roles and play again. Play four games. The player with the most points wins.

Success Goal = Score the most points _____

Success Check
- Engage and give _____
- Stick head on ground _____
- Balance and body control _____
- Correct grip for tackles _____
- Timing of steal _____
- Contact lower half of ball _____

To Increase Difficulty
- Increase size of goal line.
- Increase AR1's start distance.
- Increase number of games.

To Decrease Difficulty
- Start attack player from 3 yards.
- Decrease goal-line size.
- Reduce playing time.

3. Engaging Distance and Give

Set up a goal 6 yards wide using two cones or spot markers. Position yourself as a Defense Role 1 player between the goal. A teammate dribbles at you from a distance of 20 yards. Quickly move forward to engage and give to establish your distance to AR1. Assume a proper defensive posture to keep the dribbler in front. Attempt to tackle the ball to stop AR1 from penetrating the goal. Repeat the drill 10 times, then switch roles with your teammate. Award yourself one point for each successful stop or tackle of the ball.

Success Goal = 8 of 10 possible points _____

Success Check
- Engage and give _____
- Keep ball in front _____
- Maintain low center of gravity _____
- Balance on power points _____
- Head of stick on the ground with proper grip _____
- Contact lower half of ball _____

To Increase Difficulty
- Increase size of goal.
- Increase AR1's distance.
- After tackle, pass to a target.
- Increase number of repetitions.

To Decrease Difficulty
- Decrease goal size.
- Decrease AR1's distance.
- Reduce number of repetitions.

4. Jab the Cone

Set up two 7-inch or smaller-sized cones 1 yard apart. Balance a hockey ball on top of the second cone. Start behind a line 1 yard from the vertical row of cones. Grip your stick for the jab tackle and move toward the cone with the ball. Jab the cone by poking the bottom of the cone with your stick. If done correctly, the ball will drop straight down on the ground. Keep your stick on the ground and quickly recoil your stick so the back of it hits the first positioned cone. Immediately go to control the ball. Repeat 20 times. Award one point for each successful jab tackle that contains the three parts: jab bottom of second cone; balance body and recoil stick to hit first cone; control ball.

Success Goal = 16 of 20 possible points _____

Success Check
- Maintain balance with lead foot _____
- Keep stick head on the ground _____
- Jab technique with recoil _____
- Contact lower half of ball _____
- Control ball _____

To Increase Difficulty
- Increase distance of start line from cones.
- Increase number of repetitions.
- After controlling ball, pass to target.
- Add partner who stands behind second cone with ball on top. After you jab second cone, partner pushes the dropping ball toward your feet. Recoil quickly to touch first cone and protect your feet from pushed ball.

To Decrease Difficulty
- Reduce number of repetitions.

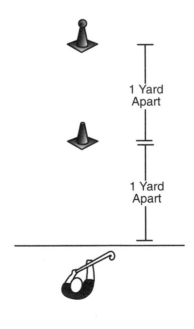

1 Yard Apart

1 Yard Apart

5. Block the Ball

A teammate dribbles at you from a distance of 10 yards. Quickly move forward and give to establish proper distance from AR1, assume proper balance and stick position, and attempt to block tackle the ball. You may tackle with the forehand or the reverse depending on AR1's angle of approach. Repeat the drill 20 times, then switch roles with your teammate. Award yourself one point for each successful block tackle.

Success Goal = 16 of 20 possible points _____

✔ Success Check

- Engage and give _____
- Body balance and stick control _____
- Timing of block tackle _____
- Contact and control of ball _____

To Increase Difficulty

- Increase distance to 15 yards.
- Use only forehand block tackle.

To Decrease Difficulty

- Reduce distance to 5 yards.
- Require AR1 to walk.

6. One-on-One Hockey Grid

Compete against an opponent within a 10-yard-by-20-yard grid. Position yourself with a ball on one end line of the grid while the opponent starts on the opposite end line. Serve the ball to your opponent, who receives it and immediately attempts to dribble the length of the grid. Your objective is to prevent AR1 from dribbling past your end line and to win ball possession. Play at game speed. Use either the block tackle or jab tackle techniques to dispossess the dribbler. You can earn two points for a successful block tackle and one point for each time you jab the ball off AR1's stick. AR1 receives one point for dribbling the ball over DR1's end line. Play one-on-one for five minutes using transition from DR1 to AR1 and vice versa. The player scoring the most points wins.

Success Goal = Score more points than opponent _____

✔ Success Check

- Engage and give footwork _____
- Low center of gravity and body balance _____
- Stick head on ground _____
- Eyes on the lower half of the ball _____
- Tackling technique _____
- Do not overcommit _____

To Increase Difficulty

- Increase field width so DR1 has more space to defend.
- Place 2 small goals on the end line behind DR1 to provide dribbler more scoring options.

To Decrease Difficulty

- Reduce field width.

7. Tackling From Recovery

Set up a 20-yard-long-by-15-yard-wide grid with a 3-yard-wide goal on the back line. The attack player starts with the ball 20 yards from the goal by dribbling toward the goal. Position yourself as the DR1 player 10 yards in front of the goal with your back turned to the dribbler. As soon as you see AR1 pass your right or left side, quickly run to the goal side of AR1 and attempt to tackle the ball before AR1 dribbles the ball through the goal. The defender scores one point for successfully tackling the ball using a jab or block tackling technique. The dribbler scores one point for dribbling the ball across the goal line. Repeat 10 times and then switch roles. The player with the most total points wins.

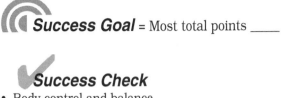

Success Goal = Most total points _____

Success Check
- Body control and balance _____
- Speed of recovery on goal side _____
- Tackling techniques _____
- Ball control after tackle _____

To Increase Difficulty
- Increase size of goal.
- Add another goal on the back line.
- Defender starts from another position—from one knee or by picking up stick lying on ground.
- After the tackle, defender passes through a set target.

To Decrease Difficulty
- Decrease distance to dribbler.
- Decrease size of goal.
- Defender starts even with AR1.

TACKLING SUCCESS SUMMARY

Winning the ball cleanly while tackling provides a team with one of the best opportunities to create a counterattack. A counterattack often finds the opponent out of position and finds its own teammates unmarked. Tackling requires as much concentration, technique understanding, footwork, balance, and self-discipline as any other skill in hockey. When contesting for possession of the ball, the player who owns the better balance and ability to keep the ball in front will probably win it! Tackling techniques are competitive and fun to practice with a teammate because ball control and dribbling are also practiced.

Ask a coach, your parent, or a teammate to observe your execution of the Defense Role 1 tackling techniques and evaluate your overall performance by using the checklists in figures 4.1 through 4.3.

STEP 5

ATTACK AND DEFENSE TACTICS: UNDERSTANDING ROLE 1

Field hockey is a fast and exciting team game consisting of a series of problem-solving situations. Attacking players work to create and use space, and defending players work to block and control the space. Although hockey is a "team" sport, every game includes a series of one-against-one battles to either maintain possession of the ball or regain it. To successfully perform these one-against-one encounters around the ball, you must understand and execute Attack and Defense Role 1 tactics. These tactics are your decisions or plans to command individual confrontations. With a thorough understanding and execution of your Role 1 responsibilities, your field hockey team can be a group of players who think and play together.

Because each player spends less than a third of a 70-minute game encountering one-on-one confrontations near the ball, your ability to make good decisions and apply the correct technique at the right moment is primary. The Attack or Defense Role 1 player is the leader who is responsible for executing good decisions for the start of team attack and team defense.

Why Are Role 1 Attack and Defense Tactics Important?

All players must be able to both defend and attack. In field hockey, when you have possession of the ball, you are the Attack Role 1 player (AR1); when the nearest opponent has the ball, you are the Defense Role 1 player (DR1). Your success in the first roles of attack and defense depends in part on your ability to choose the best option to solve game situations. As the *leader* of the attack and defense, Role 1 players must make good decisions. Good decisions are based on useful guidelines and responsibilities and lead to a higher quality of skill performance. Being attentive to the location of the ball, your teammates, and your opponents helps make a decision with or without the ball.

How to Execute Role 1 Attack Tactics

When you have the ball, you are the leader of the attack team who must execute the attack strategy while taking care of the ball. AR1 has the assignment to pass the ball that initiates team attack play. As the player with the ball, you must decide how, where, and when to pass it. You pass the ball to a teammate for three basic reasons—to penetrate the opponent's space in behind and to goal; to gain an advantage by moving closer to the opponent; and to secure possession of the ball by using a safe or possession pass. A good AR1 player will first look to deliver the *killer pass*, which penetrates through and behind the opponent. If the penetration pass is unavailable or too risky, then AR1 looks to gain ground by using an *advantage pass*. An advantage pass goes forward toward the goal but not necessarily behind the defense. If the advantage pass is too risky to a teammate, the AR1 should maintain possession by using the space behind the ball. Because of the greater distance from the defender's goal line and immediate pressure, the back space gives the attack an effective chance to change the point of attack.

Maintain Ball Possession

Although you are primarily a passer when in AR1 position, it remains vital to maintain possession of the ball as you look up to pass. You must value your team's ownership of the ball and work hard not to lose it. If you cannot complete a penetrating pass or an advantage pass, maintain possession of the ball so that you can change the point of attack. Change the point of attack by using a *possession pass* to pass the ball back to a support teammate who has more time and space to switch the ball to the other side of the field.

Cut the Ball Into Free Space

You become a better field hockey player simply by creating space for yourself and for your teammates. The more space between you—the AR1 player—and the DR1 opponent, the more time you will have for decisions to execute passing skills to lead your team's attack. *Cut* or diagonal dribble the ball with speed into free space on the field to create space and time for yourself. Cutting the ball changes the point of attack and usually makes the opponent move laterally after the ball—opening "through" spaces to the opponent's goal.

Go One-on-One—Take on the Role 1 Defender

Forcing the DR1 player to make a decision to either commit to tackle the ball or hold and give to delay penetration is commonly referred to as going *one-on-one*, or *taking on a defender*. Your objective is to keep possession of the ball as you attempt to move the DR1 player and get the ball in behind her. If you draw a wrong decision from the DR1 player, you will have created a dangerous attack penetration, which may lead to a scoring opportunity. Attempt to draw a commitment from the opponent by cutting the ball diagonally forward outside DR1's stick reach. Use body fakes and change-of-pace movements with the ball to mislead or unbalance the opponent.

Go one-on-one only in areas where the potential to create a scoring opportunity far outweighs the risk of losing possession of the ball, which would provide the opponent an immediate scoring chance. The best area to use your dribbling skills to take on the DR1 player is in the attacking zone of the field, nearest to the opponent's goal. Loss of possession in this area is not as critical as losing possession in your defensive zone of the field. Think safety first in your own defensive half of the field and avoid dribbling to take on your opponent.

When cornered or outnumbered by the opponent in a tight space, keep possession of the ball by drawing or producing a foul for a free hit. A free hit will allow you more time and space to examine your options.

Penetrate the Shortest Line to Goal

Once you have successfully beaten and eliminated a defender, keep him on your backside and penetrate the shortest line to the goal. You should never have to beat the same defender twice on your path to the goal.

ROLE 1 ATTACK TACTICS SUCCESS STOPPERS

Most errors that occur with Attack or Defense Role 1 tactics are caused by poor judgment of what to do and when to do it. No matter how skilled or talented you may be, you will not enjoy much success if you consistently make the wrong decisions in one-on-one situations. Common errors are listed here, along with suggestions for avoiding or correcting them.

Error	Correction
Role 1 Attack Tactics	
1. The DR1 steals the ball away from you.	1. Keep the ball next to your stick as you look to pass. When pressured, cut the ball to free space or change the point of attack immediately.
2. You hesitate when going one-on-one against the DR1.	2. Be decisive and diagonal dribble the ball with controlled speed to commit the defenders.
3. The defender you just beat using a dribble has recovered to the goal side to again block the dangerous space to goal.	3. After successfully eliminating a defender, go at maximum speed and take the shortest route to the goal. Keep the defender behind you.
4. You lose the ball when attempting to change the point of attack.	4. Use sudden change of direction or a drop step to create space between you and DR1. Avoid changing the point of attack without first creating space in which to pass.

How to Execute Role 1 Defense Tactics

Your purpose as the defender is to keep the ball in front of you, to prevent the opponent from penetrating forward with a pass or dribble to your goal. When you are the defender nearest to the ball, you are the leader of the defense team and must initiate the team's defense strategy by pressuring the ball. Playing the DR1 requires you to command the defense tactics of your team and apply one-on-one tackling techniques.

When you recognize that you are the nearest defender to the ball, you must decide how to immediately block and slow AR1's penetrating attack. This action is referred to as *pressuring the ball*. Use the following list of responsibilities to guide your decisions and actions when defending in a one-on-one confrontation.

Position to Block Dangerous Space

Your position in relation to the opponent, the ball, and the goal begins your team's defensive tactics. Placing immediate pressure on the ball allows your teammates time to drop back and organize defensive help. Always position *goal side* to block the dangerous space to goal. Goal side is the position between AR1 and the goal you are defending. The *dangerous space* is the forward space between the ball and the goal you are defending. From this position, keep the ball and opponent in your view at all times to deny a penetration dribble or any through and diagonal forward pass by AR1.

It is to your team's advantage to always position to shut off AR1's most direct route to goal. To execute this maneuver effectively, you need an accurate determination of your distance from the ball for engaging your approach to the ball.

Engaging Distance to the Ball

As soon as you see that AR1 is about to receive the ball, quickly engage your distance to the ball (see figure 1.9). Close the space to the ball as the ball is in flight. Typically you should arrive at the area of the ball at the same time the ball does. Slow your approach as you near AR1 by using breakdown and give footwork to maintain ideal balance and body control. The less space you allow for AR1 to receive and control the ball, the less time she will have to make attack decisions and play the ball. As a general rule, when the ball is on AR1's stick and in control, DR1 must be in control of her engaging movement, defensive stance, and playing distance.

Defensive Stance

For the defensive stance, take on a partly crouched posture with knees flexed and a low center of gravity (see figure 1.4). Use a staggered stance with a lead foot slightly forward and both feet a comfortable distance apart on the power points of your feet. The head of your stick is low or on the ground to prevent the ball going into your feet or through to the goal you are defending. From this position you can instantly change direction in response to AR1's movements.

Playing Distance

DR1's *playing distance* is the distance that purposeful pressure is applied to the ball. How close should you begin to pressure the AR1 player? Base your decision on the following factors:

■ *AR1's ability.* Evaluate AR1's speed and quality of ball control. Give more space if AR1 has great speed and quickness. This will prevent AR1 from merely pushing the ball forward and outracing you to the ball. Move closer within your stick reach to the ball if AR1 relies on a high degree of ball-control skills rather than speed and quickness. Position yourself to deny AR1 adequate time and space to use ball-control skills to beat you.

■ *Area of the field.* As a common principle, the closer the ball is to your goal, the closer you must be to defend. An opponent within scoring range of your goal must be denied the opportunity to shoot, dribble, or pass the ball forward.

■ *Position of the opponent in relation to the ball.* Be aware of the position of your opponent(s) as you are engaging your playing distance from the ball. If AR1 has unmarked teammates in the immediate area for attack support, maintain more playing space from the ball until your teammates equal the number and mark up.

■ *Position of your teammates in relation to the ball.* Be aware of the position of your nearest (DR2) teammates(s) as you are engaging your playing distance from the ball. Pressuring the ball to enable your teammates to help get possession of it is the essence of "team" defense.

Control and Balance

AR1 will use deceptive body and stick-fake movements to unbalance you or draw a commitment. Strive to maintain your playing distance with good balance and body control at all times. Keep your weight centered over the power points of your feet. Attempt to break up the play or steal the ball in a controlled manner. Do not commit or crash in after the ball and thus risk being eliminated. If the ball is passed before you are able to set up effective pressure, do not chase the pass but drop step to a ball-side and goal-side position and reorganize your new defense role.

Forcing or Channeling

DR1's immediate priority is to deny penetration. Force or channel the opponent to areas of the field where space is limited, such as the sideline or into a nearby teammate (Defense Role 2), or force AR1 to pass the ball square (lateral line across the field) or back toward her own goal. When the ball is in the center of the field or on the field's right side, pressure the ball by forcing or channeling it to your forehand side. When AR1 is positioned 10 yards or less to the left sideline, force the ball toward the sideline.

If you can delay penetration, forcing AR1 to back pass or dribble, your teammates will have time to recover to positions goal side of the ball to support you in defense.

Tackle the Ball

With patience and control, see when AR1 has allowed the ball to get out of her range of control. Time the execution of a hard block or jab tackle and gain possession of the ball.

Finish your tackle by controlling the ball and delivering a strong, accurate attack pass.

ROLE 1 DEFENSE TACTICS SUCCESS STOPPERS

Common DR1 tactical errors are listed here, along with suggestions to avoid or correct them.

Error	Correction
Role 1 Defense Tactics	
1. AR1 passes a *killer* pass into the dangerous space behind you.	1. Engage to a closer distance from the ball to deny through and diagonal forward passes. Apply immediate pressure on the ball to force the attacker to pass square or back to a supporting teammate.
2. AR1 successfully cuts the ball forward into free space.	2. Check your playing distance and position closer to deny AR1 space to dribble forward.
3. You overcommit in an effort to tackle the ball and are beaten on the dribble.	3. In a one-on-one confrontation, prevent penetration as your first priority—gain possession as your second priority. Force or channel the ball to limited space or toward a teammate. Challenge for the ball when a teammate is covering the space immediately behind you and/or when you are sure you can execute a successful tackle.
4. AR1 pushes the ball forward and outraces you to the ball.	4. Give more space if AR1 has great speed and quickness.

ROLE 1 ATTACK AND DEFENSE TACTICS—DRILLS

1. Receiving Box

Use four cones or spot markers to define a square—receiving box—5 yards by 5 yards. Play with a partner, who is the passer 15 yards opposite the receiving box's back line. Position yourself 5 yards away from either the right or left side of the box. Use changes of direction and speed to run into the box and receive a 10-yard pass from your teammate. Receive and control the ball and immediately cut dribble the ball away from the back line, which represents space being blocked by an "imaginary" defender. Attempt to control and cut dribble 10 passes and then switch roles with your partner. Award one point for each successful attempt that you receive, control, and cut dribble away from the back line of receiving box without error.

Success Goal = Score 7 points out of 10 attempts ____

Success Check
- Maintain ball control and body balance ____
- Maintain space between ball and back line ____
- Use sudden changes of direction and speed ____

To Increase Difficulty
- Place an active defender on back line of box.
- Score 10 of 12 attempts.
- Decrease size of receiving box.
- Place a 3-yard target 15 yards behind the back line. AR1 passes the ball through the target after cut dribbling.

To Decrease Difficulty
- Increase the size of receiving box.
- Reduce number of attempts.

2. Protect Area

Set up a goal 5 yards wide to represent dangerous space. Play against a teammate. Position yourself as the defender between the cones and start the game by passing the ball to the attacker, who is 5 yards away. Award yourself a point each time you steal the ball or break up the play by pushing the ball out of the play area. The AR1 player uses sudden changes of speed and direction with ball-control and dribbling skills to attempt to unbalance you. Award one point to the attack player each time she moves the ball in control through the cones. To restart play after a point is scored, the defender passes the ball to the attack player. The first player to score five points wins the game. Switch positions and play more games.

Success Goal = Win most games ____

Success Check

AR1 player
- Keep stick on lower half of ball ____
- Maintain space between ball and defender ____
- Use sudden changes of direction and speed ____

DR1 player
- Maintain balance and body control ____
- Limit space available to attacker ____
- Do not overcommit ____

To Increase Difficulty
DR1 player
- Increase size of goal.
- Increase distance the AR1 player starts with ball.
- Award 2 points for AR1 penetration through the cones.

To Decrease Difficulty
- Decrease the start distance of AR1.
- Reduce size of goal to 4 yards.
- Add sideline boundaries.

3. Receiving With Pressure

Play with two teammates within a 10-yard-by-20-yard area. Position yourself near one end line of the area as the AR1 player; a teammate positioned 2 yards behind you on goal side assumes DR1. The third player, positioned outside at the opposite end, acts as a stationary passer and serves balls to you. Receive a pass from the server while DR1 challenges you from behind. Use sudden changes of direction and speed to receive and control the ball. Try to maintain possession of the ball for a 10-second round, then return it to the server. Repeat 10 rounds. Award yourself one point if you can maintain possession of the ball within the area for 10 seconds. Award the defender one point each time he tackles the ball from you. Players rotate after 10 rounds. Continue until each player has taken a turn as the defender and the attacker.

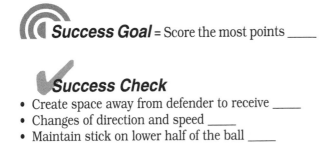

Success Goal = Score the most points _____

Success Check
- Create space away from defender to receive _____
- Changes of direction and speed _____
- Maintain stick on lower half of the ball _____

To Increase Difficulty
- Decrease size of playing area.
- Award 1 point for a 15-second possession time.
- Require AR1 to get ball in behind the defender within 10 seconds.

To Decrease Difficulty
- Passer can join to possess the ball or get ball in behind DR1.
- Increase size of playing area.
- Award 1 point for a 5-second possession time.

4. Three-on-One Passing Game

Set up a play area 15 yards wide and 20 yards long. Position one defender on each 15-yard-wide goal and one defender inside the play area. The defender on each goal line may take only one step forward off the goal line to play the ball. Three attack players try to score by maintaining ball possession in and behind the defense and over the goal line. Award one point for each completed pass or penetration dribble that the attack successfully moves over the goal line. When the attack scores, possession is maintained by the scoring team by taking a free hit 5 yards behind the goal line where the goal was scored. The attack team now attacks in the other direction. Loss of possession occurs when the defender steals the ball and when the ball travels outside of the area. Play nonstop for five minutes. Players alternate from attack to defense after five minutes and play again for another five-minute period. The team with the most points wins the game.

Success Goal = Score the most points _____

Success Check
- Receive and control of ball _____
- Priority is pass, then dribble _____
- Create space between ball and defender _____

To Increase Difficulty
- Play for 10 minutes nonstop.
- Decrease size of playing area.
- Decrease size of goal line.
- Only play with 2 attack players.

To Decrease Difficulty
- Shorten playing time to less than 5 minutes.
- Increase goal-line size.

5. Attack Dangerous Space

Set up two 10-yard-by-20-yard areas using cones to mark the attack half zone and the defense half zone, which represents dangerous space. Play with six teammates. Position as the AR1 player in the attack zone where three stationary passers are positioned on the outside—one along the left sideline (P1), one at the top (P2), and one along the right sideline (P3). Place one attack player (AR2) in the defense zone or dangerous space who may not enter the attack zone where AR1 starts. One defender (DR1) starts between the zones and may engage her distance to the ball when P1 passes the ball to AR1. AR1's objective is to receive the ball and successfully move the ball into dangerous space via the pass to AR2 or by dribbling. Score one point for each time AR1 successfully beats DR1 by passing or dribbling into the defense zone. AR1 gets three total balls from the attack passers. Switch roles with teammates so everyone has three opportunities to play the AR1 player. The player with the most points wins.

Success Goal = Score the most points ____

Success Check
- Receive ball and maintain space between ball and DR1 ____
- Changes of speed and direction ____
- Maintain close ball control ____

To Increase Difficulty
- Decrease size of playing area.
- Receive and control lofted passes.
- Require AR1 to attack dangerous space within 5 seconds after receiving ball.
- Reward 2 points for entering dangerous space from a completed pass to AR2 player and 1 point for a dribble.
- DR1 player can start by positioning next to AR1 player.
- Add another defender in dangerous space zone.

To Decrease Difficulty
- Increase size of playing area.
- DR1 starts farther away from AR1 in the dangerous space zone.
- Add another attack player in the defense zone.

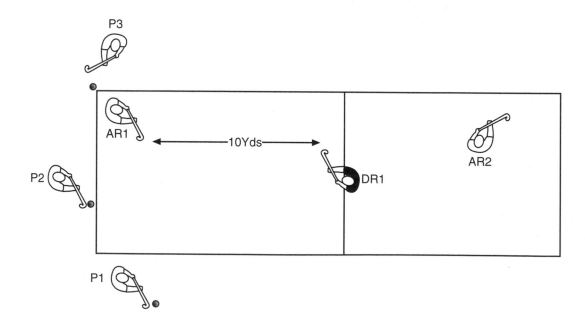

6. Two-on-One Continuous

Set up a 10-yard-by-15-yard area using four cones or spot markers. Play two-on-one, two attack against one defender. Position a defender in front of the goal line with substitute defenders in a waiting line out-of-bounds. Two attack players start with the ball 15 yards opposite the goal line with substitute attackers behind waiting for attack turns. While maintaining ball possession, attack players attempt to pass or dribble the ball in behind the defender and over the goal line. Award one point for each time the attack dribbles or completes a pass over the goal line. When the ball goes out-of-bounds or the defender steals the ball, a new pair of attack players starts with a ball and attacks against a new defender who rotates into the grid. Play is directional and continuous for five minutes. Switch roles and play another five minutes. The player with the most points wins the game.

Success Goal = Score the most points _____

Success Check
- Take on defender at speed _____
- Use sudden changes of speed and direction _____
- Pass and receive with control _____

To Increase Difficulty
- Decrease size of grid.
- Place a 2-yard goal on the back line.
- Play for 10 minutes nonstop.
- Award defender a point for each tackle.

To Decrease Difficulty
- Increase width of grid.
- Require defender to start on goal line.
- Shorten playing time to 3 minutes.

7. Pressure/Cover

Place four cones or markers to create a grid of 10 yards by 15 yards with a back line at each end and sidelines. Position one attack player at each corner of the grid who cannot move from her cone area. Position two defenders to defend the inside space of the grid. The defensive objective of the game is to block or prevent the attack players from successfully completing a *through pass* or a *diagonal forward pass* that penetrates through the grid to attack players at the opposite back line. Award one point to the attack for each successful pass that travels through the defense on a diagonal or through line. Defense scores one point for each successful tackle or interception. Play continues for three minutes. The team to score the most points after three minutes wins the game.

Success Goal = Score more points than the opponent _____

Success Check
- Maintain position to block forward space _____
- DR1 executes a drop step when ball is passed _____
- Keep ball in front _____
- Maintain balance and body control _____
- Feet positioned with lead foot _____
- Time tackle with purposeful pressure _____

To Increase Difficulty
- Increase width of grid.
- Increase size of grid.
- Increase playing time.

To Decrease Difficulty
- Decrease size of grid.
- Reduce width of grid.
- Reduce playing time.
- Reduce number of attack players.

8. Forcing in a Direction

Play with a teammate against one attacker. Use markers to divide a 30-yard-by-30-yard area into two 15-yard-by-15-yard zones. Set up three 4-yard-wide goals on each back line. You position as the DR1 player in the front zone and your teammate as the defender in the back zone. AR1 player also starts in the front zone. Position a passer along each sideline of the front zone to begin the game by passing the ball to the AR1 player. AR1 receives the pass and attempts to beat the defense by scoring through the cones using a dribble, a hit, or a push pass. The defender in the back zone must stay in the back zone and position to play DR1's directional forcing. Apply the field hockey rules. If the defense successfully tackles or intercepts the ball, it can counterattack and score through any of the three goals on the back line of the front zone. Award a point to the attack for each shot through the goal(s). Play nonstop for five minutes.

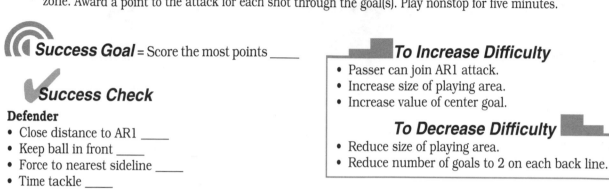

Success Goal = Score the most points _____

Success Check

Defender
• Close distance to AR1 _____
• Keep ball in front _____
• Force to nearest sideline _____
• Time tackle _____

Attacker
• Take on DR1 at speed _____
• Use sudden changes of speed and direction _____

To Increase Difficulty
• Passer can join AR1 attack.
• Increase size of playing area.
• Increase value of center goal.

To Decrease Difficulty
• Reduce size of playing area.
• Reduce number of goals to 2 on each back line.

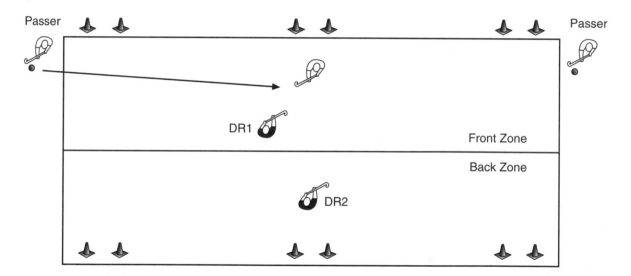

ATTACK AND DEFENSE TACTICS SUCCESS SUMMARY

The prime purpose of any game of field hockey is to create time and space in the opposition's area to create a scoring opportunity. You must do this more than your opponent, who has the same objective. Role 1 tactics deal with the creation and denial of time and space, which are directly related to the level of individual techniques you acquire within a team. Playing one-on-one is very competitive, physically demanding, and fun to practice because individual battles examine your ability to perform skills that require quick decisions under game-related conditions.

Ask someone who is knowledgeable about field hockey tactics to analyze your execution of AR1 and DR1 tactics. An observer's helpful advice will improve your one-on-one play and provide input to whether you are executing your Role 1 responsibility to *lead* your team's effort to think and play together.

STEP 6

SHOOTING: FINISHING THE ATTACK

Although scoring a goal is most often the result of a team effort, field hockey players who can finish a successful attack acquire noteworthy fame. Experienced players and coaches know that goal-scoring players increase the confidence of their team. Each hockey position requires its own specialization with a sound tactical understanding of the sport, which includes being familiar with the roles of attack and defense. However, the skills of stickwork, ball control, and good passing are common to all good shooters. Attack Role 1 techniques and tactics deal with similar requirements for shooting, which is merely the act of passing the ball in behind the defense and toward the opponent's goal. The aim of a good shooter is to develop an understanding of which techniques to use effectively.

Because shooting is a specialized skill that needs daily practice, your success as a goal scorer depends on several ingredients: (1) basic ability, (2) field position and awareness, and (3) integration of team play. The capability to move the ball for an angled shot so that the opposing goaltender cannot position behind the line of the shot is very important. The ability to accurately shoot early and follow up the shot for rebounds under all conditions is essential. Because the opposing defenders are expected to possess stickwork and mobility equivalent of Attack Role 1 players, scorers must be proficient in all skills. Quick footwork and balance will develop the ability to use all types of shots.

During a game, you will have little time to look at your target before shooting, so developing a visual image of the goal cage will allow you to shoot without looking up. Remain in a low position as you apply discrimination and imagination to guide your use of dribbling and passing. To prepare to take advantage of scoring opportunities, you must realize that swift and early passing produces the maximum speed to advance into scoring position.

Movement into position without the ball—Attack Roles 2 and 3 (see Step 8)—creates a dangerous attacking unit and develops team combination play resulting in scoring chances. No matter how gifted a scorer you may become, remember to regard yourself as a member of the team.

Why Is Shooting Important?

The aim of every attack is to score a goal, and all players enjoy scoring goals. Players who often play in the attacking third of the field are expected to execute the roles of attack to achieve penetration for the opportunity to shoot. It is here that attack players are charged with the most difficult task of all—the scoring of goals. Top scorers can execute shooting techniques from all angles, no matter where the ball arrives in relation to their feet. To score on a consistent basis, a player must be able to shoot under actual game pressures of restricted space, limited time, physical exhaustion, and aggressive opponents. The essence of shooting is the release speed of the shot, the surprise or deception of the shot, and the placement of the shot.

How to Execute Shooting

A goal scorer learns how and where to execute her shots on goal. You must learn to create space for your shot by changing speed and direction to commit a movement by the opposing defender or goalkeeper. Timing is vital to a shooter who is without the ball but wants to shoot the ball. To become a shooter in this situation, you must always move into the shooting space to coincide with the arrival of the ball. The defenders will always try to force you to shoot from a disadvantageous position—from the circle edge that is the greatest distance to the goal, from narrow angles, and at a hurried pace. A successful shooter learns to hit, flick, push, chip, and deflect the ball in the direction of the goal regardless of body position. The shooter must also concentrate on her objective while coping with restricted time and space and while being marked or unmarked. Most importantly, an accomplished shooter learns when a shot is impossible and when to pass to a teammate in a more advantageous scoring position (see figure 6.1).

The higher the level of play, the less time you have to execute an accurate shot on goal. A successful shooter can get the ball to the goal quickly using the one- or two-touch method. As a shooter, you must value the

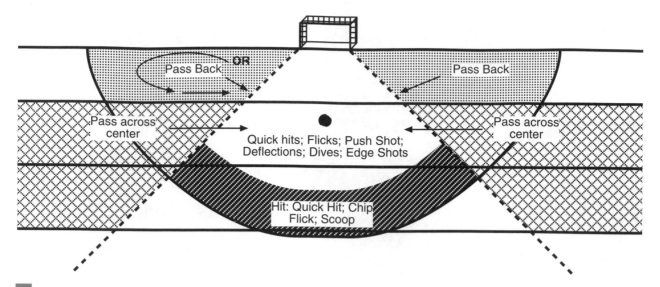

Figure 6.1 Shooting areas of circle.

need for accuracy because shots on goal, although saved by the opponent's goalkeeper, may provide another opportunity to score. Because goalkeepers may not catch, hold, or cover up the ball, an accurate shot can produce a rebound or a goal.

Because many goals are scored from the rebounds off the goalkeeper, you must learn *rebound positioning* to follow up shots by first positioning your body outside the shooting lane so you do not get hit by the initial shot. Anticipate where the ball will rebound and position to collect the rebound by moving toward the goalkeeper and into the clearing or passing lane. With your hands apart on the stick ready to touch the ball, break down your footwork into a ready position *before* the ball is rebounded. If the goalkeeper wears foam kickers and leg guards, your ready distance from the goalkeeper is at least five yards or more. The hockey ball bounces farther when it hits foam than when it hits leather or cane kickers and leg guards. In addition to winning rebounds for extra scoring chances, a high level of concentration and anticipation will enable you to press the opposing defenders in their defense zone to make receiving and passing errors.

Experienced shooters develop a sense of where the opponent's goal is without looking up before shooting. Learn to vary your shots depending on whether the ball is rolling or bouncing by developing your footwork and shortening or eliminating your backswing to shoot the ball from either your forehand or the reverse sides. Practice and repeat shooting until you are accurate with your body weight over either foot. In addition to the passing techniques described in Step 2, basic shooting skills include the quick hit, redirection or deflection, the dive, the edge, and the chip shot.

To execute shooting, move to the ball and receive it in a ready position with your hands on the stick in a "shake

hands" grip. To receive a pass from your right, point your left shoulder to the target; for a pass from your left, point your right shoulder to your target. Keep the head of your stick on the ground. Your legs are shoulder-width apart, and your center of gravity is low and evenly balanced. Keep your eyes on the lower half of the ball ready to apply any of your shooting techniques. Keep your head down and steady with a photo image of the goal cage's primary targets throughout your shooting action. Finish by transferring your weight to your front leg.

The Quick Hit

Defenders rarely give you time to prepare to hit the ball before shooting. Because of the lack of time to lift your stick to hit the ball, push shots and flicks are frequently used. But when faced with limited time, successful goal scorers need a more powerful shot than the push or flick. The quick hit or "short-grip" technique (figure 6.2) provides a fast hit rather than a hard hit whereby your hands slide together partly down the stick handle. The quick, short backswing enables you to instantly strike the ball with pace. To execute the quick hit, position your body to hit the ball by pointing your left shoulder to goal. Your left foot is in line with the ball, and your knees are bent for balance. Keep your feet 12 inches apart to assist your balance. Speed up your backswing by using the *clip grip* to slide your left hand down to your right hand. Gripping your stick slightly lower down will develop a shorter backswing. Your forearms accelerate the head of the stick through the lower half of the ball. Transfer your body weight to the front leg to assist in generating stick speed. Keep your head steady and your eyes on the lower half of the ball. Do not look up until you see your stick strike the lower half of the ball. Finish with your arms and stick in line to your target and return quickly to a ready position.

FIGURE
6.2 **KEYS TO SUCCESS**

THE QUICK HIT

a   b   c

Preparation

1. Aware of goal and opponent ____
2. Short steps, quick footwork ____
3. Lead shoulder to target in goal ____
4. Front foot in line with ball ____
5. Balanced with flexed knees ____
6. Head down and over ball; eyes focused on ball ____

Execution

1. Change to *clip grip* ____
2. Weight transferred on backswing ____
3. Head remains over ball ____
4. Short, quick backswing using forearms/wrists ____
5. Weight transfer to front leg on downswing ____
6. Align hands with wrists before contact and contact lower half of ball ____

Follow-Through

1. Keep head down and see ball leave stick ____
2. Momentum forward through front leg ____
3. Knees remain relaxed and bent ____
4. Arms and stick finish in line to target ____
5. Return to ready position ____

The Deflection Shot

A deflection shot is a shot in which the path of the passed ball is altered without the shooter actually stopping or trapping the ball. Often attack players are closely marked by defenders inside the shooting circle, which means that shooters may need to execute a one-touch shot on a pass to deflect the ball to the opposition's goal. Sometimes referred to as the redirection shot, the *deflection* is an effective shot used on hard, fast surfaces to shoot centering passes or free hits into the circle and in long hit situations. Learning to execute the deflection shot will promote confidence in many goal-scoring situations.

To execute the deflection (figure 6.3), firmly grip your stick using the shake hands grip. Artificial turf, where the playing surface is smooth, allows you to lay your stick horizontally to deflect the pass toward the goal. The horizontal stick dropped to the ground offers the largest possible surface area to play the ball. The de-

flection shot can also be executed using a more vertical stick. Use the head of your stick to jab firmly into the line of the approaching ball. Whether using a horizontal or vertical stick, keep your head in line with your stick and the ball. The critical element of this challenging shot is to correctly angle the left side of the stick so when the lower half of the ball hits your stick, the ball takes on a new path to the opposition's goal. To execute a successful deflection shot, it is crucial that you place your stick inside the shooting angles to the goalposts. Do not swing your stick to perform the deflection. Always firmly grip your stick and guide the ball by establishing the correct stick angle with the face of your stick. Aim for the near post because your deflection shot has less distance to travel when at maximum speed.

Much practice is needed to execute accurate deflections on both your forehand and reverse stick. It is a scoring weapon that requires excellent timing and a great deal of hand-eye coordination, but it is a very effective way to score!

FIGURE 6.3 **KEYS TO SUCCESS**

THE DEFLECTION SHOT

Preparation

1. Aware of goal and opponent ____
2. Short steps, quick footwork ____
3. Lead foot and shoulder point to target ____
4. Firm shake hands grip ____
5. Horizontal or vertical stick position ____
6. Angle stick face to target and approaching ball; block path of ball ____
7. Weight balanced and centered with eyes on lower half of ball ____

a

Execution

1. Transfer weight forward through front leg ____
2. Contact lower half of ball ____
3. Guide shot in target direction ____

b

Follow-Through

1. Generate momentum through the ball ____
2. Head kept in line with ball path ____
3. Extend stick and arms to target ____
4. Return to ready position for rebound ____

c

The Dive Shot

The sight of a shooter diving fully extended to shoot the ball is one of the most exciting and acrobatic skills in field hockey. Players who play regularly on water-based artificial surfaces enjoy performing this advanced form of a deflection called the *dive*, or slide, shot. Most players find the dive shot a more difficult shot to execute than any other shooting technique because it requires precise timing as well as correct technique to deflect a rolling ball. Sliding your body in a horizontal position—head leading—along a watered surface will give you a greater reach to the ball. The watered-artificial surface protects your body from possible injury. Dive shots can be executed on your forehand and reverse stick (figure 6.4).

The diving mechanics are very similar to those used by a base runner in baseball who sprints and dives to reach the base with his hands. The primary difference in hockey is that you reach for the ball with your stick face correctly angled to deflect the ball toward the goal. The initial diving movement begins from short, quick running strides or a ready position with vision focused on the rolling ball. Keep your eyes focused on the lower half of the ball to judge the distance and speed that the ball is traveling. As with the deflection shot, hold your stick firmly using the shake hands or receiving grip. Your judgment of ball speed and distance from your stick reach will assist your decision to begin your dive. You must coordinate the movement of your legs and upper body to vault toward the space when you can intercept with your stick the path of the approaching ball. Move the foot nearest the ball in the direction you are going to dive. Push off that foot to begin your dive; for example, push off your right foot when diving to your right. Your opposite leg follows to generate additional momentum. Extend your arms and correctly angled stick toward the ball, maintaining your hands/stick, eyes, and head position to the ball. Contact the ground by sliding on your side. To deflect the ball to the goal, angle your stick toward the target and keep your wrists firm. When diving on the reverse stick or left side, the mechanics are the same except for the grip of the stick. To obtain maximum reach, only your left hand grips the stick using a firm reverse grip. To deflect the ball upward and forward to the goal, always contact the lower half of the ball with a slightly open stick.

FIGURE 6.4 KEYS TO SUCCESS

THE DIVE SHOT

Preparation

1. Aware of goal and opponent ____
2. Short steps, quick footwork ____
3. Square shoulders to oncoming ball ____
4. Lead foot and shoulder point to target ____
5. Assume slightly crouched position with weight balanced and centered on power points ____
6. Firm shake hands grip on stick ____
7. Angle stick face to target and approaching ball; keep eyes on lower half of rolling ball ____

a

Execution

1. Dive toward space to intercept the ball ____
2. Push off near foot of dive direction ____
3. Side of body parallel to ground ____
4. Extend arms and horizontal stick forward ____
5. Eyes on lower half of ball ____
6. Contact ground sliding on side ____
7. Firm wrists ____
8. Deflect ball on stick angled to goal ____

b

Follow-Through

1. Momentum forward with contact ____
2. Jump to feet ____
3. Return to ready position ____

c

The Edge Shot

Good shooters learn to execute shots despite the restriction of time and space. There are occasions when the shooter must find a way to strike a ball that is rolling away from the shooter's stick. The modern game of field hockey, which is played primarily on artificial surfaces, has adopted the *edge shot* to shoot a "runaway" ball. With the edge shot, the player strikes the ball on the forehand or reverse sides using the edge of the horizontal stick (figure 6.5). Your stick must be positioned horizontally on the ground with the flat side facing the sky. For a successful edge shot that travels accurately along the ground, it is crucial to lower your left hand to the ground to place the handle of your stick on and parallel to the ground to expose a larger surface edge to sweep at the ball.

To execute the edge shot, square your shoulders to the runaway ball and maintain a crouched position with your weight on the power points of your feet. Your lead or front shoulder must point toward your target. Bring your hands together on your stick for greater reach to the ball and to prepare to hit the edge shot. Keep your eyes on the lower half of the ball to prepare your horizontal stick position along the ground. Using a short backswing with the flat side of your stick facing upward and parallel to the ground, contact the lower half of the ball with the edge of your stick shaft or the edge of the stick head. Return to a ready position for rebounds.

FIGURE 6.5 | **KEYS TO SUCCESS**

THE EDGE SHOT

Preparation

1. Aware of goal and opponent ____
2. Short, quick footwork ____
3. Square shoulders to ball rolling away ____
4. Front shoulder points to target ____
5. Shake hands grip ____
6. Assume crouched position; weight on power points of feet ____
7. Eyes on lower half of ball ____

a

Execution

1. Slide hands together on stick ____
2. Horizontal stick behind ball ____
3. Flat side of stick faces upward ____
4. Short backswing ____
5. Weight transferred to foot nearest target ____
6. Align hands with wrists/forearms on contact ____
7. Contact lower half of ball with stick edging ____

b

Follow-Through

1. Weight transfer through front foot ____
2. Knees remain relaxed and bent ____
3. Head down to see ball leave stick ____
4. Arms/stick finish in low line to target ____
5. Return to ready position ____

c

The Chip Shot

Experienced shooters realize that the hit and the quick hit are prerequisites to the powerful aerial hit—the chip shot. The *chip shot* is an advanced shooting technique (figure 6.6) used to beat the low-sliding goalkeeper or to place the ball in the upper part of the goal. By hitting the ball with a partially opened stick head from both your forehand and reverse sides, you can loft the ball off the ground to various heights and distances. A chip shot should only be used after you learn to control its outcome.

The chip shot execution is similar to the hit with the exception of the slightly opened stick face on contact and ball position. The ball is controlled a little far-ther in front of your lead foot. To hit with an open stick face, turn your stick head slightly clockwise to no more than a two-o'clock position. Slide your hands together on your stick as you begin the backswing and transfer your weight to the back leg. Keep your eyes on the lower half of the ball. Lower your right shoulder and transfer your weight to the front leg and hip on the downswing. While your hands remain behind the ball on impact, see your open stick contact the lower half of the ball. The follow-through of your stick will determine the line of accuracy of your shot. To hit a chip shot that has maximum backspin for greater distance and elevation, strike the ball and the ground behind the ball.

FIGURE 6.6

KEYS TO SUCCESS

THE CHIP SHOT

a   b   c

Preparation

1. Aware of goal and opponent ____
2. Short steps, quick footwork ____
3. Lead shoulder points toward target; head down and over ball ____
4. Split shake hands grip ____
5. Prepare ball beyond front foot ____
6. Knees bent with crouched body ____
7. Eyes on lower half of ball ____

Execution

1. Slide hands together ____
2. Open stick face ____
3. Weight transferred to back leg on backswing; lower right shoulder ____
4. Weight transfer to front leg/ hip on downswing ____
5. Hands behind the ball on impact ____
6. Contact lower half of ball with open stick ____

Follow-Through

1. Fluid transfer of weight through front foot ____
2. Knees remain relaxed and bent ____
3. Head down and see ball leave stick ____
4. Arms/stick finish in line to target ____
5. Return to ready position ____

SHOOTING SUCCESS STOPPERS

Your objective when executing the various shooting techniques is accuracy with a quick release. If you consistently fail to achieve one without the other, you probably will not score many goals. Common shooting errors are listed here, along with suggested corrections.

Error	Correction
Shooting Areas of Circle, Primary Shooting Targets	
1. The pass to you in a shooting area of the circle is intercepted by the opposing defender.	1. Time your arrival to coincide with the approaching ball. When you arrive too early or arrive too late, the defender can successfully mark you and intercept passes.
2. You mishit the ball.	2. Keep your head down with eyes on the lower half of the ball instead of the target.
3. You shoot to a nonexisting target.	3. Without looking up, select a target from your memory image. Square your shoulders to the ball and point your lead shoulder to the goal target.
The Quick Hit, Edge Shot, Chip Shot	
1. You undercut or slice the ball when attempting the quick hit.	1. Keep your feet shoulder-width apart and position the ball 9 inches in line with your front foot. Face of stick must be flat at moment of impact.
2. You top the ball when attempting an edge shot.	2. Bend your knees and adjust your body in a low, crouched position. Lay stick horizontally on the ground behind the ball to begin your sweep to the ball. Keep your left hand on the ground to maintain a parallel stick throughout the swing. Strike the lower half of the ball with edging of your parallel stick.
3. The quick hit is choppy.	3. Position the ball in your control box off the front foot instead of near the back foot and follow through after impact.
4. The quick hit has little power or accuracy.	4. Check your grip to make sure hands are together and not split. Use and coordinate forearms/wrists on downswing and transfer of weight.
5. The edge shot is bouncing.	5. Edge of stick must be square to the lower half of the ball on contact.
6. Chip shot is wild and uncontrolled.	6. A complete follow-through motion is necessary for the chip shot. Discipline your follow-through by always finishing in line to your target. Adjust your grip before starting your backswing and swing your arms freely and in unison away from your body. Avoid wrist movement.

Error	Correction
Deflection Shot, Dive Shot	
1. Ball hits your feet when trying to redirect the ball.	1. Stick and hands too close to your feet. Keep your eyes on the lower half of the ball to judge the speed and distance of the rolling ball.
2. Height of your deflection shot is too low.	2. Contact the lower half of the ball with face of open stick, which will deflect the ball upward.
3. You have poor accuracy with your deflection shot.	3. Front shoulder and foot point to the target and your stick angle follows line toward the target.
4. Your dive shot lacks power and accuracy.	4. You mistimed your dive and failed to keep your stick firm as the ball contacted your stick. Contact the ball on the flat surface of your stick.
5. You get the wind knocked out of you as you contact the ground after diving for the ball.	5. You may be so intent on diving to the space to deflect the ball that you forget to cushion your fall to the ground. Extend your stick and arms forward and downward as you slide on your side along the ground. This stick and arm movement not only provides added momentum to your dive but also enables you to cushion your dive on the side of your body.

SHOOTING DRILLS

1. Shooting the Rebound

Use a goal cage with an 18-inch backboard, or place rebound boards side by side to create the width of a 4-yard goal. Use masking tape or chalk to mark three targets on the left, center, and right front of the backboard. From a distance of 10 yards, apply a quick-hit technique to shoot a stationary ball to the center goal target. Return to ready position and use any shooting technique from the forehand or reverse stick to shoot the rebound accurately to the left or right target. Award yourself one point for each rebound shot on the left and right targets. Take 30 quick hit shots with follow-up rebound shots.

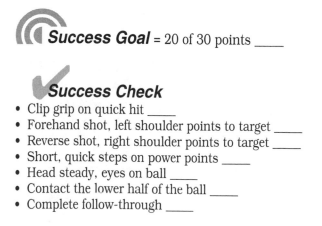

Success Goal = 20 of 30 points _____

Success Check
- Clip grip on quick hit _____
- Forehand shot, left shoulder points to target _____
- Reverse shot, right shoulder points to target _____
- Short, quick steps on power points _____
- Head steady, eyes on ball _____
- Contact the lower half of the ball _____
- Complete follow-through _____

To Increase Difficulty
- Increase quick hit distance.
- Reduce size of chalk targets.
- Shoot the quick hit from a dribble.
- Shoot all rebound shots from the forehand.
- One-touch rebound shots.

To Decrease Difficulty
- Reduce quick hit distance.
- Allow three touches to shoot the rebound.
- Increase size of targets.

2. Deflect the Pass

Position in the shooting circle and have a teammate pass a ball to you from 15 yards away. Deflect the passed ball to the goal using the deflection technique. From a distance of 15 yards, take 10 balls from the right direction, 10 balls from the center direction, and 10 balls from the left direction. Award yourself one point for each ball deflected accurately into the goal cage.

Success Goal = 20 of 30 points _____

Success Check

- Lead shoulder points to target _____
- Use short, quick steps on power points of feet _____
- Ball played in control box _____
- Stick remains still with firm grip _____
- Head down, eyes on ball _____
- Contact lower half of the ball _____
- Complete follow-through _____

To Increase Difficulty

- Increase distance from passer.
- Increase velocity of served pass.
- Take all deflection shots on reverse stick.
- Reduce size of goal target.

To Decrease Difficulty

- Decrease distance from passer.
- Take all deflection shots on the forehand side.
- Increase goal target.
- Server reduces velocity of pass.

3. Pressure Shooting From the Top of the Circle

Play on one end of a regulation field. Position a goalkeeper in goal and a pass server with her back to the goal on the center of the 17-yard line. You stand directly in front and face the server with a supply of hockey balls. Start the shooting activity by pushing the ball to the server. The server one touches the ball ahead of you near the circle edge. Quickly sprint to the ball, shoot to score, and sprint back to your original spot. Repeat the same sequence for six balls, trying to one touch or two touch your shot. The server alternates passing balls to your left and right sides. Take six shots, then switch positions with the server and repeat the round. Award two points for each goal scored and one point for each shot on goal saved by the goalkeeper. Play three rounds as the shooter and three as the server.

Success Goal = 6 points or more per round _____

Success Check

- Short, quick steps on power points of feet _____
- Point lead shoulder to target _____
- Head steady and eyes on ball _____
- Prepare grip _____
- Contact lower half of ball _____
- Complete follow-through _____

To Increase Difficulty

- Increase passing distance from server.
- One touch every shot.
- Take 10 shots per round.

To Decrease Difficulty

- Reduce passing distance to the server.
- Decrease speed of repetition.
- Reduce number of shots per round.
- Play without a goalkeeper.

4. Shooting—Two-on-One Game

Set up a playing area 25 yards wide by 40 yards long. Place goals on each back line. Using eight or more players, divide into two equal teams. Start with three players from each team—one is positioned in the defense half of playing area and the other two players start in the attack half of the playing grid. The players must remain in their assigned zones or 20-yard half. The coach starts play from outside the midline area by passing a ball to one of either team's two attack players.

The two attack players receive the ball and attack against the opposing defender in an attempt to shoot and score. If the defender tackles or intercepts, she immediately passes the ball to the two attack teammates who create a two-on-one to goal in the opposite direction. When the ball goes out-of-bounds, the coach passes the next ball into play. Apply field hockey substitution rules where players depart and enter the playing field at the midline area. Score one point for each shot that scores. Play for 10 minutes. The team with the most goals wins the game.

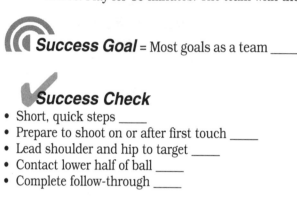 **Success Goal** = Most goals as a team _____

 Success Check
- Short, quick steps _____
- Prepare to shoot on or after first touch _____
- Lead shoulder and hip to target _____
- Contact lower half of ball _____
- Complete follow-through _____

To Increase Difficulty
- Add a goalkeeper at each goal.
- Allow one attacker to drop back in defensive half of grid to help defend with teammate—two-on-two.
- Increase playing time.
- Allow shooter two touches to control and shoot the ball.

To Decrease Difficulty
- Decrease playing time.
- Allow defender to counterattack and join two attack teammates to create a three-on-one.
- Allow shooter three touches to control and shoot the ball.

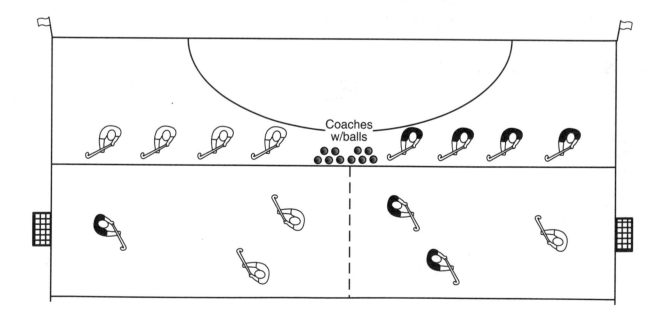

5. Through-the-Gate Shooting

Use the attack third of the field with a regulation goal to set up your shooting practice. Place two spot markers in front of the goal to represent the gate where centering passes are served and shot. One gate marker is placed 4 yards and the other is place 8 yards from the center of the goal line. On the right side of the field, set up a diagonal line of three cones from end line to sideline, 2 1/2-yards apart, starting 5 yards from the back line and outside of the shooting circle. In the same area but 5 yards inside the shooting circle, set up another diagonal line of three cones 2 1/2-yards apart. Place a stationary passer (P #1) with a supply of hockey balls in the center of the 20-yard area. P #2 positions on the 30-yard area opposite P #1 to receive the first pass. P #3 positions near the right sideline on the 30-yard area to receive a pass from P #2. A line of servers are positioned near the sets of cones to receive a pass from P #3. The server receives the ball from P #3 and dribbles around the cones in the direction of the end line and serves the ball by hitting or pushing the ball through the gate markers. As a shooter who starts outside the shooting circle on the left side, time your run through the gate to coincide with the arrival of the ball. Using any shooting technique, take 20 shots. Play until each player completes 20 shot attempts. Award one point for each shot that scores.

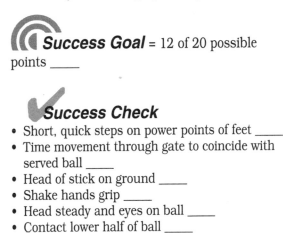

Success Goal = 12 of 20 possible points ____

✔ Success Check
* Short, quick steps on power points of feet ____
* Time movement through gate to coincide with served ball ____
* Head of stick on ground ____
* Shake hands grip ____
* Head steady and eyes on ball ____
* Contact lower half of ball ____
* Complete follow-through ____

To Increase Difficulty
* Require shooter to execute first-time shot.
* Place a goalkeeper in goal.
* Require servers to increase velocity of passes through the gate.
* Add a defender to defend gate area.

To Decrease Difficulty
* Allow three-touch shooting.
* Require servers to push pass the ball through the gate.

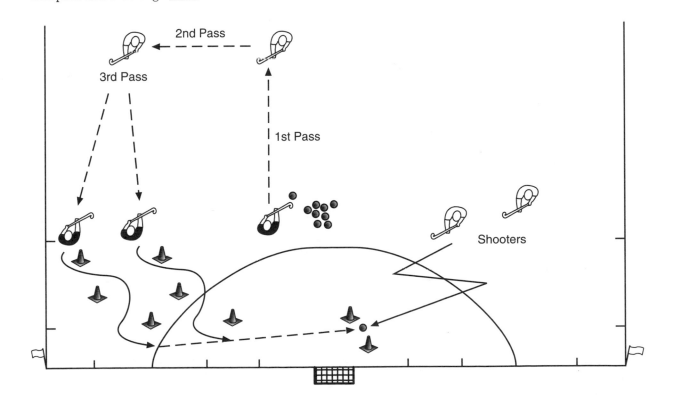

6. Skeletal Shooting

Place a supply of hockey balls in four areas at one end of a regulation hockey field: P1—the center of the 25-yard line; P2—on the 10-yard line, 10 yards outside the shooting circle on the right side of the attack area; P3—on the 10-yard line, 10 yards outside the shooting circle on the left; P4/5——behind the back line, 8 yards from the right goalpost. Stationary servers are positioned at P1, P2, P3, and P4/5. At the 25-yard line (P1) with a shooting partner, begin the skeletal shooting exercise by moving toward the edge of the shooting circle while passing the ball back and forth with your partner. The player who has possession of the ball when entering the shooting circle shoots the ball on goal. Your shooting partner positions for a rebound shot. After a score, a missed shot, or a rebound that goes outside the circle, you and your partner prepare to shoot a second ball crossed into the circle from P2. Try to control each crossed ball with your first touch, then shoot to score with your second touch. Perform the same for the crossed ball from P3. From behind the back line, two consecutive balls are served from P4/5 into the shooter's gate. Using the shooting technique of your choice, perform five repetitions of the five-ball round. Award you and your partner one point for each ball that is controlled and shot into the goal using only two touches or fewer. Do not use a goalkeeper.

Success Goal = 15 or more points ____

Success Check
- Short, quick steps on power points of feet ____
- Stick head on ground ____
- Prepare ball with first touch ____
- Head steady and eyes on ball ____
- Contact lower half of ball ____
- Complete follow-through ____

To Increase Difficulty
- Add a passive defender.
- Add a goalkeeper.
- Shoot first time without controlling the ball.
- Increase velocity of crossed balls.

To Decrease Difficulty
- Reduce distance of crossed balls.
- Allow shooter three touches to control and shoot the ball.
- Require servers to push all crossed balls.

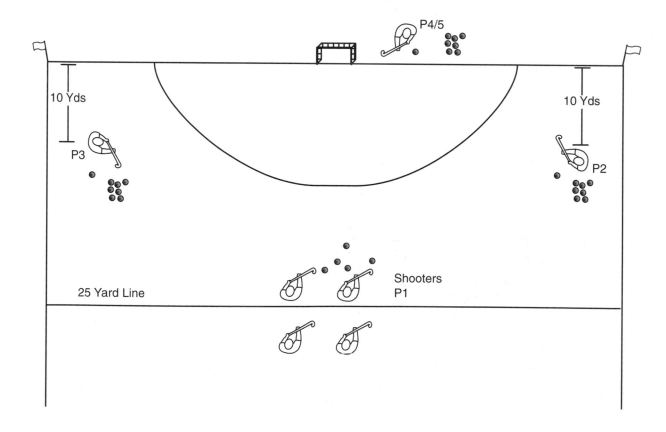

7. Cut, Receive, and Shoot From the Dribble

Position a goalkeeper in the goal and use the attack area inside the 30-yard line to goal. Play with six or more teammates. Set up on a diagonal line two four-cone dribbling obstacles outside the shooting circle on the right and left sides. The first cone is placed 2 1/2 yards outside the shooting circle and 5 yards to the outside of the line of the near goalpost. The subsequent cones are placed 2 1/2 yards apart on a diagonal line toward the sideline. On the center of the 20-yard line with a bucket of hockey balls, position a player facing the 50-yard line to start the passing sequence. Three players who face the shooting circle are evenly spaced along the 30-yard line. The center player receives the first pass and passes a square (flat-lined) pass to either player positioned on the right or left sides of the 30-yard line. After the outside player receives the second pass, she prepares to make the third pass to the shooter. As the shooter, you position near the cone farthest from the shooting circle and cut to receive the third pass. Immediately control the ball and dribble the ball around the four cones. Using any shooting technique to score, prepare to shoot the ball from the forehand side of the body. When the shooter begins dribbling around the first cone, the next ball should be passed from the bucket of balls to the other side of the field. Take five shots from each shooting line, then switch positions with one of the passers and repeat the round. Award two points for each goal scored and one point for each shot on goal saved by the goalkeeper.

Success Goal = 12 or more points per round _____

Success Check

- Short, quick steps on power points of feet _____
- Head of stick on the ground _____
- Control and dribble lower half of ball _____
- Left shoulder and leg point to target in goal _____
- Head steady and eyes on ball _____
- Ball positioned in control box, in line with front foot _____
- Contact lower half of ball _____
- Complete follow-through _____

To Increase Difficulty

- Allow shooter only two touches to control and shoot the ball.
- Take 10 shots from each shooting side.
- Shoot using the reverse stick.
- Require shot to be taken between 10 and 16 yards from the goal.
- Increase speed of repetition.

To Decrease Difficulty

- Reduce shooting distance to inside the 10-yard area.
- Decrease speed of repetition.
- Allow the shooter three touches to control and shoot the ball.
- Eliminate the goalkeeper.

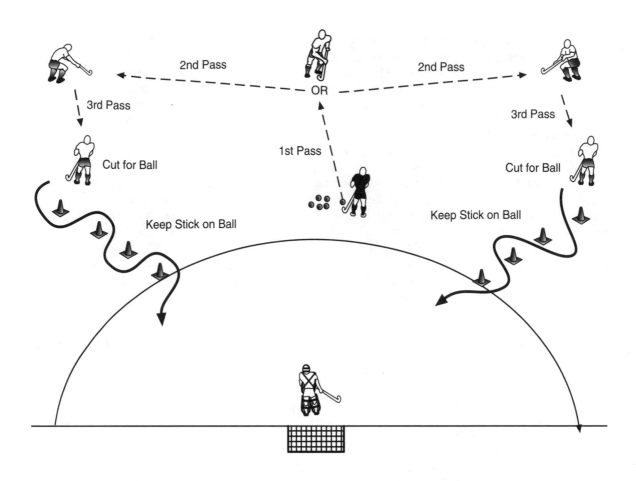

2nd Pass

OR

2nd Pass

3rd Pass

3rd Pass

Cut for Ball

1st Pass

Cut for Ball

Keep Stick on Ball

Keep Stick on Ball

8. Three-on-One Shooting With Recover Player

Play with two teammates on one end of a regulation hockey field. Designate three servers to pass balls from three areas: center at the 40-yard area, the right-side long hit mark, and the left-side long hit mark. The defensive team has three players: a goalkeeper in goal, a defender near the 25-yard area, and a defender near the 40-yard area who recovers to help after the third ball. Three attack players position between the 40- and 25-yard area. Play is started by server "A" passing a ball to the three attack players. The objective of the three attack players is to execute quick penetrating passes that will enable a shot or score. Award one point for a shot that scores. When the ball goes out of play or in the goal, server "B" passes a ball to the attack team from the right long hit mark. When this ball is out of play, server "A" passes another ball to the attack team. It is on this ball that the recovery defender joins the defensive play to create two defenders against the three attack players. After a score or the ball is out of play, server "C" passes the fourth ball into play. Repeat a second round of four balls, then rotate different attack, defense, and servers, and repeat the drill. The attack team scoring the most goals after two rounds each wins the competition.

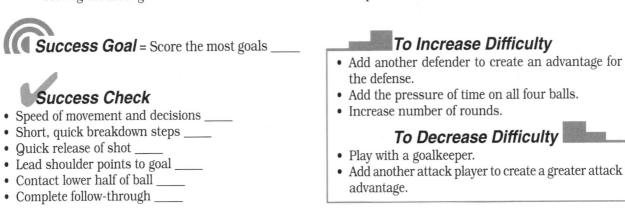

Success Goal = Score the most goals _____

✔Success Check
- Speed of movement and decisions _____
- Short, quick breakdown steps _____
- Quick release of shot _____
- Lead shoulder points to goal _____
- Contact lower half of ball _____
- Complete follow-through _____

To Increase Difficulty
- Add another defender to create an advantage for the defense.
- Add the pressure of time on all four balls.
- Increase number of rounds.

To Decrease Difficulty
- Play with a goalkeeper.
- Add another attack player to create a greater attack advantage.

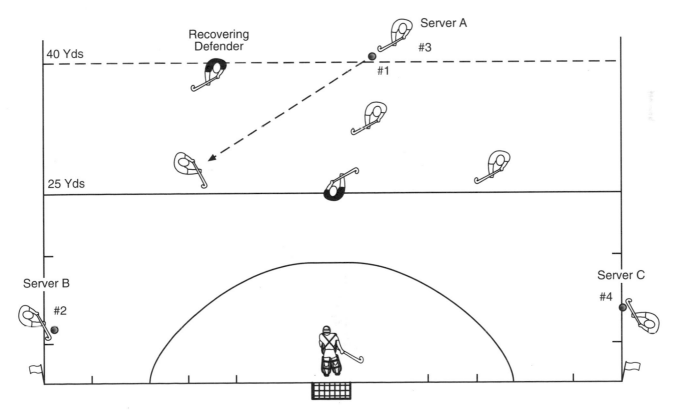

9. Two-on-Two Shooting Game

Divide into two teams of four field players each with one goalkeeper on each team. Use cones or flags to outline a 35-yard-by-40-yard field area with a regulation-size goal at each end line. The field area has two 20-yard zones divided by a midline. Each team defends a goal and tries to score in opponent's goal. Each team positions two attack players and two defense players in each of the two zones. Begin the game with a pass from the center of the midline. Regular hockey rules apply except that the ball may only be passed over the midline. Once the ball is passed from zone to zone, one of the defense zone players may join the attack teammates to create a three-on-two in the attack zone. Use any type of shooting technique to shoot from anywhere in your attack zone. Award two points for a goal scored and one point for a shot on goal saved by the goalkeeper. Play for 10 minutes. Rotate different players in the attack and defense zones.

Success Goal = Score the most points _____

Success Check
- Lead shoulder and leg point to target _____
- Use quick, balanced footwork _____
- Stick head on the ground _____
- Prepare proper grip _____
- Contact the lower half of ball _____
- Complete follow-through _____

To Increase Difficulty
- Require first-time shots.
- Increase playing time.
- Do not permit dribbling.

To Decrease Difficulty
- Do not use a goalkeeper.
- Allow shots from any distance and from both zones.
- Do not allow defenders to tackle, only intercept passed balls.

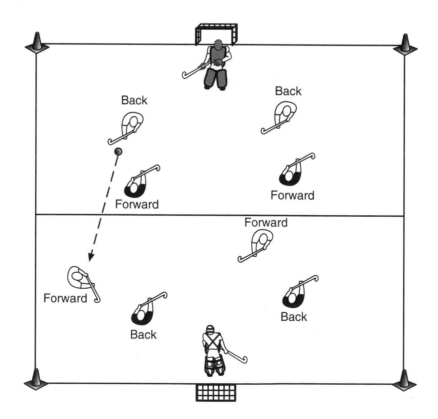

10. Chip Shooting to Score

Position yourself 16 yards front and center of a regulation goal. Position a server on the side area with a supply of hockey balls. The server crosses balls into the shooting circle for you to control and chip shoot on goal. Try to control each crossed ball with your first touch, adjust your feet and grip, then chip shoot to score with your second touch. Perform 20 repetitions—receiving 10 balls from each side. Award yourself one point for each crossed ball that you control and chip into the goal using only two touches. Do not use a goalkeeper.

Success Goal = 12 or more points ____

Success Check

• Face crossed ball with lead shoulder pointing to goal target ____
• Use quick, balanced footwork ____
• Prepare feet and ball on first touch ____
• Adjust grip ____
• Contact the lower half of ball with slightly open stick face ____
• Complete follow-through ____

To Increase Difficulty

• Add goalkeeper or rebound boards.
• Increase velocity of crossed balls.
• Increase number of repetitions.

To Decrease Difficulty

• Reduce shooting distance to 12 yards.
• Allow shooter three touches to control and shoot the ball.
• Reduce number of repetitions.

SHOOTING SUCCESS SUMMARY

The ultimate goal of every field hockey team is to play as a unit to score more goals than the opposition. To achieve this goal, each team member must possess solid shooting skills. There will always be a time when a player will have a chance to win a game. For this reason alone, every player, regardless of her playing position, should be able to finish an attack. Beginners should start by shooting without the pressure of restricted time, opponents, and space limitations, which will permit a higher concentration on the correct skill. Develop your ability to shoot first with accuracy and then power. Ask your coach or teammate to observe and analyze your shooting techniques during practice sessions. As your technical skills improve, progress to more game-related training by adding limited pressure of time and opponent(s) and begin to restrict space for shooting. Eventually you will be able to execute shooting skills in the full-sided game.

STEP
7
GOALKEEPING: PROTECTING THE GOAL

The field hockey goalkeeper needs as much mental, physical, technical, and tactical preparation as the field player. To play as a goalkeeper, you must be able to *block* or *save* all types of shots, which can travel at speeds in excess of 90 miles per hour. At times you will have to dive in the air or on the ground to save shots to either side. You may even have to deny an opponent on a one-on-one breakaway. To make a save of a shot is only half the expected skill. You must also *clear* the ball safely and skillfully. Teammates must know that if a deep pass penetrates the defense, the goalkeeper will clear or control the ball with coordination and purpose.

Goalkeeping requires a special type of athlete who uses protective, lightweight equipment similar to gear worn by ice hockey goaltenders. With this equipment, the hockey goalkeeper is the only player allowed to use the hands, feet, and body to play the ball and can do so only within the team's own shooting circle. Comfortable and protective equipment worn by the field hockey goalkeeper is very important to ensure confidence against injury when playing the ball. Artificial surfaces and stiffened sticks that produce powerfully hit shots enhance higher playing standards and faster play. It is vitally important for goalkeepers who rely on tremendous reflexes, outstanding agility, and an enormous desire to perform to be totally protected. Because extensive goalkeeping attire can be expensive, the dependable goalkeeper must practice good habits and pride by following instructions on proper equipment care to prolong the life of her equipment.

The goalkeeper who possesses excellent physical and mental qualities breeds confidence in her team. Physically, you must develop the ability to use either foot, your hands, or the stick to block and clear the ball. This requires a high degree of eye coordination to your body parts. The maintenance of strength, flexibility, and stamina will promote good body balance and footwork, which enable you to perform reliable goalkeeping techniques and quick reflexes. The goalkeeper's mental attributes consist of courage, reliability, and determination. It is a primary requirement for the goalkeeper to remain aggressively calm and make decisions to play the ball while under pressure.

Goalkeeping requires that a player have a complete understanding of the roles of defense. Within the roles of defense, the goalkeeper plays a specialized position with a formidable responsibility to protect the goal. To be a good goalkeeper, you must develop the ability to "read" the game because you have the best position to view the entire defensive plan. The advanced goalkeeper must combine Defense Role 1's engage-and-give technique with sliding stack tackles to handle the dangerous one-on-one breakaway. Understanding the roles of defense will enhance your ability to organize your defensive unit with leadership and apply the proper techniques to protect your goal.

As the last player who can prevent the ball from going into the goal, the goalkeeper must master technical skills that are entirely different from those used by the field players. Young players (under 12 years of age) should not specialize in the goalkeeper position but instead should split time between the playing in the goal and in the field. Although a team usually designates one or two players specifically as goalkeepers, all players should understand goalkeeping skills. Goalkeeping techniques include the basic stance (the *ready position*), methods of *blocking* or saving low ground shots and aerial shots directly at and to the sides of the goalkeeper, and clearing methods using various kicking techniques and the occasional stick clearing pass.

Why Are Goalkeeping Skills Important?

The aim of every defense is to prevent a goal. Good positioning and timing will result in successful defensive skills. Players who often play in the defending third of the field are expected to execute the roles of defense to prevent penetration for the opportunity to shoot. It is here that defense players and the goalkeeper work together to block dangerous space to goal.

The essence of goalkeeping is understanding the roles of defense, positioning in the space from the ball to the center of the goal line, using correct balance and footwork to ensure good save-clear-recovery techniques, and maintaining a determined attitude to execute goalkeeping skills in a confident and correct manner. No team wants a goalkeeper who is showy and brilliant one minute and embarrassingly unreliable the next. Understanding the roles of defense will allow you to dominate the situation and influence the way in which AR1 attempts to shoot at goal. The goalkeeper works with her teammates to force the AR1 player to shoot as far away from the goal as possible and from as narrow of an angle as possible. Forcing the opponent into errors of hurried shooting mechanics allows the goalkeeper to handle a weaker shot. The goalkeeper who can direct his teammates to force a delayed shot will gain more time for proper positioning to narrow the shooting angle and make the save. A successful goalkeeper will learn to anticipate where shots are going to be made and position to save them.

A good goalkeeper is qualified in many specialized goalkeeping techniques. The technique used by the goalkeeper depends on three factors: 1) the type of equipment worn; 2) the speed of the shot; and 3) the position of the opponent. As the goalkeeper, you must choose between the *block and clear* and the one-time clear often used on artificial surfaces and higher levels of play. The *one-time clear* is a save and clear all-in-one touch movement. Being that more goals are scored from rebounds off the goalkeeper than from direct shots, it is essential to develop the ability to control and clear your rebounds with accurate and powerful kicks with either foot. Good goalkeeping techniques that require mobility, quick reflexes, and balance will raise your skill level and can only be achieved with top physical conditioning

and proper technical training. Goaltending is a position in which technique development initiates success.

The Goalkeeper Stance

When an opponent has the ball within shooting distance of your goal, assume the balanced goalkeeper stance, or *ready position*. From the ready position (see figure 7.1), you will be able to move quickly in any direction by getting behind the line of the ball. The goalkeeper's balance is a crucial aspect of successful skill execution. All skills start from the classic position of readiness, with a return to the ready position after the clear. The first rule of goalkeeping is to get the head in the correct position to establish body balance and feel comfortable with it. Subsequent goalkeeping techniques are controlled from the position of the goalkeeper's head, no matter if the body is set in control or in a movement pattern.

To execute the ready position, square your shoulders to the ball with feet approximately shoulder-width apart. Keep your head and upper body forward and steady behind the line of the ball. Center your body weight forward on the power points of your feet with your heels off the ground. Your knees remain bent with the back slightly crouched. The goalkeeper must remain relaxed, yet alert. Keep your chin beyond your knees and your knees beyond your toes. Both arms are alongside the body with palms of the hands open and the "pinkie" fingers touching the outside of the knees. Your right hand holds your stick midway down the shaft, producing an extension of your right arm. Keep your head steady and your eyes focused on the lower half of the ball.

Figure 7.1a   Front view stance.

Figure 7.1b   Side view stance.

Positioning—Covering the Angles

Although defense of the circle area is a group responsibility, goalkeepers often are beaten because they are out of position. The circle is the goalkeeper's boundary and base. As the goalkeeper, you are a vital part of a cover system that is the last line of defense. To play the goalkeeper position successfully, you must develop an understanding of where to prepare your ready position to save a direct shot at goal. Shots at goal come from a variety of angles and distances up to 16 yards varying from 90 degrees at the top of the shooting circle to zero degrees along the back line. The aim of the goalkeeper is to give AR1 the smallest view of the goal. The movement of the goalkeeper to position and cover these shots is referred to as *covering the angles.*

By drawing an imaginary line from the ball, through the goalkeeper's legs and to the center of the goal line, the goalkeeper becomes a barrier who must narrow the scoring angle available to the Role 1 attack player. As the AR1 approaches the attack area, you must move using quick, short steps to maintain a ready position between the ball and the center of the goal. When the ball is passed, you must take up a new position relative to the ball and the center of the goal (see figure 7.2).

Positioning is essential for good goalkeeping. You must always know where you are in relation to the goal to enable you to discriminate between simple and difficult shots. Experienced goalkeepers who are familiar with the angles do not have to make spectacular saves because they know where to position. The well-positioned goalkeeper will also know whether a shot is on goal or wide without having to look around and behind. Referring to the zones of the circle (see figure 7.3)

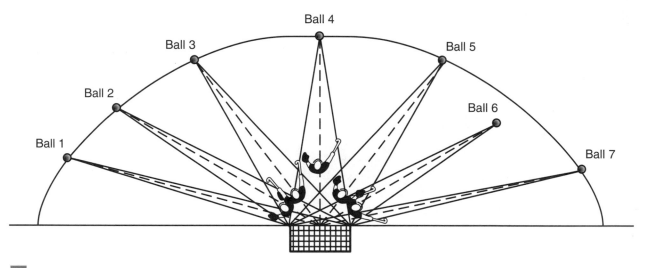

Figure 7.2 Positioning: covering the angles.

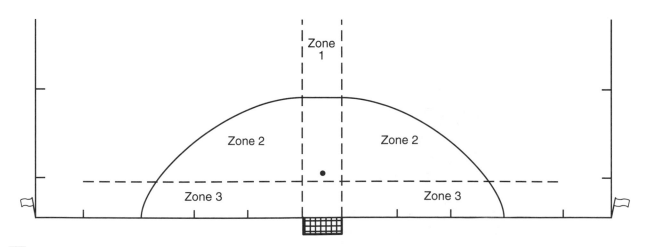

Figure 7.3 Zones of the cricle.

will assist your positioning to cover angles to the goal. When the ball is in zone 3 near the back line, keep your eyes on the ball and search for the goalpost with your stick on the right side and your glove on the left. Position against the goalpost nearer to the ball and make sure there is no gap between your legs and between your body and the post. No shot from this zone should be successful. When the ball moves into zone 2, you must use quick shuffle steps to stay in line with the ball and the center of the goal. The shooting angle is greater than in zone 3, so you must move forward from the goal line to increase the goal coverage. In zone 1, AR1 has maximum view of the goal. To defend this angle, you must position at the extremity of the arc from one goalpost to the other. To successfully cover the angles, develop speed of movement around a three or four yard arc in front of the goal and between the posts.

If advancing to play the ball, you must do so with shouted directives to your defenders. Never interfere if another defense teammate is tackling or harassing an opponent. Wait for the developments in a ready position to save the shot or advance to a new position.

How to Block Ground Balls

The goalkeeper's fundamental saving techniques to block ground balls are the same for grass surfaces as for artificial surfaces. Because of the faster pace and higher standard of play on artificial turf, the goalkeeper will more often use her entire body to block the ball. Making a routine save on a consistent basis is just as important as making an occasional spectacular play. If teammates execute the roles of defense, most of your saves will be routine—shots at the goal along the ground. Depending on the nature of the shot, you will use either the upright or the horizontal position to stop or block the ball. Remember, every ball stopped by the goalkeeper should be cleared away from the goal quickly and safely.

Ball Rolling Directly at the Goalkeeper

When addressing a shot, the goalkeeper must decide to stop/control the ball or redirect (one-time) the rebound elsewhere. On artificial surfaces and with higher levels of play, the experienced goalkeeper will almost always make the save and clearance in one action. Performance of the one-time or save-clear requires good head positioning and good timing that, in turn, are developed only through repeated training of the basic ready position.

The Block Save

Controlling the rebound is critical when stopping a ball hit directly at you. Always move your head and body behind the line of the ball and apply the basic principle of *blocking*—let the ball come to you. A novice goalkeeper learns to block or stop the ball with both legs together and body weight forward on the power points of the feet. Both knees are slightly bent to confine the rebound into the control box. The block save can also be executed with a *single-leg stop* against those shots that are coming hard at pad height. The *double-leg stop* is also used for shots that are bouncing or slightly lofted and on hard, uneven grass surfaces.

To execute the block save, position your head and body in behind the line of the ball. From a ready position, be prepared to give with the shot in the same manner as when the stick absorbs the impact of the ball when trapping or receiving. Keep your leg guards together and watch the ball come to you. At the moment the ball strikes the pads, knees are bent over your toes with your head over the ball and chin over your knees. The stick is held in your right hand and the left hand is open with the palm side to the ball. Maintain a low center of gravity for speed into your next movement (see figure 7.4).

FIGURE
7.4

KEYS TO SUCCESS

THE BLOCK SAVE

a

b

c

Preparation

1. Short, quick steps behind ground ball line _____
2. Relaxed, ready position _____
3. Leg guards kept together _____
4. Eyes on lower half of ball _____
5. Let ball roll to legs/feet _____

Execution

1. Bend knees beyond toes as ball hits legs _____
2. Direct rebound downward _____
3. Head over ball and beyond knees _____
4. Lower center of gravity _____

Follow-Through

1. Keep eyes on ball _____
2. Return to ready position _____
3. Clear the ball _____

Ball Rolling to the Side of the Goalkeeper

Very often in field hockey, the ball comes toward the goal at a pace that does not allow you time to move your whole body behind the line of the ball to execute a block save. With this type of shot, you must learn to move your leg with your head in a side direction to meet the line of the ball.

The Lunge Save

The lunge technique (see figure 7.5) is a reflex save that allows you to save the ball from entering the goal by stretching out the leg and foot that correspond to the direction of the ball. The inside of your lunge foot is placed in a direct line with the ball and your head must be over your lunge knee. If using kickers other than high-density foam, a close rebound off your kicker is your objective. To execute the lunge save, the goalkeeper must first identify the direction of the ball shot toward the goal and then time the save. From the ready position, move your leg corresponding to the direction of the ball directly into the ball's path to goal. Transfer your body weight onto the saving leg with the inside of your leg facing the shot. The ball contacts the inside of your saving foot slightly in front of the body. Complete the lunge by pushing into the upright position as fast as possible and clear the rebound. Return to a ready position.

FIGURE 7.5 **KEYS TO SUCCESS**

THE LUNGE SAVE

a

b

c

Preparation

1. Position between ball and goal ____
2. Short steps, quick footwork ____
3. Assume ready position ____
4. Identify ball direction ____
5. Eyes on lower half of rolling ball ____

Execution

1. Lunge leg/foot in direct line of ball ____
2. Transfer body weight on saving leg ____
3. Head over lunge knee and ball ____
4. Contact ball with inside of lunge foot/leg ____
5. Control a close rebound ____

Follow-Through

1. Push up into upright position after contact ____
2. Clear rebound ____
3. Return to ready position ____

The Split Save

When a fast shot along the ground is too wide for the lunge technique, the goalkeeper must use a reflex technique—split save—to save the shot. Before practicing the split save, thoroughly stretch the groin and hamstring muscles. To execute the split save (see figure 7.6), you must keep your eyes on the ball while in your "set" ready position. From the ready position, judge the direction and width of the shot so that you can make the correct reflex decision to lunge or split. Get your head as close to the flight of the ball as possible. Fall into a hurdle-seat position with the leg corresponding to the path of the ball outstretched and the trail leg tucked up behind in support. On contact with the ground, the hands remain close to the knees and the saving foot points to the sky. The back of the calf muscle of the extended leg saving the ball is directly on the ground. Stretch the corresponding hand of the split leg behind and beyond the knee while bringing your head over your saving knee. On a right side split, the stick is placed behind the right leg to extend the reach of the right foot. On the left side, the glove hand extension from the knee increases the height of the pad. Contact the ball with the inside of the foot, which is in an upright position. Keep your opposite hand close to your tucked knee. Recover to a ready position in one action. Use both hands/arms to push off the ground by placing the corresponding hand of the split leg behind your hip as the opposite hand is placed in front of your hip. While beginning the push action with the arms, pull in the extended leg and push upward with the tucked leg. Return to a ready position to play your rebound.

Figure 7.6 The split save: Push off nonsaving leg, fall into hurdle-seat position by extending saving leg and tucking support leg, and contact ball with inside foot of extended leg. Keep stick hand in contact with outside of extended leg and head close to ball. Recover to ready position in one action.

The Stick Dive

Balls that are out of reach and wide of the goalkeeper's split distance can be intercepted with a stick dive in lateral directions. The stick is used like a racquet to become an extension of the goalkeeper's right arm for blocking and saving wide balls. Situations that may require you to perform the stick dive to the right and the *reverse stick dive* to the left include accurate shots wide of your split reach, interception or breakup of centering passes through the shooting circle to prevent a shot on goal, and as a tackle in a one-on-one to break up AR1's attempt to dribble around you.

To execute the stick dive, start from a ready position and focus on the ball. Coordinate the movement of your legs, head, and upper body to vault toward the spot where you can intercept the ball with your extended stick. When diving to your left, extend both arms to the ball with a reverse-stick position in your right hand. The feet and knees face the front and arms remain at your sides as you take a step with the foot nearest the ball in the direction you are going to dive.

Transfer your body weight over that fully flexed leg nearest the ball and push off that foot to begin your dive. To generate additional momentum, let your opposite leg and arm follow. Extend your stick (right arm), head, and shoulders toward the ball's flight path. With the reverse stick dive, keep your left glove hand behind your stick and block the ball with reverse stick and palm of your left glove. When possible, place your head behind the ball with the palms of your hands facing the ball. Contact the ground on your side, not on your stomach. Keep your right wrist firm and angle your stick to *block* or deflect—not swing—the ball away from the goal. Upon landing, your outer thigh contacts the ground first, followed by the hip, rib cage, and finally the shoulders. Your head remains between the arms, eyes focused on the lower half of the ball as you watch the ball meet your stick (see figure 7.7). Immediately move your head and upper body behind the ball and pull both knees to your chest so that recovery to an upright position to clear the ball is possible.

FIGURE
7.7 **KEYS TO SUCCESS**

THE STICK DIVE

Preparation

1. Position between ball and goal ____
2. Assume set ready position ____
3. Judge direction and width of shot/pass ____
4. Eyes focused on ball ____
5. Prepare right hand stick grip ____
6. Step with near foot to ball's flight path ____
7. Transfer weight on flexed leg nearest ball ____

a

Execution

1. Push off near foot and extend leg/foot ____
2. Vault toward spot to intercept ball ____
3. Side of body parallel to ground ____
4. Extend stick/arm, head, shoulders to ball's path; opposite leg and arm follow ____
5. Contact ground on outer thigh, hip, ribs, and shoulder ____
6. Head between arms; firm right wrist ____
7. Block or redirect ball with angled stick ____

b

Follow-Through

1. Eyes focused on lower half of ball ____
2. Momentum forward through point of contact with ball ____
3. Pull knees to chest and jump to feet ____
4. Return to ready position ____

c

BLOCKING GROUND BALL SUCCESS STOPPERS

Most errors that occur when blocking ground balls are caused by improper positioning of the head, knees, and feet. It is important that you move into position as quickly as possible and prepare to block the ball before it arrives.

Error	Correction
Positioning—Covering Angles	
1. You attempt to save a direct shot from zone 2 and it passes close to your feet and into the goal.	1. Position in line with the ball and the center of the goal line. Move forward from the goal line to increase the goal coverage.
2. While playing a shot from zone 3, the ball goes off your pads and over the back line.	2. Be sure your pads are slightly in advance of the goalpost and together. Position against the goalpost and make sure there is no gap between your body and the goalpost. Keep your eyes on the ball instead of the target.
The Block Save	
1. You attempt to make a block save but the ball passes under or close by your feet and into the goal.	1. Do not jump forward to meet the ball. Position your head and body behind the line of the ball with your feet and pads together. Keep your eyes focused on the ball and let the ball come to you.
2. You have a poor rebound when executing the double-leg block save.	2. Position your head and body behind the line of the ball and let the ball come to you. At the moment the ball strikes your pads, bend both knees slightly forward beyond your toes to trap and control the ball.
Lunge and Split Save	
1. You attempt to lunge save a shot to your right side and the ball glances off your kicker and into the goal.	1. Transfer your body weight onto your right leg and place the inside of your right foot in a direct line of the ball. Keep your right knee beyond your toes and head over your knee.
2. The ball hits your calf on a split save attempt.	2. The ball is too close to your body for a split. Keep your eyes focused on the ball and instantly judge the direction and width of the shot. Use a stand-up skill such as the lunge save.

Error	Correction
Stick dives	
1. You slide on your stomach when attempting to stick save a shot along the ground. You fail to reach the ball with your stick and you watch it roll into the goal.	1. Vault toward the spot where you can intercept the ball with your extended stick. Transfer your body weight onto your corresponding leg and to the direction of the ball. Contact the ground on your side while facing your feet, pads, and chest protector to the ball.
2. Recovery to a ready position after a stick dive is slow.	2. Maintain forward momentum through point of contact with the ball. Lead with your head as you pull your knees to your chest and push off your hands and feet. Jump to your feet and return to a ready position.

How to Block Aerial Balls

The goalkeeper must also be able to block balls that arrive through the air. For shots above leg-guard height, you use the glove or stick to block the ball—never swing your stick or arms at the speeding ball! Using both hands equally well—for powerful chip shots, fast-spinning or high-lofted flicks, and aerial deflections shots—requires a high degree of hand-eye coordination. Field hockey rules permit only the goalkeeper while in her respective shooting circle to kick the ball and stop the ball using the body and hands. But the goalkeeper is not allowed to catch or hold the ball or propel the ball dangerously forward. The rules also permit only the goalkeeper to stop the ball above the shoulders with the stick. By using your body, arms, and hands/stick, you can successfully save aerial shots of various heights, direction, and speed.

The key to blocking aerial balls is to always position your hands, eyes, head, and chest in line with the ball as you receive it. Follow the flight of the ball into your body, hands, or stick. Absorb the shot's power and redirect or "bunt" the ball downward for a kick or stick clearance. The harder the shot, the more give or cushion you must provide to keep the ball from rebounding away from you. Remember, to successfully defend against aerial shots of various heights, direction, and speed, you must be able to position your head/ body in the ball's flight path and execute solid blocking technique or safely redirect the ball.

To execute aerial saves, you must be in a ready position with your left hand close along the side of your body. The right hand holds the stick midway down and remains close to the right hip and above knee level. Eyes remain focused on the ball to determine direction and width, height, and speed of the shot. It is crucial that your head remain as close as possible to the line of the ball. Your objective is to concentrate on coordination and control, which will enable you to block or redirect the aerial ball and to clear in one smooth motion. No matter the height and direction of the aerial shot, it is vital to watch the ball onto and off your glove, stick, or body.

As you control the aerial shot, work on your peripheral vision to decide where to clear the ball after the completed save. Proper positioning of the hand and head will allow you to easily play a ball away from the danger area of an approaching opponent. Some aerial shots are lofted over the goalkeeper's head, dropping down dangerously toward the goal. When this situation occurs, you must use quick, short footwork to recover to the goal line. Execute a drop step with the corresponding leg closest to the direction of the ball. During your foot movement back to the goal line, keep your opposite shoulder facing the oncoming ball. The hand closest to the ball's flight path blocks or deflects the ball.

Aerial Glove Saves

When saving an aerial shot directly at you or close to your body on either side, the left glove hand plays the ball by bunting the ball downward. For aerial shots above your waist and chest, point your left glove fingers up and block the ball. Position the left hand so fingers point down for aerials below waist height. To save an aerial shot above your head or wide and high to your left, stretch or lunge to block the ball downward with your left glove hand. Depending on height and speed of the shot, you can also redirect the ball around the goalpost or over the crossbar. With the wide and high aerial shot to your left, bring your hands together by moving your right hand across the body with the toe of the stick pointed down in a reverse-stick position. Save the ball with your left glove hand and clear the ball safely to the outsides of the field. Any aerial ball close to your right side is also played with your left glove, which is moved across the front of the body and above your stick. In this position, keep the left palm facing the ball and contact the ball on your glove with your head and chest as close to the line of the ball as possible.

To execute the aerial glove save (see figure 7.8), position yourself in line with the ball in the ready position. Keep your fingers of the glove hand pointed up-

ward and palm facing forward. About waist high, hold your stick with the right hand halfway down the stick. Keep your eyes focused on the ball to determine direction, speed, height, and width of the aerial shot. With elbows slightly flexed, extend your left hand, head, and chest behind the line of the ball. Block or redirect the ball on the palm and fingers of the glove hand. Withdraw the glove from the ball and control the ball to the ground. Clear the ball and return to a ready position.

FIGURE 7.8 KEYS TO SUCCESS

AERIALS—THE GLOVE SAVE

a   b   c

Preparation

1. Position yourself in line of ball ____
2. Assume ready position ____
3. Palms forward, elbows flexed ____
4. Eyes focused on ball ____
5. Determine direction, height, speed of aerial ____

Execution

1. Extend left hand, head, chest behind ball ____
2. Palm facing ball ____
3. Watch ball onto glove ____
4. Position head close to ball line ____
5. Block or redirect ball with palm of glove ____

Follow-Through

1. Withdraw glove from ball ____
2. Maintain body balance and head behind ball ____
3. Control ball to ground ____
4. Clear the ball ____
5. Return to ready position ____

Aerial Stick Saves

For aerial shots high and away from the right side of the body (see figure 7.9), the stick alone has to be used to block the ball. Usually a ball shot high in this direction will require a reflex response with the goalkeeper's stick. The stick is held with the toe pointing up and, if time allows, the left arm is brought to a position above the stick with the palm facing the ball. To execute the aerial stick save, face the oncoming ball in a ready position. Keep your head steady and focus on the ball to determine flight and direction. Shift your body weight

over the right leg and lower your center of gravity by flexing both knees. Extend your stick toward the ball as you push off and extend your right leg. Pull your left leg upward in the direction of the ball. Keep the front of your body facing the oncoming ball and contact the ball on the flat facing of the stick. Position your head between the arms to view contact of the ball to your stick. When diving in the air, land on the outside of your right thigh, hip, rib cage, and shoulder while maintaining a head-to-ball position with your stick behind the ball. Clear the ball and return to a ready position.

FIGURE
7.9

KEYS TO SUCCESS

THE AERIAL STICK SAVE

Preparation

1. Face oncoming ball ____
2. Assume ready position; palms forward, elbows flexed ____
3. Toe of stick pointed up ____
4. Determine flight and ball direction ____
5. Head steady and focus on ball ____
6. Shift body weight over right leg ____
7. Lower center of gravity by flexing both knees ____

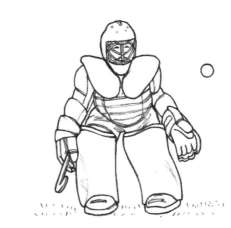

a

Execution

1. Take off and extend right leg ____
2. Extend stick toward ball ____
3. Pull left leg upward in direction of ball ____
4. Contact ball on stick facing ____
5. Left glove hand above stick, palm facing ball ____
6. Head between arms to view ball contact ____

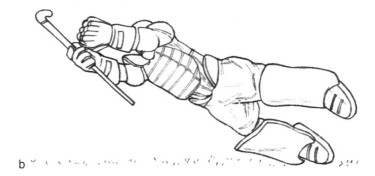

b

Follow-Through

1. Keep eyes focused on ball ____
2. Land on right side ____
3. Maintain stick behind ball ____
4. Return to ready position ____

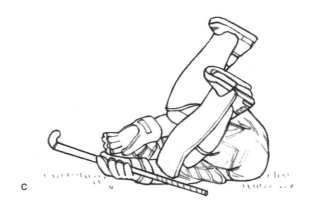

c

BLOCKING AERIAL BALL SUCCESS STOPPERS

Most errors that occur when blocking aerial balls are caused by improper positioning of the head/body or hands, poor timing of the jump, or both. Common problems are listed here, along with suggested corrections.

Error	Correction
Blocking Aerials With Glove and Stick	
1. The aerial ball tips off your fingers of the glove hand and flies into the goal.	1. Keep your eyes focused on the ball and watch it onto the upper palm area of the glove to control your rebound.
2. In an attempt to block a high-lofted ball, the ball goes over your head and into the goal.	2. Face the ball and judge its flight path. Move toward the oncoming ball or drop step backward toward the goal line in preparation to jump. Wait until the last possible moment, then use a two-leg takeoff to leap upward and block or redirect the ball at the highest point of your jump.
3. While attempting to block an aerial shot above the waist, the ball bounces off your chest protector and out of your control.	3. Round your shoulders and jump back a few inches as the ball arrives to absorb its impact.
4. The ball slips through your stick and glove hand when attempting to save a medium-height ball close to your right side.	4. Position your glove hand and stick hand close together (thumbs and forefingers should almost touch) behind the ball and save the ball with the palm of your glove hand. Keep your eyes focused on the ball and watch the ball onto your glove and off your glove.

How to Clear the Ball

Every shot stopped by the goalkeeper must be redirected or cleared away safely. There are two goalkeeping methods of clearing the ball from the circle area: kick clears and stick clears. Using your stick with an occasional push or hit pass (see Step 2, figures 2.1 and 2.3) can be a quick and safe means of clearing the ball while under pressure from an upright or a "grounded" position. The push can also be used to pass to a teammate. The hit is seldom used by the goalkeeper except in situations in which the goalkeeper loses her kicking privileges when intercepting outside the circle. From here, the goalkeeper uses the hit to clear the ball over the sideline and away from the opponent. Clearing the ball with the feet is the most frequently used method to direct the ball wide into space or to pass to teammates. To execute a successful clear following a rebound off your glove or stick, body, and pads, remain calm and control your weight transfer before kicking. Although you have a privilege of being able to use your feet in addition to your stick to clear the ball away, you must be conscious of safety. You cannot clear a ball in any manner that is dangerous or that can lead to dangerous play. On higher levels of play, shots can travel in speeds up to 100 miles per hour largely because of the fast artificial turf, stiffer sticks, and quality execution of shooting skills. This environment presents an opportunity for the goalkeeper to redirect or onetime the ball, especially if using modern goalkeeping equipment consisting of lightweight, high-density foam that helps to create a quick and powerful rebound.

Once you develop an understanding of proper body positioning and movement for making block saves, you are well prepared to execute various kicking techniques without first stopping the ball—*jab, crossover jab,* and *punch clear.* The *dropkick* and *punt kick* are used to kick aerial glove saves. While under pressure, the goalkeeper kicks to distribute the ball to space, to a narrow shooting angle parallel to the back line, or to the nearest sideline to put the ball out of play. Kicking techniques are also used to distribute a controlled pass to a teammate. The complete goalkeeper must be able to kick with the right and left foot equally with accuracy and power. Favoring one kicking foot will lead to miskicking across the line of the body and to poor balance, resulting in weak skill performance. Always kick through the line of the body to contact the ball with as much foot as possible. Proper positioning with a balanced stance will permit kicking a rolling ball in one fluid movement.

The Jab Kick

On artificial surfaces or hard fast ground, it is necessary to save and clear all in one movement. The *jab kick* is a redirected rebound or "save-clear" used by the goalkeeper to accurately pass the ball to a target from a ground shot. It requires no backswing of the foot, so the goalkeeper can make contact with a hard shot and with proper timing be assured that the ball will be quickly thrust 20 to 40 yards away. The ball is cleared to the nearest sideline with the foot aligned with the oncoming ball. Using a one-touch jab action with the inside of the foot thrust in front of the body requires good head positioning and good timing. Correct positioning will enable you to turn and angle your foot to rebound the rolling ball onto the inside wall of your kicker and direct the ball swiftly away.

To successfully perform the jab technique, (see figure 7.10), position between the ball and the center of the goal. Assume a ready position with your weight balanced and your eyes on the ball. As the ball approaches, keep your head in line with the ball and push the foot that is in the direct line of the ball forward to meet the ball. Turn or angle both your hip and the inside of your kicker to the target. Keep your head over your knees and knees over your toes as you contact the ball with a firm foot in front of the body line. Transfer your body weight through the power points of the jab foot, and to maintain balance, keep your palms facing forward and the pinkie fingers on the outer sides of the knee. Generate momentum through the ball with your head well forward. Follow the ball from your foot with your eyes and bring your legs together to complete your follow-through to a ready position.

FIGURE 7.10 **KEYS TO SUCCESS**

THE JAB KICK

a b c

Preparation

1. Position between ball and center of goal line ____
2. Assume ready position ____
3. Arms along side for balance ____
4. Palms face ball ____
5. Head steady in line of ball ____
6. Determine ball direction and target ____
7. Eyes focused on ball ____

Execution

1. Body over ball ____
2. Push contact foot forward ____
3. Keep jab foot firm ____
4. Face hip and contact foot to target ____
5. Meet ball in front of body line ____
6. Contact lower half of ball with inside surface of foot ____

Follow-Through

1. Transfer body weight onto jab foot ____
2. Head beyond knees, knee beyond toes ____
3. Keep palms forward, pinkies next to knee ____
4. Generate momentum through the ball ____
5. Eyes follow ball ____
6. Bring legs together ____
7. Return to ready position ____

Crossover Jab Kick

When the shot is hit hard directly at the goalkeeper's feet, the *crossover jab* kick enables the goalkeeper to save-clear the ball parallel to the back line and toward the sideline. The "jab" action of the crossover is to the side of the oncoming ball and across the line of the ball. The mechanics are the same as the jab kick except for the placement of the foot at the contact point. Your toes of the contact foot face forward as you place the foot out in front of the support or back foot. Keep your head directly over the ball and on contact with the ball onto the inside of the foot, move through the kick and return to the ready position (see figure 7.11). The foot placement consists of no backswing, only a sharp jabbing action through the ball. The timing of the contact foot is crucial for a proper rebound that runs parallel to the back line.

FIGURE 7.11 **KEYS TO SUCCESS**

THE CROSSOVER JAB KICK

a b c

Preparation	Execution	Follow-Through
1. Position between ball and center of goal line ____	1. Body over the ball ____	1. Transfer body weight onto jab foot ____
2. Assume ready position ____	2. Push contact foot forward in front of nonkicking foot ____	2. Head beyond knees, knee beyond toes ____
3. Arms along side for balance ____	3. Keep crossover jab foot firm ____	3. Keep palms forward, pinkies next to knee ____
4. Palms face ball ____	4. Keep toes of contact foot facing forward ____	4. Generate momentum through the ball ____
5. Head steady in line of ball ____	5. Meet ball in front of body line at point across ball line ____	5. Eyes follow ball ____
6. Determine ball direction and target ____	6. Contact lower half of ball with inside surface of foot ____	6. Keep legs together ____
7. Eyes focused on ball ____		7. Return to ready position ____

The Punch Clear

A powerful and useful technique that goalkeepers at all ability levels must master is the *punch clear*. The punch clear is a well-suited skill for tackling the ball away from the ballcarrier and more frequently for sliding and clearing away a loose ball out of the shooting circle. The sliding action is similar to a baseball slide into a base or a soccer slide tackle that is initiated foot first on the side of your body. Use of the punch clear must be based on good distance judgment from the ball. Because you leave your feet to challenge for the ball, you are briefly in a poor position to recover from a missed punch. While sliding into a punch clear, the lower leg and sole of the punch foot thrust out at the ball and, on contact, clear with power. Especially on watered artificial surfaces, the punch clear is an effective and powerful means to intercept or win the first touch on an unsecured ball.

To execute the punch clear (see figure 7.12), you must judge the speed of the ball and advance quickly in a pretackle position to time your slide the moment the ball becomes loose. Advance toward the ball, and when approximately one or two yards from the ball, allow your body to fall to the ground on the side of the punch leg. The leg about to punch the ball is well bent at the knee while the knee of the rear leg is also bent slightly. The pace is absorbed by the arm on the side nearer to the ground and the punch leg. With the outside ankle and little toe of your punch foot facing the ground, bring the sole of the punch foot in contact with the ball. Rotate your body in the direction of the punching leg during your slide down and forward to the ball. During the rotation of your body, the outer part of the shin of the punch leg is the first to touch the ground, followed by the hip and the side of the trunk, which slide along the turf. For balance, bring the opposite arm from the punch leg up and forward to the ball. The sliding action of the punch clear should be continuous and gradual. Keep your eyes focused on the ball, and after punching the ball, immediately position your head in line with the cleared ball and recover to a ready position.

FIGURE 7.12 **KEYS TO SUCCESS**

THE PUNCH CLEAR

Preparation

1. Approach between ball and center of goal line ____
2. Judge speed and distance of ball ____
3. Assume crouched position as you near ball ____
4. Head in line of ball ____
5. Maintain balance and body control ____
6. Eyes focused on loose ball ____

a

Execution

1. Leave feet; slide on side of punch leg ____
2. Rotate body on side of punch leg ____
3. Catch fall with arm nearer to ground ____
4. Opposite arm of punch leg up and forward to ball ____
5. Extend sliding punch (lower) leg to ball ____
6. Extend sole of punch foot ____
7. Flex opposite leg at knee ____
8. Snap punching leg/foot into ball and contact ball on sole of foot ____

b

Follow-Through

1. Generate momentum through the ball ____
2. Keep outside of punch foot facing ground ____
3. Place opposite arm out in front of punch leg ____
4. Head well forward and eyes follow the ball ____
5. Line head and hands to rebound ____
6. Jump to feet ____
7. Return to ready position ____

c

The Dropkick and Punt

Two common kicking techniques that the goalkeeper can use after blocking an aerial ball are the dropkick and full volley punt. The kicking mechanics are nearly identical, but rarely does the goalkeeper have time to execute the more difficult *punt*, which requires more space to safely volley the ball directly out of the air. The *dropkick*, or half volley, is a useful alternative to the punt because it requires less space and time to execute. Although less accurate than jab kicking, the *dropkick* can be used as a powerful distance clear along the ground or high into the air by contacting the ball just as it hits the ground.

To execute the dropkick (see figure 7.13), stand erect and face your target. Block the aerial ball with your hand/stick and anticipate where the ball will drop. Move to that spot and step forward with the nonkicking foot. Keep your head steady. Draw your kicking leg back, and at the instant the ball contacts the ground, fully extend your kicking foot to strike the ball with the instep. For a low clear, contact behind the lower half of the ball, and for a high clear, lean back and use the instep of the kicking foot to contact the bottom of the ball. With your hips and shoulders square to the target, use a complete follow-through motion of the kicking leg.

The punted ball must be kicked high over the heads of all players to eliminate the possibility of danger. To execute the punt kick (see figure 7.14), face your target and drop the ball from the palm of your glove opposite your kicking foot. Extend your glove hand forward so the ball is approximately waist level. Keep your head steady and always watch the ball. Step forward with your nonkicking foot as you release the ball, then punt the ball out and high into the air using a complete follow-through motion of the kicking leg. Square your shoulders and hips to the target, and contact the lower half of the ball with the instep surface of your punting foot. Your punt foot must be firmly extended at the moment of contact with the ball. Proper foot and knee position is required to control the height of the punt.

Figure 7.13 The dropkick: Block ball, step forward, and strike ball with instep at the instant ball contacts ground. Keep steady and use complete follow-through motion of kicking leg.

Figure 7.14 The punt kick: Step forward with the nonkicking foot, drop ball from glove, contact ball on instep of kicking foot. Use a complete follow-through motion.

CLEARING SUCCESS STOPPERS

Accuracy is more important than distance when clearing the ball from your defensive circle. It doesn't matter how far you can kick the ball if it goes to the opponent. You can vastly improve your clearing skills by practicing your kicking techniques with emphasis on body balance, footwork, and hand-eye/foot-eye coordination. Common errors that occur when clearing the ball are listed here, along with suggested corrections.

Error	Correction
Stick Clearances	
1. You run outside the circle to clear the ball, and you kick it over the nearest sideline. The umpire awards a penalty corner against your team.	1. When outside the shooting circle, the goalkeeper must use the stick to play the ball.
Jab Kick, Crossover Jab Kick	
1. You have poor rebound power and control when jab clearing.	1. Contact the ball in front of the body line instead of level.
2. The ball rises up dangerously when you attempt a jab kick.	2. Your legs are stretched too far reaching for the ball, or you are leaning backward on your nonkicking leg. Place your body weight on the power point of your contact foot. Keep your head forward to keep the ball along the ground.
3. You lose your balance when jab clearing and mistime the save-clear.	3. Bend more at the waist and saving knee to get your body weight over the ball. Keep your eyes on the ball so that you avoid extending the leg and pushing your upper body back from the ball.
4. During a crossover jab kick, the ball hits the support leg.	4. Focus on the ball so your timing to push the contact foot forward in front of the nonkicking foot is early enough to redirect the ball parallel to the back line. Meet the ball in front of body line at a point across the ball's flight line.
Punch Clear	
1. You land hard on your buttocks when attempting a punch clear.	1. Rotate your body to the side of the punching leg and fall to the ground with both knees flexed. Catch your drop into a slide with the arm nearest to the ground.
2. Your punch leg slides over the ball.	2. Judge the speed of the ball and advance to time your slide about 1 or 2 yards from the ball. Keep your eyes focused on the ball and contact the ball with the sole of your foot.
Dropkick, Punt	
1. Your dropkick lacks accuracy.	1. Step toward the target with your nonkicking foot. Square your shoulders and hips to the target. Contact the ball with the full instep of your kicking foot.
2. Your punt lacks height and distance.	2. Lack of height and distance is usually due to insufficient follow-through of the kicking motion. Keep your foot firmly positioned and kick through the point of contact with the ball. Your kicking foot should swing upward to waist level or higher.
3. Your kick clears generally lack power.	3. Complete your follow-through, and keep your head over the ball, foot, and knee.

Goalkeeping Specialties

Although it can only be obtained through experience, the ability to read the game of field hockey is one of the most important aspects of the goalkeeper's development. The goalkeeper is a vital member of the team who plays in the defensive spotlight in three special situations: one-on-one breakaway, penalty corner (discussed in Step 10), and the penalty stroke. A good performance in specialties makes as much of a difference in victory as a poor performance makes in defeat.

One-on-One With the Goalkeeper

Because of talented attackers on fast artificial turf surfaces and the elimination of the offsides rule, the one-on-one breakaway against the goalkeeper is a frequent occurrence in today's game. If the AR1 breaks away from other field players and moves dangerously toward the shooting circle, the goalkeeper has no other choice than to confront the ballcarrier. As the last line of defense, your one-on-one mission is to block or tackle the ball and prevent an easy scoring chance. To be successful, it is crucial to master the "engage and give" before using stick dives (see figure 7.7) to tackle the ball or attempting a more advanced one-on-one goalkeeping block tackle—the double-leg stack. The *double-leg stack* is an advanced skill that requires the goalkeeper to decide whether to remain in her footwork to block space or to slide and smother the ball to prevent a shot. The aim of the double-leg stack is to tackle the AR1 player by using the pads to block or prevent a powerful shot at goal. In these one-on-one situations with the goalkeeper, the basic standing block save (see figure 7.4) is a not an effective means of stopping or preventing the shot. When the goalkeeper is the nearest defender to the AR1 player who is about to enter the shooting circle, the goalkeeper has to tackle the ball to prevent a scoring opportunity.

To execute goalkeeping one-on-one defense, you must advance to the ball from the seven-yard area fast, with confidence and determination to take the ball off the attacker. Although AR1 players are more mobile on artificial surfaces, it remains essential to close down space keeping your body between the center of the goal line and the ball. Close down space by running fast and controlled. A goalkeeper who charges madly or is hesitant is easily beaten. Force AR1 to take a side that you prefer, which is usually your open stick side and the attacker's reverse stick side. Attempt to move toward AR1 so that you reach near the top of the circle at the same moment as the ball. From your DR1 position, your judgment is crucial to timing your tackle. Refuse to allow the ball to get around you as you maintain a playing distance on your feet that will enable you to block a shot or tackle a

loose ball! Stay on your feet as AR1 starts to dodge or pull the ball to a side direction beyond the line of your head and shoulders. If you have engaged using short, quick footwork within the proper playing distance, you are in a position to time a stick dive tackle when AR1 loses control of a ball pulled to your right side. Always slide on your right side with your stick stretched forward to the ball. If the attacker pulls the ball to your left, stay on your feet and maintain your playing distance to time a reverse-stick tackle or a double-leg stack. When using stick dives to tackle or a double-leg stack to block, always try to slide through the ball and AR1's stick to clear the ball at the same moment.

To execute the stack (see figure 7.15), you must be close enough to slide into the ball before the shooter can get a shot away at goal. Depending on your ability to establish a playing distance to pressure the ball, a goalkeeping tackle such as the stack requires execution from five yards or closer. Attempt to move toward AR1 to reach the top of the circle at the same time as the ball. You must avoid a hesitant decision in your initial movement toward the ball. Step forward on the shooter's take-away swing and initiate the slide into the stack when the shooter begins his downswing. Always position yourself so that you can time your slide into the ball with your pads stacked on top of each other to create a wall. The pads face the attacker's stick as your head remains steady in line with the ball. During the slide, the slightly bent right leg becomes the first leg onto the ground. The bent left leg should fall on top the right leg, which is also presenting the front pad to the ball. The right arm and stick are behind the upper body to push up through the slide on the moment of contact.

Figure 7.15 The double-leg stack: Close distance within 3 to 5 yards of ball, line pads and head to ball, step forward on the shooter's take-away swing, slide into stack on shooter's downswing, drop on bent right leg and stack bent left leg on top, and contact ball on center of pads. Use a complete follow-through motion by bringing hands and head in line to the blocked ball.

Error	Correction
Stack Saves	
1. AR1 drags the ball around you as you attempt to stack the ball.	1. You are going down into a double-leg stack too early. Focus on the ball and step forward to the ball on the shooter's take-away swing. Time your downward slide when the ball is being hit.
2. You attempt to stack tackle and miss the ball but instead slide into the AR1 player. The umpire awards a penalty corner against your team.	2. Advance toward the Role 1 attacker to reach the top of the circle to coincide with the ball. Position yourself as DR1 to tackle the ball and prevent a shot from happening. Keep your pads open to the attacker and head in line with the ball. Time your slide into the ball as the ball is being hit.

The glove hand guards the space above the left leg on contact. Eyes remain focused on the lower half of the ball. During the recovery into a ready position, bring your head and hands to the front of your body in the direction of the ball and push up to your feet.

Defending the Penalty Stroke

The goalkeeper is the only defender who can defend against an awarded *penalty stroke*. When the defending team in the circle commits an unintentional or intentional foul that prevents the probable scoring of a goal, the umpire will whistle for a penalty stroke. Also, the umpire will award a penalty stroke for any continuous early running off the back line by defenders at penalty corners. Many tournament structures provide for a penalty stroke competition to determine a winner if overtime play proves fruitless. As the goalkeeper, you must be prepared for a one-on-one push or flick from seven yards out. It is crucial to watch the ball, determine the ball's flight direction, and commit yourself one hundred percent to the save.

To defend against the penalty stroke, stand on the center of the goal line in a ready position. A lower center of gravity will allow easier and swifter movement upward than the downward movement with a higher center of gravity. The rules do not permit you to leave the line or move your feet until the ball has been played. With your heels over the front portion of the goal line, balance your body weight forward. Learn to react to the direction of the ball with eyes focused on the ball. Even though your legs are longer, your hands are quicker, so be prepared to dive to save the shot with your hands. Remain relaxed and confident as more pressure is on the stroker to complete the score.

GOALKEEPING DRILLS

1. Drill Blocking

Without your helmet and gloves, face a rebound board or wall 5 yards away and hold a tennis ball in your left hand. Toss the ball hard off the backboard/wall and move to block the rebound with your feet and pads before it passes you. Repeat 50 times.

Success Goal = 40 of 50 tosses blocked ____

Success Check
- Short, quick shuffle steps in behind the line of the ball ____
- Leg guards kept together with bent knees ____
- Eyes on ball ____
- Let ball come to you ____
- Head beyond knees, knees beyond toes on contact ____

To Increase Difficulty
- Ask a teammate to bounce or hit the tennis ball very hard off the board.
- With entire goalkeeping gear, have teammate hit hockey balls off the rebound board or wall for you to block.

To Decrease Difficulty
- Use a larger ball such as a soccer ball.

2. Aerial Blocks With Glove Hand

Wear gear except for your stick and helmet, and stand facing a teammate 6 yards away. Your teammate tosses an aerial tennis ball to the right or left of your chest or head. Block the ball with the upper palm section of your glove hand and bring your head behind the ball. Attempt to direct the ball down into the control box in front of your feet. Then toss the tennis ball to your goalkeeping partner to block in the same manner. Attempt to block 40 tosses each.

Success Goal = 30 of 40 tosses blocked successfully to the ground ____

Success Check
- Head steady ____
- Use short, quick shuffle steps on power points of feet ____
- Focus on ball ____
- Glove hand, eyes, head aligned with the ball ____
- Fingers of glove hand pointed correctly ____
- Contact ball on upper palm of glove hand ____
- Complete follow-through ____

To Increase Difficulty
- Fully dressed in goalkeeping gear, increase velocity of tennis ball.
- Perform drill while shuffling sideways.
- While fully dressed, toss hockey balls.

To Decrease Difficulty
- Toss ball softly.

3. Block and Kick

Play with two teammates who act as servers. The servers, each with a ball, face one another 12 yards apart while you position midway between them. Servers alternate turns pushing the ball along the ground to you. Block save each ball from a ready position and return it to the server by kicking the ball with the inside of your foot. Immediately turn and block a push pass from the opposite server. Block 30 balls using the upright blocking technique, then switch places with one of the servers and repeat the activity. Award one point for each ball blocked without a rebound and accurately kicked back to the servers.

Success Goal = 28 of 30 possible points ____

Success Check
- Position behind the line of the ball ____
- Leg guards together in a ready position ____
- Allow ball to roll to feet or leg guards ____
- Head steady, eyes on ball ____
- Block ball, head forward and knees bent ____
- Return to standing position ____
- Place nonkicking foot along side of ball ____
- Contact ball on inside of firm kicking foot ____
- Return to ready position ____

To Increase Difficulty
- Increase velocity of serves.
- Increase speed of repetition.
- Increase numbers of repetitions.

To Decrease Difficulty
- Decrease number of repetitions.
- Decrease velocity of serves.

4. Jab Kick to Target

Use markers or cones to set up two targets, one in each zone 2 of the circle. The targets are 2 yards wide, approximately 12 yards from the back line and angled to the sideline. Play in front of a regulation goal and select a teammate to act as a server. The server has a pile of 20 balls around the 7-yard spot and begins by pushing a ground shot toward the goal. Position as the goalkeeper in a ready position to jab kick the ball through the targets. Return to a ready position and repeat 20 times.

Success Goal = 15 of 20 balls jab kicked through the target ____

Success Check
- Short, quick footwork on power points of feet ____
- Align body with oncoming ball ____
- Transfer body weight through saving leg ____
- Contact ball with inside of foot ____
- Accuracy and correct pace of jabs ____
- Return to ready position ____

To Increase Difficulty
- Increase velocity of serve.
- Decrease width of targets.

To Decrease Difficulty
- Increase distance of push serves.
- Servers roll ball to goal.
- Increase width size of markers.
- Reduce distance of markers from goalkeeper.

5. Positioning Footwork With Save and Clear

Five servers, each with two balls, position themselves an equal distance apart 10 yards from the center of the goal line. Position as the goalkeeper next to one of the goalposts facing server 1 in zone 3. Server 1 pushes a ball that you return using a block-clear technique such as a jab or lunge. Shuffle across the front of the goal along a 3- to 4-yard arc as server 2 in zone 2 pushes a ball at you. Jab or lunge at the ball and return it to server 2. Continue to shuffle sideways to zone 1 and block-clear a ball from server 3. Continue the drill in the same manner to servers 4 and 5 located on the opposite side zones 2 and 3. When you reach the opposite post from the start, clear server 5's ball and block a second ball from server 5. Repeat the drill, shuffling in the opposite direction.

Continue shuffling back toward the original post until you save and clear 10 balls.

Success Goal = 7 out of 10 balls saved and cleared _____

Success Check
- Short, quick side-shuffle steps _____
- Position head and body between goal and in line with the ball _____
- Assume ready position with palms of hands facing ball _____
- Transfer body weight onto saving leg _____
- Contact ball with inside of kicking foot _____

To Increase Difficulty
- Increase speed of side-shuffle movement.
- Increase velocity of serves.
- Decrease distance of servers.
- Clear all shots through space to the sideline.

To Decrease Difficulty
- Servers roll ball to goal.
- Increase distance of serve.

6. Split Save

Play in front of regulation goal. Select a teammate to act as a server who positions 7 to 8 yards from the center of the goal line. Position as the goalkeeper in a ready position. The server pushes a straight ground shot to a point either side of the goalpost. Using a split save, save the ball and return to a ready position. Repeat 10 times.

Success Goal = 7 of 10 balls saved _____

Success Check
- Position between ball and goal _____
- Assume ready position _____
- Push strongly on nonsaving leg _____
- Fall into hurdle-seat position _____
- Corresponding hand behind leg on right; above leg on left _____
- Head close to ball _____
- Contact ball with inside of foot _____
- Complete recovery to ready position _____

To Increase Difficulty
- Increase velocity of serves.
- Increase speed of repetition.
- Increase number of repetitions.
- Add another teammate to shoot the rebound from the split.

To Decrease Difficulty
- Decrease number of repetitions.
- Decrease speed of repetition.

7. Punch Clears

Position at or around the 7-yard mark in front of a regulation goal. Select a teammate with a pile of balls at the top of the circle to roll a ball to the goalkeeper. Move with speed toward the ball and fall into the slide to punch clear the ball out of the circle. Return to a ready position and repeat 10 times, five with each leg. Award one point for each correctly executed punch clear.

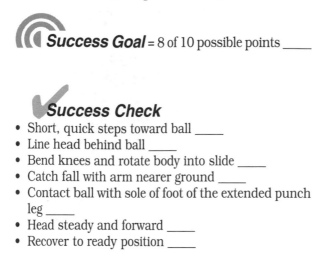

Success Goal = 8 of 10 possible points _____

Success Check
- Short, quick steps toward ball _____
- Line head behind ball _____
- Bend knees and rotate body into slide _____
- Catch fall with arm nearer ground _____
- Contact ball with sole of foot of the extended punch leg _____
- Head steady and forward _____
- Recover to ready position _____

To Increase Difficulty
- Increase velocity of serve.
- Increase distance of ball from goalkeeper.
- Use a teammate to loosely dribble into the circle.
- Increase number of repetitions.

To Decrease Difficulty
- Decrease number of repetitions.
- Punch a stationary ball.

GOALKEEPING SUCCESS SUMMARY

The ultimate goal of every field hockey team is to play together as a unit to prevent the opposition from scoring. To achieve this goal, each team must have a dependable goalkeeper. As the protector of the goal, you can shut out an opponent and guarantee that your team will not lose. To master the skills needed to become a solid goalkeeper requires a great deal of time and effort. Field and match-related goalkeeping skills demand the cooperation of three or more field players. Beginners should start by positioning and blocking shots without the pressure of restricted time, opponents, and the limitation of clearing space. Focus on the basic techniques and gradually increase the speed of repetition of the movements until you are confident and comfortable, which will permit a higher concentration on the correct skill. Develop your ability to clear first with accuracy and then develop power. Eventually, you will progress to more challenging game situations. Ask your coach or goalkeeper-teammate to observe your execution of the saving and clearing techniques discussed in Step 7. Regular evaluation of your performance will provide helpful feedback for improvement. Let the enjoyment of hockey continue as you use the drills described in Step 7 to achieve your objective to be a proficient goalkeeper. Don't ever turn your back on the goal line or your skills!

STEP
8

TEAM ATTACK: EXECUTING ATTACK ROLES 2 AND 3

Field hockey is a team sport that demands a high level of technical and tactical interaction among players. During a 70-minute game, players will be without the ball about 65 minutes. Most of this time is devoted to supporting the Role 1 player. Although each player must be able to execute Role 1 techniques and tactics discussed thus far, the team will not be successful unless all players are thinking and working together to achieve the same objective. With a thorough understanding and execution of your *Attack Role 2* and *Attack Role 3* responsibilities, your field hockey team can be a group of players who think and attack together.

To effectively play without the ball requires attacking players to react intelligently in transitional play to find space. By immediately running into open spaces, passing, dribbling, and finishing techniques can be incorporated to achieve a potent team attack. Because Attack Role 2 (AR2) players, or *helpers*, are nearest to AR1, their prime responsibility is to help the leader of the attack with support movement and combination play. The *assistant helpers* of the attack are the Attack Role 3 (AR3) players. As AR3, your responsibility is to create and use spaces of greater width and depth from the ball and to provide movement to support AR2 and the ball. With proper support movement from AR2 and AR3 to unbalance the opponent's defense, your team can create combination play or passing combinations to maintain possession of the ball, to achieve penetration, and to score goals.

The attack players without the ball are responsible for executing good decisions for the continuation of team attack. To be a successful problem solver within team tactics, you must be aware of key information—the whereabouts of the ball and quality of pressure around the ball, the whereabouts of your teammates, and the whereabouts of the opponent. Understanding Attack Roles 2 and 3 will give you a greater opportunity for increased contact with the ball and for involved decision making with teammates—a formula for successful team play.

Why Are Roles 2 And 3 Attack Tactics Important?

All field players must be able to attack when ball possession is secured. Team-attack tactics create time and space, provide attacking players with an assortment of possibilities, trigger an advantage in numbers during attack situations, and, of course, broaden scoring opportunities. Understanding the relationship of time and space on the hockey field is crucial to the execution of team attack. The more space available to you, the more time you will have to receive, control, pass, or shoot the ball. For a team to be successful, the ball must move from player to player. Roles 2 and 3 attack responsibilities provide the tactical means for the ball to move from player to player and essentially create a "team" attack.

The tactical responsibility of Attack Roles 2 and 3 is movement to create spaces and to use these spaces to provide support for the ball. Off-the-ball attack players must create and use three types of spaces—possession space, advantage space, and dangerous space. *Possession space* is alongside and behind the ball where ball possession is more easily maintained. *Advantage space* is forward space in between the ball and the opponent blocking penetration to goal. *Dangerous space* is the space in behind the opponent and closer to the goal line. Dangerous space is most desirable to attack tactics because of the penetration and scoring opportunities it holds. Each AR2 and AR3 player must move to create an entry for the ball or for other teammates into one of these three spaces.

How to Execute Role 2 Attack Tactics

It is fundamental that AR1 have several passing options both in possession-style offenses and, especially, in fastbreak-style attack play. The moment your team wins possession of the ball, rapid counterattacks into space behind the defense characterize the transition into team attack.

Attack Role 2 players create two basic attack tactics for nearby passing options: support in attack and combination play. It is AR2's responsibility to decide, communicate, and execute runs into the immediate spaces around the ball to create passing lanes for the ball.

AR2 Support Movement

To effectively support the ball, you must create spaces or passing lanes where AR1 can pass you the ball. The creation of passing lanes is a primary responsibility of AR2. The *passing lane* is the space that the ball can travel safely to you from AR1. The basic passing lanes include behind the ball, alongside the ball, and in front of the ball. To create passing lanes, you must execute *movement* toward the ball, away from the ball, back behind the ball, and, if already positioned in front of the ball, diagonally forward. Effective movement must include deceptive change of direction and speed in addition to readiness to receive the ball. Proper support enables your team to consistently create greater numbers than the opponent in the vicinity of the ball. A lack of support for AR1 leaves your leader isolated and increases the chances that she will lose possession.

Organizing capable support for AR1 depends on several factors, including the (a) number of AR2 players, (b) angle of support, (c) distance of support, and (d) communication of support.

■ *Number of AR2 support players.* The number of AR2 helpers near the ball is critical. Too few players limit AR1's choices. Too many AR2 teammates near the ball can also be a disadvantage because they attract additional opponents to the area. When space around the ball becomes congested, executing passing combinations and maintaining ball possession become more difficult. As a guideline, three AR2 teammates should support AR1. An AR2 player should be positioned to each side, working the spaces to establish passing lanes ahead and alongside the ball. The third AR2 player should work the space behind the lateral line of the ball.

■ *Angle of AR2 support.* As a general rule, AR2 players should position themselves from AR1, the opponent, and other AR2 players to form angles that will allow a pass to be made and received with relative ease. As the AR2 player, your angle varies according to the position of the opposition and your teammates. The wider the angle of support, the more difficult it becomes for the DR1 player to challenge the ball. Narrow support angles allow the DR1 player to pressure the ball and cover the passing lanes. If you position directly behind AR1, there is no advantage in your position because the range of passing possibilities is severely reduced—AR1 has restricted vision of where you are providing support, and you have limited vision of the field. If you position **directly** alongside AR1, there is limited attack effectiveness because of the lack of depth between you and the ball. A pass to you has a greater chance of being intercepted by a covering opponent. Also, you have little chance of covering the opponent's AR1 player if possession is turned over to the opposition. Too much ground would have to be covered in a limited time to effectively move from Attack Role 2 to Defense Role 1.

When moving into a support angle in space in front of the ball, always try to win the ball-side position in the passing lane so that AR1 can easily see your stick's readiness to receive the ball. When providing angles of support in space behind the ball, position on the goal side of AR1 in the event AR1 loses the ball. This positioning is especially important close to your own defensive goal because a safety pass is assured, a defensive role can be applied quickly if required, more passing possibilities are available, and AR2's vision of the field is enhanced with more time and space.

■ *Distance of AR2 support.* Generally AR2 helpers are positioned one pass away from the ball. The distance of AR2 is very often determined by where the ball is positioned on the field (see figure 8.1) and the opponent's positioning in the vicinity of the ball. Usually when the opposition is applying immediate pressure, AR2 must take a closer position to AR1 to provide a quick and easy pass to maintain ball possession. In the attacking third of the field, AR2's distance from the ball is from 5 to 10 yards because of the restriction of space and time. In this area of the field, you must offer immediate help for AR1.

Because of the availability of more space in the midfield area of the field, the distance of AR2 support is from 10 to 15 yards. This area is often referred to as the building or transitional area from offense to defense and vice versa. The correct presence of AR2 players in this area provides a series of options that can change the direction and speed of team attack play.

In the defensive third area, the distance is from 10 to 30 yards. The threat from the opposition determines the exact distance of AR2 support. If there is little chance of immediate pressure, a wide-angled support position can be used. AR1 then has the opportunity to switch play in the opposite direction by passing the ball to AR2 angled in the space behind the ball, who has time to change the point of attack to the opposite side of the field where two attack advantages exist—open space and up-numbers. Without AR2's correct distance and angle of support help, a cross-field pass in the defensive area of the field by AR1 could prove very costly.

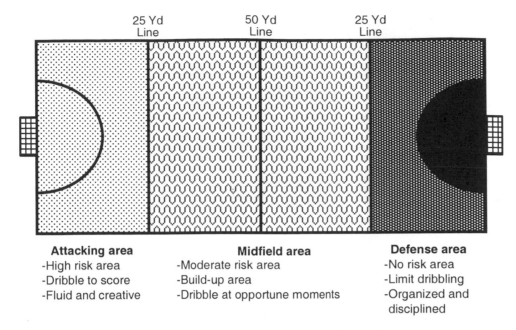

| 25 Yd Line | 50 Yd Line | 25 Yd Line |

Attacking area
-High risk area
-Dribble to score
-Fluid and creative

Midfield area
-Moderate risk area
-Build-up area
-Dribble at opportune moments

Defense area
-No risk area
-Limit dribbling
-Organized and
 disciplined

Figure 8.1   Three areas governing principles of hockey.

AR2 players must achieve a balance between being too close or too far away from the ball. If you are too close, crowded space can restrict the amount of time available to execute a skill should you receive the ball. When you are rushed to receive, control, and pass, loss of ball possession is likely. If you are too far away, AR1's pass could be intercepted. The opponent also is given the opportunity to reorganize quickly as the pass travels a greater distance away from the space alongside and behind AR1. AR2 has an immediate defensive duty if AR1 loses the ball. If you are too far away from the ball when possession is lost, there is more ground for you to cover if your role switches to DR1.

■ *AR2 communication with AR1.* The ability to move and receive the ball at the right moment—commonly referred to as "cutting" or "leading" to the ball—is an integral part of teamwork. Players without the ball must know where to cut, when to cut, and how to breakaway from a defender who is marking them. Key elements of cutting include eye contact with AR1 and AR2 players, the use of your stick by pointing the hook in a direction where you want the ball, the position of your stick near to or on the ground when the ball is in your area, and the calling out of verbal information for immediate decisions. Calling out helpful information to assist AR1 is as important as the execution of technical skills. Communication by AR2 must be brief, loud, and to the point. Verbal directives such as "With you," "Left," "Right," "Time," "Trouble," "Yes, square," "Here," "I have you covered," "Through," or "Now" delivered quickly and loudly during play will build AR1's confidence in AR2's readiness to play the ball. Players who communicate effectively will think and attack together.

Combination Play—Two-on-One

The most fundamental AR2 attack tactic with AR1 is the creation of *combination play*, which is two attackers versus one defender—two-on-one. Combination play uses the give-and-go tactic—the wall pass and the double pass—between AR1 and AR2 to achieve penetration into the dangerous space behind DR1. In hockey, the give-and-go passing combination from AR2 back to AR1 can be executed with a one-touch pass, commonly referred to as a *wall pass*, and with a two-touch pass, referred to as the *double pass*. The primary concept of the give-and-go combination (see figure 8.2) requires AR1 to be a threat with the ball by gaining a commitment from DR1 to step forward to tackle the ball. As soon as the defender commits, AR1 passes the ball to a nearby AR2 teammate and sprints into the space behind the defender to collect a return pass. For the give-and-go tactic to work, both AR1 and AR2 must fulfill their responsibilities. Precise technical execution, correct timing of pass and run, and a quick-sighted understanding of the basic tactics are essential for combination play success.

■ *The wall pass.* To execute the wall pass in a two-on-one situation, AR2 must move into a position near the ball and recognize the opportunity for a give-and-go combination. Position yourself five yards to the side of DR1 at a 45-degree angle from AR1. Place your stick in a horizontal position on the ground as the wall. Your stick is positioned to redirect the ball along the ground similar to the deflection shot described in Step 6 (see figure 6.4). Use an open stance and face AR1 with a lead foot behind your angled stick. Redirect the pass from AR1 by executing a one-touch pass into the space behind DR1. Immediately sprint forward to support AR1 after passing the ball as another give-and-go combination could develop.

■ *The double pass.* The *double pass* is the most common give-and-go combination play for penetration in a two-on-one attack. By directing a forward "through" ball to execute the double pass in a two-on-one situation, AR2 is in a nearby support position behind the ball.

Position yourself at a 45-degree angle approximately five yards behind AR1. Be ready to receive a diagonal back pass from AR1. Two-touch a return through pass into the space behind DR1. Occasionally this through pass can be lifted over DR1's stick or lofted high over DR1's head for AR1 to run onto. After passing the through ball, sprint forward and look for another give-and-go opportunity.

FIGURE 8.2

KEYS TO SUCCESS

THE GIVE AND GO

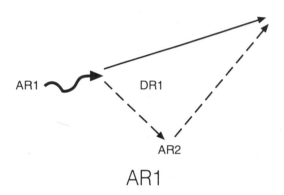

AR1

Preparation

1. Face DR1 ____
2. Recognize dangerous space ____

Execution

1. Cut dribble outside DR1's lead foot ____
2. Commit defender to you ____
3. Release pass using push pass technique ____
4. Pass to stick of AR2 player ____

Follow-Through

1. Sprint forward into space behind DR1 ____
2. Receive wall/double pass from AR2 behind DR1 ____
3. Advance toward goal ____

AR2

Preparation

1. Move to position near ball ____
2. Position 5 yards to side of DR1 (wall pass) or 5 yards behind AR1 (double pass) ____
3. Recognize dangerous space ____
4. Watch ball in ready position to receive ____
5. Maintain open passing lane to AR1 ____

Execution

1. Extend stick to receive ____
2. Position stick at proper angle ____
3. Keep stick firm ____
4. Head and lead foot behind line of pass ____
5. Contact ball on flat side of stick ____
6. Wall or double pass ball into space behind DR1 ____

Follow-Through

1. Sprint forward ____
2. Look for another give-and-go opportunity ____

Transition Play of AR2

Transition play of AR2 consists of two basic areas of execution—the ability to interchange the roles of attack and the ability to counterattack and counterdefend. Interchanging the attack roles refers to moving smoothly and effectively from AR2 to AR1 or AR3. Based on the awareness of the situation, constant swift decisions have to be made to execute attack tactics during transition play. While AR2 scans the area to read the *Big Three* keys of information—(1) the position of the ball and quality of ball possession exhibited by AR1, (2) the position of the opponent and quality of defensive pressure, and (3) position of your teammates—smooth role interchanging can occur.

When your teammate wins possession, it is referred to as the *counterattack*. The attack fastbreak is the ultimate tactical weapon used to counterattack or surprise the opposition, especially against pressure defenses and against a retreating defense whenever there is significant space behind the defense. As the AR2 player during the attack fastbreak, you have several transitional responsibilities the moment your leader secures the ball—recognize that AR1 is looking to immediately pass a forward penetrating ball; sprint into open space immediately and if a penetrating pass is not available, help to move the ball to the other side of the field with quick support movement and two-touch passing; and refrain from dribbling, which slows your team's chances to penetrate quickly. Taking risks is necessary for scoring success;, subsequently, losing the ball is to be expected. Attack players, regardless of position, must quickly assume a role on defense to win back ball possession, which is typically regarded as *counterdefense* (discussed in Step 9).

With attack transition, speed is the essential ingredient—speed of skill, speed of vision, and speed of communication. Through repeated practice in tactical situations, you will learn to execute AR2 transition hockey and improve your ability to interchange attack roles with effective counterattacks and counterdefenses.

How to Execute Role 3 Attack Tactics

Attack players need to make intelligent runs to cause confusion and to destroy the balance that the opposition's defense aims to achieve. If you are not in the group around the ball, you must be aware of space because you are one of many assistant helpers who have three primary functions: stretch the defense by staying spread out, create space for other teammates by making runs, or make runs into spaces where you can receive the ball. With these Attack Role 3 (AR3) players, your team attack tactics begin to take form with unlimited and creative outcomes that unbalance the defense.

The chief responsibility of all AR3 players is to create space and use space two or more passes away from the ball. AR3 can effectively create and use space by *running* toward the ball, away from the ball, around and behind the ball, and through and diagonally forward from the ball. Effective AR3 movement must include deceptive change of direction and speed in addition to readiness to receive the ball. You must make the opposition's defender(s) worry about whether to play the ball, play the space, or defend the player in the space. AR3's decisions to create and use space are also based on knowledge of the *Big Three*—the position of the ball and quality of ball possession exhibited by AR1, the position of the opponent and quality of defensive pressure, and position of your teammates. You must decide where you can do the most good by simply staying wide or deep and stretching the defense, by making a run to create a space, or by running into created space with intentions to receive the ball. By creating greater width and depth space from the ball through coordinated team play, AR3 can open up an area to be used by AR1 or AR2. By using space through coordinated team play, AR3 or AR2 can receive passes that maintain ball possession from player to player. To be successful as one of the AR3 players, be prepared to assume and execute the technical and tactical skills of AR2 and AR1, as well as the roles of defense.

AR3 Width and Depth Support— Stretching the Defense

To maintain flowing and dangerous attack play, your team needs to create space within the opposing team's defense by stretching itself vertically up and down the field and horizontally across the field. AR2 players and AR1 need to have immediate deep and wide support from the AR3 players. *Width* is the space between the ball and attackers across the field. Proper width produces various chances—it creates more space for each attacker to work; it stretches opponents, which makes covering and engaging distance more difficult; and it creates gaps in defense for through passes or AR1 runs. *Depth* in attack will increase the number of passing options and provide a method of safely changing the point of attack without risking loss of possession. Depth in front of the ball often draws a defender out of the line of defense and creates space behind the defender to be used by all attack roles. Penetration is gained only with effective use of width and depth attack movement.

Organizing AR3 width and depth support in space for AR2 and the ball depends on several factors, including the (a) number of AR3 players, (b) angle of AR3 support, (c) distance of AR3 support, and (d) AR3 communication with AR2 and AR1. AR3 must always concentrate on the next move, react quickly, and execute sharp runs with one- and two-touch attack play.

■ *Number of AR3 players.* Depth in attack establishes a minimum of one or two AR3 players ahead of the ball and one or two AR3 players behind the ball. The function of the AR3 player behind the ball is to provide depth in the attack and to do what AR1 is not able to do—pass the ball forward. The front-running AR3 players spearhead the attack, playing as deep targets ready to move into AR2 or AR1 position.

Maintaining width in an attack forces the defending team to cover a larger field area and can create gaps within its defense. Players in Role 3 attack position on the side of the field nearest the ball, and to some extent, the weakside or farside AR3 players position on the opposite side of the field to provide width. Usually one or more AR3 players provide width on each side of the field.

■ *Angle of AR3 support.* AR3 players should position themselves to form angles from the nearest AR2 player, the opponent, and AR1. Your angle varies according to the position of the opposition and your teammates. The wider the angle of support, the more difficult it becomes for the DR3 player (see Step 9) to defend the space. Narrow support angles allow DR3 to intercept the long direct pass. If you position directly behind AR2, there is no advantage in your position because the range of space is severely reduced—AR1 has restricted vision of where you are providing deep or wide support, and you have limited vision of the field. If you position directly alongside AR2, there is limited attack effectiveness because of the lack of depth between teammates and the ball. A long-distance pass made from AR1 to you has a greater chance of being intercepted by a covering opponent. Providing correct angles of width and depth will enhance your recovery into a defensive role if possession is lost.

When moving into a support angle in space in front of the ball, always try to win the ball-side position in the passing lane so that AR1 can easily see your readiness to receive the ball. When providing angles of support in space behind the ball, position on the goal side of AR1 and on a 45-degree angle to AR2 teammates in case AR1 loses the ball. This positioning is especially important close to your own defensive goal because a safety pass will change the point of attack, a defensive role can be applied quickly if required, a greater range of passing possibilities is available, and AR3's vision of the field is enhanced with more time and space.

■ *Distance of AR3 support.* As a general rule, there should be no more than 50 to 60 yards between the last field player in behind the ball and the deepest AR3 player in front of the ball. Because the hockey field is 60 yards wide, AR3 players providing width should use the 35- to 50-yard guideline between one another. Generally, AR3 assistant helpers are positioned two passes away from the ball, which is approximately 30 yards.

AR3 has an immediate defensive duty if AR1 loses the ball. It is crucial to drop back to a ball-side position in the passing lane on nearest opponent in your area of the field. Often AR3 players find themselves far away from the area where possession was lost. It is vital for successful team defense to sprint from AR3 to recover into a defensive role.

■ *AR3 communication with AR2 and AR1.* Although talking is an important part of effective AR2 support movement, AR3's communication is of less importance because of the greater distance from the ball. However, communication between two or more attackers who understand each other's plan and respond together remains a very important part of attack tactics in hockey. You are working the spaces far from the ball, so calling for the ball would not be very effective because defenders would have time to organize. As an AR3 player, you must communicate by calling whenever AR1 has her head down or whenever AR2 and other AR3 players are not aware of your presence. Seventy percent of human communication is nonverbal body language. AR3 communicates her intentions not just by words but by gestures, head position, positioning of the ball, stick position, posture, and even by the direction she faces. These same elements can be used to deceive opponents.

Effective AR3 communication with AR2 and AR1 will achieve ball penetration. Penetration is gained only with successful use of width and depth in attack. It is AR3's responsibility to arrive in the space at the same moment the ball arrives; that is, if you arrive before the ball, you will quickly become marked by the defense, and if the ball arrives before you, it is usually picked up by a cover defender or allowed to roll over the back line for a 16-yard defense hit. Another factor apart from width and depth that helps contribute to successful attack penetration includes the short, sharp fake cuts before cutting or leading to receive the long through pass. Fake or dummy lateral movements by AR3 tend to drag defenders out of position, which allows the ball to be passed through into space for AR3.

AR3 Runs to Create and Use Space

Various types of runs can create and use space. Basic concepts that govern running include (a) if AR3 moves and the opponent moves with her, space is created for AR1 or AR2 and (b) if AR3 moves and the opponent does not move with her, space can be used for an immediate pass to AR3. It is important to realize that space can be created through the combined movements of two or more attack players.

Because of the recent elimination of the field hockey offside rule, the *diagonal run* (see figure 8.3) has become a tremendously effective method of movement by Role 3 attackers to penetrate through the opponent's defense in the attacking third of the field.

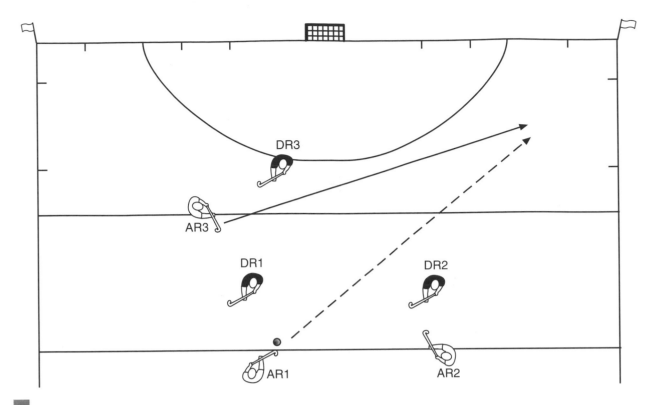

Figure 8.3 Diagonal run.

By running diagonally through the defense, you can begin your run from the outsides of the field and travel inward toward the center of the defense, or you can begin from the central area and move toward the outside of the field. In either scenario, diagonal runs penetrate the dangerous space and force the opposition to mark you, possibly drawing these defenders into bad defensive positions. A diagonal run may also clear the area of defenders, allowing AR2 or AR1 to move forward into the open area. Should you receive the ball while moving diagonally through the defense from the outside to the center, you will be in an excellent position to penetrate and shoot to score! A diagonal run from the midfield area out to the side is used to create space. A long diagonal run occupies many areas in a shorter time, causing confusion in both zone defenses and man-to-man defenses. Space in the middle of the field can be created with split diagonal runs. A *split diagonal run* (see figure 8.4) involves two AR3 players moving in opposite directions from the middle of the field to the outsides so that space is create between the central defenders. This space is then used by AR2 attackers or AR1 moving forward from deep positions.

A run that is made behind a defender is referred to as a *blind-side run*. The opponent cannot defend the run of AR3 if he cannot see him. A blind-side run (see figure 8.5) can create space by forcing the covering defender across the field to open up the area behind DR1.

The blind-side run from the middle of the field to the outside wing areas often stretches the width of the opponent's defense.

A run from behind AR1 and to the outside of the ball is referred to as an *overlap run*. As an effective run to either create or use space, it is most effective to the outsides of the field to increase attack width. Decide at what moment to make the overlap run (see figure 8.6) by determining the defensive position ahead of the ball. Accelerate your running pace to move ahead of the ball and communicate with AR1 when to hold the ball to take on the DR1 player and when to pass the ball forward to force a two-on-one.

Checking runs are short, sudden bursts of speed designed to fool the defender into thinking that you are going into space behind her. Bluff a run forward past the defender, then suddenly check back toward the ball. Use the checking run (see figure 8.7) to create distance between you and the opponent marking you, which often develops in the attacking area of the field. Because defenders attempt to maintain a goal-side position when marking or covering, the distance between you and the defender increases when you suddenly stop and check back toward the ball. The execution of the checking run enables you to take advantage of the open space to receive the ball.

Because of limited space and the pressure placed on the opponent in the attacking area of the field, combination movements with other attack players can

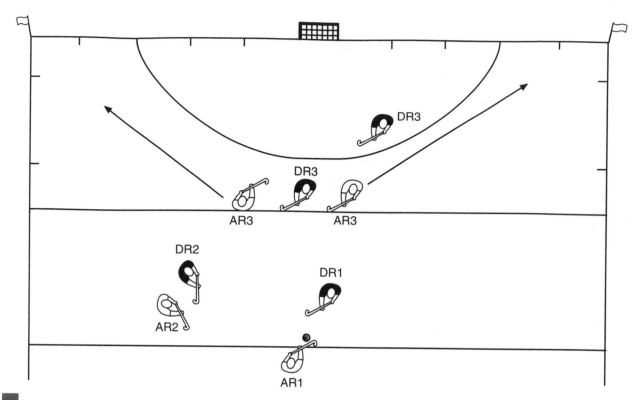

Figure 8.4 Split diagonal run.

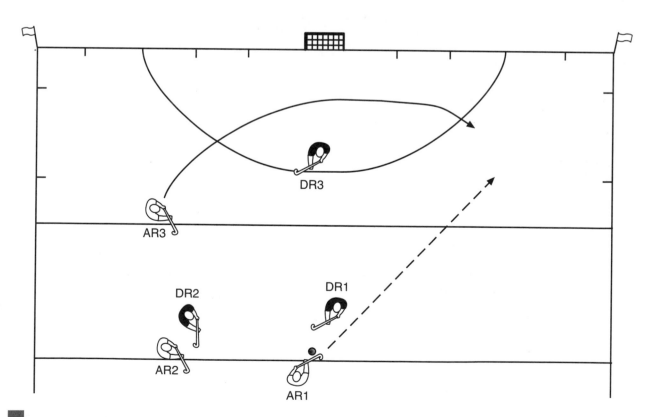

Figure 8.5 Blind-side run by AR3.

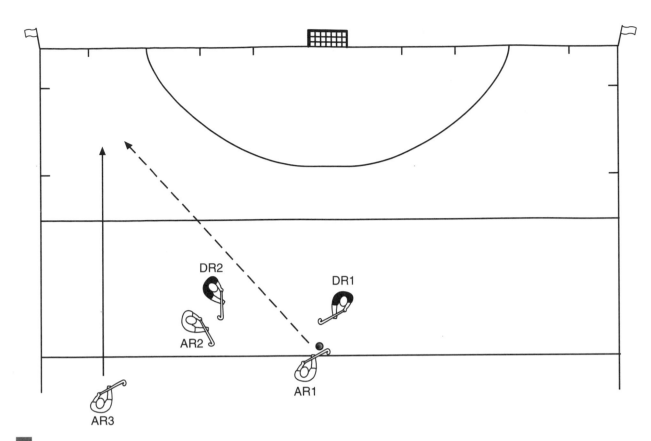

Figure 8.6 Overlap run by AR3.

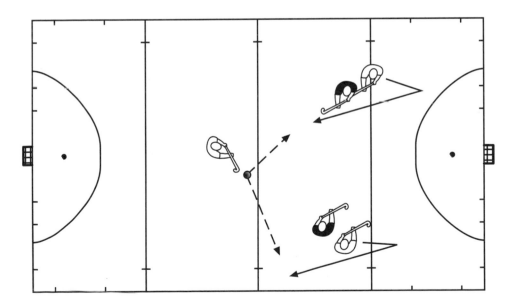

Figure 8.7 Checking runs

destroy defensive coverage. The decisions AR3 faces are Should I use space by attacking the ball? or Should I create space by taking defenders away? AR3 must concentrate on the next move and react quickly. Sharp and accurate execution of movement and combination play, which include one- and two-touch passing, will produce scoring opportunities. Keep the ball in your view at all times while you attempt to lure defenders into bad defensive positions. When using space in the attack area of the field, you must move swiftly whether unmarked or marked. Attempt to keep as wide a view of the field as possible.

AR3 players must be ready to score! AR3 prepares to get the ball from cross passes directed to the near post, far post, and middle of the shooting circle. With cross passes, it is very important to concern yourself with the angle of the run, the timing of the run, and the finish shot on goal. When receiving a crossed ball, move into the line of the ball rather than attempting to move across it. If the angle is correct, timing your run can be achieved much easier. Because of the precise timing needed to contact the ball, it is more difficult to make contact while running across the path of the ball. Timing your run is crucial for success. The run should be made late but at a fast rate. Defenders will be able to reorganize their marking assignments quickly if you move too early and wait for the ball to arrive. Finishing in the circle from a crossed ball is merely redirecting the ball to goal. A still stick must accompany your correct stick angle while timing your run into the line of the pass.

When the ball is in the midfield area, all Attack Roles must coordinate their responsibilities to control this area. Patient but quick attack execution creates penetration opportunities. As the AR3 player, constructive runs ahead of the ball are very useful in creating space. Diagonal runs in front of the opponent disrupt and stretch man-to-man and zone defenses. Blind-side runs are similar to the diagonal in the midfield area with the difference that the blind-side run has less depth. Overlapping runs can be used frequently to attack from the midfield into the attacking area.

When the ball is in the defensive area of the field, maintaining possession is very important. Playing the ball safely to the outside of the field is an appropriate team-attack tactic that emphasizes possession and safety. AR3 players must attack the opposition with combined runs to create space and use space. Usually your combined runs are made behind the opposition's defenders.

Transition Play of AR3

Even the best attacking situations can break down, and often when you have an up-numbers attack situation, the more devastating the counterattack is in return by the opposition. When your team loses possession, immediately determine which Defense Role you are to assume because you must be able to adjust to regain possession and/or break down the opponent's counterattack. The AR3 player who can effectively move from attack to defense to anticipate the opponent's most obvious attacking alternatives will often create the all important goal-scoring opportunity.

When your team wins possession of the ball, AR3's responsibility is to immediately provide forward depth or lateral width for the counterattack such as the fastbreak. A crucial part of AR3's transitional game includes the readiness to move smoothly and effectively into AR2 support or receive the ball and become the new leader! The ability to interchange your Attack Roles as the ball travels is crucial for successful team-attack tactics. Ball movement from player to player will result in longer periods of ball possession, penetration into dangerous space, and scoring opportunities—the ultimate beauty of team attack play.

ROLES 2 AND 3 ATTACK TACTICS SUCCESS STOPPERS

Tactical errors in team attack occur for a variety of reasons because both technical execution and decision making are involved in every possible situation. An inaccurate or poorly paced pass, improper movement or positioning of AR2 and AR3, failure of AR1 to gain a defensive commitment, or poor timing in the release of the pass can all result in a break down of team attack tactics. Common errors are listed here, along with suggested corrections.

Error	Correction
Role 2 Attack Tactics	
1. In preparing to set up the give-and-go combination, you fail to get a commitment from DR1 before passing to AR2.	1. Dribble diagonally outside of the defender's lead foot. As DR1 steps forward to tackle the ball, execute a pass to AR2.
2. You pass the ball to a supporting AR2 but she cannot execute the give and go with you.	2. AR2 must be positioned 5 yards or closer and to the side of the DR1 player. Support at a distance greater than 5 yards gives DR1 time to readjust his position to intercept a give-and-go pass. You must sprint forward after passing the ball to your support teammate.
3. You fail to recognize the two-on-one situation and do not attempt to combine with the give and go or wall pass.	3. Keep your head up and view the field. A two-on-one in the opponent's half of the field must be executed quickly because additional defenders are trying to recover.
4. An opponent blocks the passing lane between you and the ball.	4. Position yourself at a wide angle from the ball to create an open passing lane. Never position behind the defender or at a narrow angle where the defender can intercept the pass. Do not fill the passing lane too early.
Role 3 Attack Tactics	
1. As either a Role 2 or 3 attack player, you fail to readjust your position in response to movement of the ball.	1. When playing without the ball in attack, positioning must be in a state of constant transition. As the ball is played from one area of the field to another, readjust your position to provide passing options in the area of the ball (AR2) and in the area away from the ball (AR3).
2. Through passes to you are always being intercepted by the opponent.	2. You have arrived too early. Time your cut or checking run in the space to receive the through ball and arrive as the ball arrives.
3. AR1 cannot see you, which restricts use of space and limits her passing options.	3. Avoid positioning directly behind or directly alongside of AR2 because your position reduces the number and size of the passing lanes available for AR1. Position to form wide 45-degree angles from AR2 players so that the range of depth and width space is increased.
4. You have difficulty getting the ball from crossed passes in the attack area of the field.	4. Concentrate on the angle that you move to for receiving the ball. Time your move into the line of the passed ball. Keep your stick still and correctly angled to redirect the pass to a target.

ROLES 2 AND 3 ATTACK TACTICS—DRILLS

1. The Give and Go

Execute the give-and-go passing sequence with a teammate against an imaginary defender as you jog the length of the field. Use a one-touch wall pass the length of the field and return using a two-touch double pass. With the wall pass, try to pass the ball to the stick reach of your AR2 teammate, who redirects the ball ahead into the space behind the imaginary defender. Award yourself a point for each accurate pass to your teammate's stick. Award your teammate one point for each one-touch pass redirected forward into space behind the imaginary defender. Perform the drill at half speed the length of the field hockey field. Return performing the double pass. Award yourself a point for each two-touch pass accurately directed forward into space behind the imaginary defender. Switch starting Attack Roles and repeat.

Success Goal =
Wall pass AR1 player points _____
Wall pass AR2 player points _____
Double pass AR1 player points _____
Double pass AR2 player points _____

To Increase Difficulty
• Increase speed of execution.
• Add a defender to the drill.

To Decrease Difficulty
• Practice give-and-go passing with stationary AR2.

Success Check

AR1 player
• Dribble outside imaginary defender's lead foot _____
• Accurate push pass to AR2's stick _____
• Sprint forward into space _____

AR2 player
• Wall pass—Position 45-degree angle on front side of AR1 _____
• Double pass—Position 45-degree angle behind AR1 _____
• Wall pass—Redirect pass into space behind imaginary defender _____
• Double pass—Two-touch pass into space behind imaginary defender _____
• Move forward to support the ball _____

2. Two-Versus-One Directional

Select two teammates to participate with you; organize into teams of at least six players each. Mark off a playing area of 15 yards by 20 yards with two distinct zones of 15 yards by 10 yards. There must be one defender in each zone at all times who starts on the back lines in each of the two zones. The defender may leave the back line of his zone to play the ball when the ball enters his zone. Your attack team of three players starts in the zones to receive a pass from outside the zone. Use two-on-one dribbling, passing, and support movement to maintain possession to beat the defender in the front zone and to beat the defender by penetrating across the goal line in the back zone. Award one point for each give-and-go pass that beats a defender and one additional point for each penetration possession over the goal line. After a goal line score, next three attackers attempt to execute the two-on-one to the goal line. Defenders may substitute for each other at will. If defenders intercept or successfully tackle, they play keep away or clear the ball from the zone. Play for five minutes, then switch Attack and Defense Roles and repeat. The team with the most points wins.

Success Goal = Score more points than opponent _____

Success Check
- Take on and commit defender _____
- AR2 players must maintain clear passing lanes to AR1 _____
- Redirect pass into space behind defender _____

To Increase Difficulty
- Decrease size of grid.
- Limit attack players to 3 or fewer touches.
- Allow defender in front zone to recover and help in back zone.
- Increase playing time.

To Decrease Difficulty
- Increase size of grid.
- Add an attack player and play 4 versus 2.

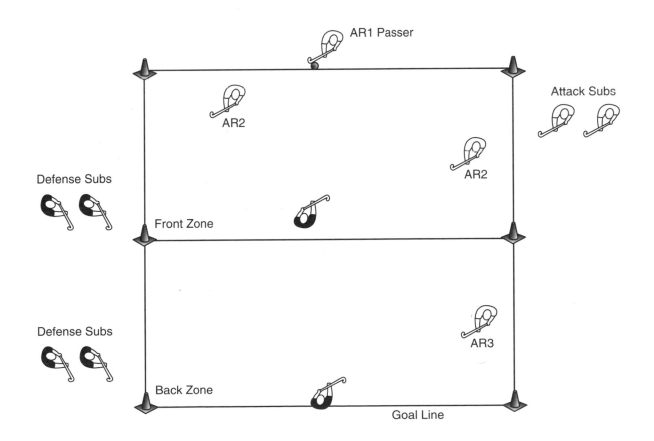

3. The Nine-Goal Game

Use cones or markers to scatter nine goals, 3 yards wide in a 50-yard-by-50-yard grid. Play with two teams of six players each. Regular field hockey rules apply except that teams are awarded points for the following:

- One point for six or more consecutive passes without possession loss.
- One point by passing the ball through the goal to a teammate or dribbling through a goal.

Play for 10 minutes. The team scoring the most points wins the game.

Success Goal = Score more points than opponents ____

Success Check
- AR2 provides support for AR1 ____
- AR3 stretches opponent's defense by creating width and depth space ____
- Maintain open passing lanes ____

To Increase Difficulty
- Decrease size of playing area.
- Limit players to 3 or fewer touches to pass and receive the ball.
- Use smaller goals.
- Play with 1 extra defender.
- Must execute a give and go in the consecutive passing series.

To Decrease Difficulty
- Increase size of playing area.
- Enlarge the goals.
- Award 1 team point for 4 or more consecutive passes.
- Play with uneven numbers: the team that loses possession drops a player and the team that wins possession adds a player.

4. Three-Versus-One Goal-Line Game

Designate one player as a defender and form a team of three attackers. Use markers to outline a 15-yard-by-20-yard grid with 15-yard goal lines where a goal-line defender is positioned. The goal-line defender may take only one step forward off the goal line to play the ball. The objective is for your team to score by dribbling over the goal line or completing a pass within the boundaries to AR2 over the goal line. Attacking team is free to move anywhere within the grid and are allowed unlimited touches to pass and receive the ball. When the defender in the playing area gains possession of the ball, she attempts to play keep away from the attacking team. Award one point for each time your attack team scores and immediately attack the other goal line. The attacking team has a 5-yard zone behind the goal line to maintain possession of the ball, turn, and attack in the opposite direction. Play for five minutes, then switch defenders and repeat.

Success Goal = 4 or more points scored in 5 minutes _____

Success Check
• Immediate support help of the ball _____
• Position wide 45-degree angles of support _____
• Correct pace and accuracy of passes _____

To Increase Difficulty
• Play for 10 minutes nonstop.
• Decrease size of grid.
• Limit attackers to 2 touches.
• Allow goal-line defenders to take more than 1 step off the goal line.
• Place a goal cage 15 yards behind the goal line to shoot to score.

To Decrease Difficulty
• Increase size of grid.
• Add another AR2 player and play 4 versus 1.

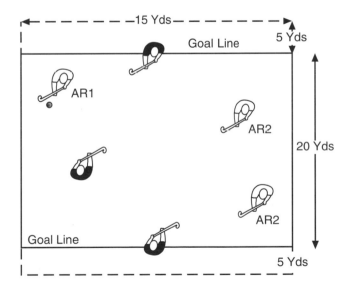

5. Rover Game—Three-Versus-Three Depth

Use markers to designate a 20-yard-by-30-yard playing area consisting of two equal 20-yard-by-15-yard vertical zones. Organize into two teams of three players each. Each team must position at least one player in each zone at all times. The team in possession of the ball scores a point by controlling the ball over the opponent's back line. One attack player—rover—may move back and forth in each zone to support the ball. The rover may switch his rover privilege with another attack teammate at anytime. Change of possession occurs when a defender steals the ball, the ball goes out-of-bounds last touched by a member of the attacking team, or a point is scored. Play for 10 minutes and keep track of points.

Success Goal = Score more points than opponent _____

Success Check
- Create depth space _____
- Immediate transition from defense to attack _____
- Take on and commit DR1 and create a two-on-one combination _____
- AR2 wide angles of support using width and depth _____
- Correct pace and accuracy of passes _____

To Increase Difficulty
- Decrease playing area.
- Limit players to 2 or fewer touches.
- Use goals and goalkeepers to finish to score.
- Increase number of players.

To Decrease Difficulty
- Increase grid area.
- Allow 3 or more touches.
- Shorten playing time to 5 minutes.
- Add extra attack player and allow 2 attack players to rove.

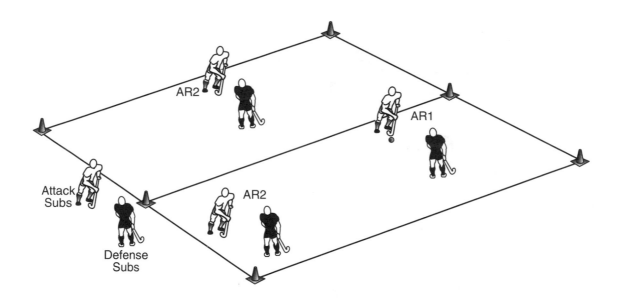

6. Three-Versus-Two Develop Balance

Use markers to create a playing area 20 yards by 20 yards. Within this area, designate three zones to include two width zones 10 yards by 10 yards and one depth zone 20 yards by 10 yards. The back line of the depth zone is the goal line. Select three teammates to participate with you on the attack team. One attack player must position in each zone until the ball is passed into the playing area by a stationary passer located on the front side of the width zones. Two defenders take on your attack team. The object is to play three versus two to create a two-on-one "give and go" to penetrate the defender's goal line. Award one point to your attack team for each possession dribbled over the opponent's goal line that is executed with three or fewer passes. After each score, the passer puts another ball into play. Play for five minutes and switch roles. Repeat the drill.

Success Goal = Score more points than opponents ____

Success Check
- Maintain open passing lanes ____
- Recognize and execute give and go ____
- Maintain depth and width balance ____

To Increase Difficulty
- Decrease size of the playing field.
- Limit attackers to 2 touches or fewer.
- Increase playing time.

To Decrease Difficulty
- Increase size of playing area.
- Allow 4 passes or fewer to score.
- Decrease playing time.

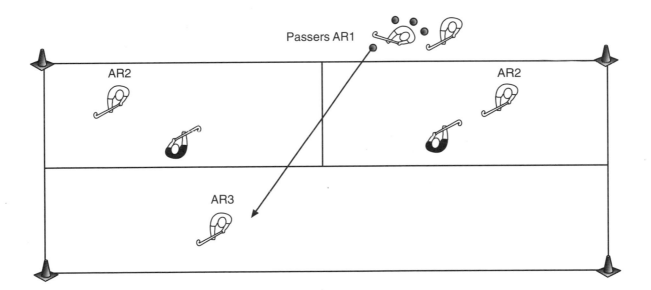

Passers AR1

AR2

AR2

AR3

7. Three-Zone Balance Game

Use markers to outline a rectangular area 20 yards by 45 yards consisting of three equal zones of 20 yards by 15 yards. On both back lines of the rectangular area, center 4-yard goals. Select three teammates to participate with you on the attack team. The defense team has only three players. Play regular field hockey rules except one attack player and one defense player must remain in each of the three zones to maintain positional balance. Score one point for each goal scored. Play for 10 minutes then switch from Attack Roles to Defense Roles. The team scoring more points wins the game.

Success Goal = Score more points than the opponents ____

Success Check
• Recognize and execute two-on-one play ____
• AR2 provides support for AR1 ____
• AR3 creates width or depth space ____
• Maintain open passing lanes ____
• Recognize and execute transition play ____

To Increase Difficulty
• Decrease size of playing area.
• Use goalkeepers.
• Increase playing time.
• Limit attackers to 2-touch passing.
• Add a defender and play 4 versus 4.

To Decrease Difficulty
• Increase playing area.
• Eliminate a defender and play 4 versus 2.
• Reduce playing time.
• Limit players to 3 or fewer touches to pass and receive.

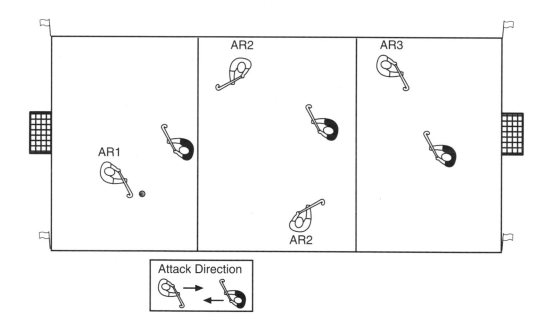

Attack Direction

8. Three-Goal Game

Play with two teams of four players each. Use markers to outline a 60-yard-by-50-yard playing area with three 4-yard-wide goals positioned evenly behind each of the back lines. Each team defends its three goals on its own back line and attempts to score in one of the opponent's three goals. Regular field hockey rules apply. Play for 15 minutes and keep track of the goals scored.

Success Goal = Score more points than the opponents ____

Success Check
• Width, depth, and penetration on attack ____
• Quick transitional play from Attack Roles and from possession change ____
• Create two-on-one combination play ____
• Recognize and execute fastbreak counterattack ____

To Increase Difficulty
• Decrease size of playing area.
• Use 2 goalkeepers to defend 3 goals.
• Increase playing time.
• Limit players to 3 touches to pass, receive, and shoot the ball.
• Defense team plays with extra defender, 4 versus 5.

To Decrease Difficulty
• Increase playing area.
• Use only 2 goals on each back line.
• Reduce playing time.
• Attack team has extra player, 5 versus 4.

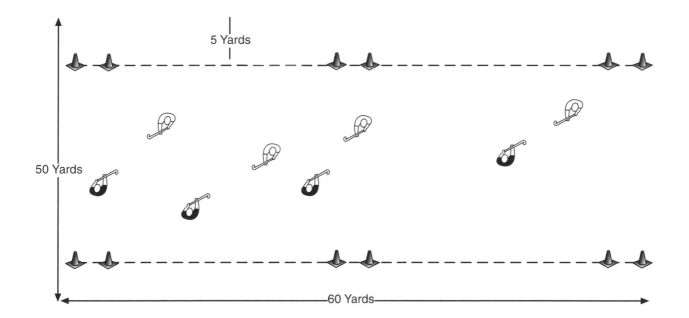

5 Yards

50 Yards

60 Yards

TEAM ATTACK SUCCESS SUMMARY

Playing off the ball is teamwork. Teamwork includes everything a player can do to help others on the team when she does not have the ball. This includes supporting, creating options, creating space, making runs to space, confusing the opponent's defense, distracting the defense, stretching the defense, and communicating. Remember, the prime purpose of any game of field hockey is to create sufficient time and space in the opposition's area, which will give you a scoring opportunity. When your team is attacking and you are without the ball, execute the responsibilities of either Attack Role 2 or Attack Role 3. You must do this more than your opponent, who has the same objective in the defensive roles.

Ask a coach, your parent, or teammate who is knowledgeable about field hockey tactics to observe and analyze execution of your Role 2 and 3 attack tactics. Helpful advice from an observer will improve your team play and provide input as to whether you are executing your Role 2 responsibility to help the ballcarrier and your Role 3 attack responsibility to create and use space for yourself and your teammates. The most important lesson is that the attack tactics employed by you and your teammates reflect the quality of skills within your team. The greater the level of skills, the more effective and varied the attack tactics available to your team. The creation of attack team tactics is very satisfying when you and your teammates think and play together.

STEP 9

TEAM DEFENSE: EXECUTING DEFENSE ROLES 2 AND 3

The aim of team defense tactics is to prevent goals through a disciplined and organized method in which two or more defenders understand each other's plan and respond with teamwork. While each player must be able to execute Defense Role 1 techniques and tactics discussed thus far, the team will not be successful unless all players are thinking and working together to achieve the same objective. To effectively play team defense, players must block the opponent's penetration efforts and control the space behind, beside, and in front of the ball. Every player needs to understand each role of defense to successfully execute the tactics and skills of team play. With a thorough understanding and execution of your *Defense Role 2* and *Defense Role 3* responsibilities, your field hockey team can be a group of players who think and defend together.

Immediate calculated pressure, coverage of the field by dropping back while evaluating, organization, and transitional flow from role to role are skills that must be incorporated into a potent team defense. Because Defense Role 2 (DR2) players, or *helpers*, are nearest to DR1, their prime responsibility is to help the leader of the defense by marking the nearest opponent and controlling space near the ball. The *assistant helpers* of the defense are the Defense Role 3 (DR3) players. As DR3, you are responsible for covering and controlling dangerous spaces of greater width and depth from the ball. Marking and covering in the Defense Roles refer to the defense of AR2 in the vicinity of the ball and to the defense of AR3 two passes or more—30 yards or more—from the area of the ball. With proper positioning and communication from DR2 and DR3, your team can create the defensive tactics it needs to block penetration, to prevent goals, and to win back ball possession.

In field hockey, the play is always changing, which presents numerous decision-making situations. Defenders not only must be physically fit and have a great deal of determination, but they also must respond with superior ability to make decisions such as when to challenge for the ball and where to position for best coverage and balance of the team's defensive undertaking. The defenders away from the ball are responsible for executing good decisions for the organization of team defense. You can improve your decision making by developing a clear understanding of how to organize and evaluate what is most important to defend—the ball, the opponent, or the space. To be a successful problem solver within team defense tactics, it remains vital that you be aware of the *Big Three* window of information discussed in Step 8. Applying the correct defensive skill at the right moment is primary to achieving organized and aggressive team play that will win back the ball. Defending away from the ball requires players to react with discipline, intelligence, and anticipation. Every player should understand each Defense Role, which will lead to good decisions for successful execution of team defense tactics.

Why Are Defense Roles 2 and 3 Important?

Defense Roles 2 and 3 create cooperation among individual players in the overall tactical strategy of the group. When you are able to blend all three roles of field hockey defense, your team will be able to influence how the opponent plays, reduce the opposition's scoring opportunities, and increase your team's chances to win back ball possession. By understanding the defense tactics of Role 2 and Role 3, you will learn to intercept passes, interrupt opponents when they change position, prevent "give-and-go" attack tactics by covering space, and shift position in the direction of the ball to provide balance. *Balance* in defense protects the open space on the side of the field opposite the ball. As with attack play, understanding the relationship of time and space on the hockey field is crucial to the execution of team defense. The less space you make available to attack players, the less time they will have to receive, control, pass, or shoot. A great deal of organization is necessary to position and effectively communicate with your teammates so that you can mark the opponent, restrict space, and cover the dangerous space. Roles 2 and 3 defense responsibilities provide the tactical organization to win back the ball.

How to Execute Role 2 Defense

It is fundamental to deny the opponent several passing options both in possession-style offenses and, especially, in fastbreak-style attack play. The moment your team loses possession of the ball, rapid counterdefenses into space behind DR1 characterize the transition into team defense. DR2 players are "helpers" who support the teammate pressuring the ball by using two basic defense tactics: controlling or restricting space and marking the opponent near the ball. It is DR2's responsibility to decide on, communicate, and execute the marking of AR2 and to control the immediate spaces around the ball to limit passing options and create narrow passing lanes. To effectively help DR1, you must control or block passing lanes one pass away from AR1. The basic passing lanes include behind the ball, alongside the ball, and in front of the ball. DR2's primary responsibility is to protect the space around DR1.

To successfully defend passing lanes that support DR1's immediate pressure, you must demonstrate the ability to mark. *Marking* is defending an opponent in the vicinity of the ball. Effective marking includes the ability to change direction and speed, as well as a readiness to challenge for the ball if it is passed to the AR2 player you are marking. In addition to DR1 skills, DR2 players need to possess vision, anticipation, and communication skills to perform the tactics of marking and controlling space. Proper positioning enables your team to consistently control the space and mark the opponent in the vicinity of the ball. A lack of help for DR1 leaves your leader isolated and increases the chances that she will be beaten. Organizing capable support for DR1 depends on several factors, including the (a) number of DR2 helpers, (b) angle of DR2 help, (c) distance of defense help, and (d) communication of defense help.

■ *Number of DR2 helpers.* The number of DR2 helpers near the ball is critical. Many DR2 players may limit AR1's choices near the ball, but too many can be a disadvantage because congestion creates chaos. When space around the ball becomes congested, players must organize marking and passing lane coverage. As a routine guideline, AR2 players must be marked if they are moving to create forward passing options such as *diagonal* and *through* passing lanes.

■ *Angle of DR2 help.* DR2 players need a clear view of the ball and the AR2 player being marked. DR2 players should position themselves from DR1, the opponent, and other DR2 teammates to form angles that will allow coverage to intercept passes and quick read-

justment to the opponent's movement. As the DR2 player, your angle varies according to the position of the pressure player and the movement of AR2. Directly behind DR1, there is no defensive advantage in your position because the range of passing possibilities by the opponent is severely enhanced. If you position directly alongside DR1, there is a lack of depth between you and the ball. Without depth, a penetrating pass in behind you from AR1 to AR2 has a greater chance of being completed. Too much depth by DR2 players is also a problem in transition because too much ground would have to be covered to effectively move from Defense Role 2 to dangerous Attack Roles.

When defending passing lanes in space in front of the ball, always try to win the ball-side position in the passing lane. When defending passing lanes in space behind the ball, position on the goal side of AR2 in the event DR1 gets beaten. This positioning is especially important close to your own defensive goal because a defensive role can be applied quickly if required, a limited range of passing possibilities is available, and AR2's vision of the field is decreased with less time and space.

■ *Distance of DR2 help.* Generally DR2 helpers are positioned one pass away from the ball. The distance of DR2 is very often determined by where the ball is on the field (see figure 9.1), the quality of DR1 pressure on the ball, and the opponent's positioning in the vicinity of the ball. Usually when DR1 is applying effective immediate pressure, DR2 must take a closer position to AR2 to control the space and size of passing lanes near the ball. In the defending area of the field, DR2's distance from the ball is from two to three yards because of space and time restrictions. In this area, you must offer immediate help for DR1 in tight defense situations. Opponents must be denied time and space in the shooting circle, especially in the vital scoring zones in the front and center.

In the midfield area of the hockey field where there is more space, the distance of DR2 help is from five to six yards. This area is often referred to as the transitional area from defense to offense and vice versa. The correct positioning of DR2 players in this area provides organization and control that can change the direction and speed of team defense play.

In the attack area, the distance can be greater than five yards because the threat from the opposition determines the exact DR2 distance for help. If there is little chance of immediate pressure, a wide-angled help position can be used. Without DR2's correct distance and angle of support help, an unsuccessful tackle by the DR1 could prove very costly. A long outlet pass executed by the opponent can result in a dangerous upnumbered fastbreak.

■ *DR2 communication.* The ability to position and intercept the ball at the right moment is an integral

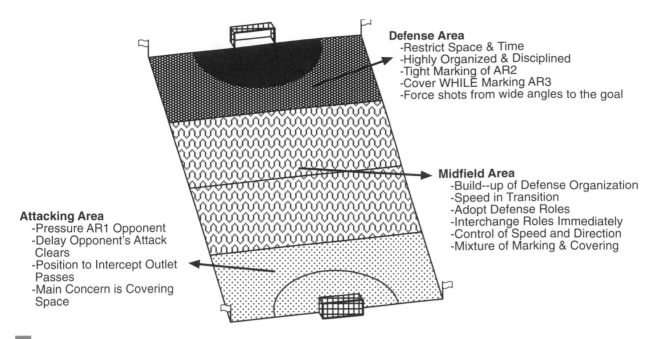

Defense Area
-Restrict Space & Time
-Highly Organized & Disciplined
-Tight Marking of AR2
-Cover WHILE Marking AR3
-Force shots from wide angles to the goal

Midfield Area
-Build--up of Defense Organization
-Speed in Transition
-Adopt Defense Roles
-Interchange Roles Immediately
-Control of Speed and Direction
-Mixture of Marking & Covering

Attacking Area
-Pressure AR1 Opponent
-Delay Opponent's Attack Clears
-Position to Intercept Outlet Passes
-Main Concern is Covering Space

Figure 9.1   Principles of defense play

part of defensive teamwork. DR2 players one pass away must position to keep the stick head near or on the ground and give verbal information about immediate defensive decisions. It is mandatory to call out helpful information to assist DR1. The communication given out by DR2 must be brief, loud, and to the point. Verbal directives such as "With you," "Force left," "Force right," "Time," "I have you covered," "Go," or "Now" delivered quickly and loudly during play will build DR1's confidence and DR2's readiness to play the ball. Occasionally DR2 players must communicate to other DR2 players when switching during marking assignments of AR2 movement around the ball. Players who communicate effectively will think and defend together. Successful performance of team defense is based on your ability to perform your DR2 responsibilities.

DR2 Controls Immediate Spaces

Everyone defends. When your team does not have the ball, all defenders assume a Defense Role to stop penetration, deny space, and regain ball possession. To control space near the ball, drop back in the space closer to your goal and slide ball side to help DR1.

■ *Drop back (recover) and slide ball side to control space.* When pressure is applied by DR1, defenders away from the ball drop back or recover to a position closer to the ball and goal. To *recover* is to move to a defensive position between the ball and the goal being defended. Dropping or falling back on defense buys time to recover and organize your team's defensive strategy to win the ball back. Always move quickly on the shortest route to protect the area in front of the goal. Evalu-

ate the situation by scanning the area to see the opponent, the ball, and your teammates. From a *goal-side* position (see figure 9.2), you will be able to keep the ball and the opponent you are marking in view while you position to provide cover and balance for your teammates. Maintaining an awareness of your goal and keeping the view of the ball and opponent in front of you will determine the space and time needed to base your decisions of how far to drop and at what angle to slide. DR2 players move to a position on the *ball side* of the opponent (see figure 9.3) to reduce the space available to AR2 players near the ball. Defenders away from the ball should slide inward toward the central area of the field as they recover. Coordinating the recovery to goal side and ball side is a collective "team" discipline that is necessary to control space.

■ *Help DR1—read pressure and cover to control space.* To achieve successful "team" defense, DR2 players help DR1 by controlling space around the ball. DR1 player is responsible for pressuring the ball to stop or slow down the opponent's forward penetration by positioning between the ball and the goal. While DR1 pressures, DR2 players fall back and organize to defend the opponent one pass away from the ball. Effective immediate pressure may force AR1 to slow and play into the defense where passes are limited. It is most important to drop back so that immediate *cover* defense can be set up before DR1 tackles or forces the ball in a direction. *Covering* is defending space behind and beside a teammate. If DR1 cannot cleanly tackle to gain possession, she should delay or slow down the attack to give DR2 teammates time to drop back and slide to ball side so they can pro-

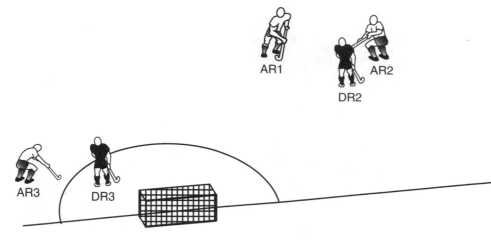

Figure 9.2 Goalside position

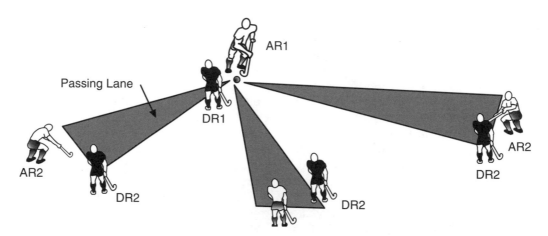

Figure 9.3 Ball side position

vide help near the ball. DR2 players help *control space* by blocking forward space available to AR2 players. When controlling space, DR2 must pay close attention to the roles relative to all other teammates, the ball, and the opponent. You must be aware of risk and priorities that affect team depth, control of space, and positional balance. By keeping the ball and the opponent in your front view, you can intercept an opponent's pass directed into the space in behind DR1. The farther you are from the ball, the deeper your position must be to view the opponent and the ball, which will enable your team to control and block the space in behind.

DR2 Marking and Covering

Defense Role 2 players are responsible for marking the opponent near the ball or one pass away from the ball. All DR2 players have a marking assignment in every area of the field (see figure 9.1) unless there is no cover player. A cover player defends space behind teammates who mark. To successfully mark, you must position to take away a passing lane to the opposition's AR2 player. While marking, DR2 must position to prevent a penetrating pass through that space and be ready to challenge the AR1 opponent if she has beaten DR1 with the dribble. DR2 must be prepared to create a double team defense with DR1. How tight you mark depends on the direction AR2 is moving, her speed, skill, closeness to goal, and closeness to ball, and the need to cover for nearby defenders. Marking is generally tighter closer to the ball, closer to goal, when AR2 is slow and unskilled, and when AR1 is turned while DR1 has excellent pressure on the ball. When the ball is on the outside of the field, mark in a ball-side position. Because of no offside in field hockey, defenders must mark in front of the attackers when the ball is in the central areas of the field.

■ *Mark while controlling space.* Marking the opponent while controlling space must be achieved to prevent goals. The open space from and center of the goal you are defending is the area from where most goals are scored. To mark and control space in the most dangerous shooting areas is a defense tactic of Role 2 defenders. While positioning to defend the space behind the defense, you must reduce the number of receiving choices available to AR2. If you tightly mark the AR2 players, then you force AR1 to attempt a longer pass, which produces a greater chance for error and an opportunity for you to intercept. If you position ball side in the passing lanes to control the diagonal forward and through passes, then you force AR1 to lift an aerial ball or pass the ball square or back to a supporting AR2 teammate. As discussed in Step 2, aerial passes are time-consuming and easier to defend. Also, flat passes directed across the field or back passes toward the opponent's own goal provide your defense team additional time to organize marking and controlling of space.

■ *Force opponent away from center.* Because a small, congested area is easier to defend than a large space, it is important to force the ball wide to limit the opponent's range of passing and to delay direct penetration to the goal. Your team should work hard to keep the ball on the side, which will minimize defensive adjustments. By restricting space, the opponent is not able to make fast cross-field passes that stretch your defense. By limiting space and forcing the opponent from the center area, a team defense can eventually gain effective control of the most dangerous scoring area.

■ *Cover to provide depth in defense.* The entire principle of cover-defense play is based upon the team skill of depth in defense. One or more DR2 teammates should provide cover or depth for DR1, the leader who is applying pressure on the ball. Depth in defense is a means of countering attack overloads by the opposition. DR2 players away from the ball should stagger their positions and maintain 45-degree angles from one another so that sufficient time and space are available to move and play the ball on the forehand side if the ball is passed forward. Depth on defense provides cover for your teammates and reduces the open space between teammates. Too much depth will allow the opponent to play closer to the goal that you are defending.

DR2 Transition Play

The ability to change roles and play effectively completes the organization of team defense. Transition play of DR2 consists of two basic areas of execution—the ability to interchange the Defense Roles and the ability to counterdefend and counterattack (discussed in Step 8). Interchanging the Defense Roles refers to moving smoothly and effectively from DR2 to DR1 or DR3. Constant decisions have to be made when interchanging roles to execute defense tactics. Your decisions are based on the awareness of the situation—position of the ball in areas of the field, the position of the opponent and quality of ball possession exhibited by AR1, and the

position of your teammates with special attention to the quality of defensive pressure by DR1.

Defending as a team must begin the moment before the opponent gains possession of the ball. When defending a counterattack, all players regardless of position must quickly assume a role on defense to prepare for an opponent coming at speed. The period that your team initially loses possession is referred to as your *counterdefense.* The tactical weapon you and your teammates are able to organize against the opposition's attack fastbreak is crucial to counterdefense play. To avoid being beaten by an opponent who outnumbers your team in transitional play, regain possession immediately if possible, slow the attack down and keep the play in front, retreat and delay your defense, force play to the outside or keep the ball in the same area of the field so that you will need less defensive organization, protect the center of the field and prevent movement and passing through the center, and, finally, approach the ball when a scoring threat is high or you are positioned at an angle to prevent centering passes.

Win the Ball

With patience and control, see when DR1 has forced the ball to your range of cover. Intercept or time the execution of a hard block or jab tackle and gain possession of the ball. Finish your tackle or interception by controlling the ball and delivering a strong, accurate attack pass.

How to Execute Role 3 Defense

One objective of attacking play is to get behind the opponent to create scoring chances. Because modern-day attacks are fast and controlled on artificial turf surfaces, defense players need to recover quickly and organize a defense that will keep the attack play in front to deny any form of penetration into the dangerous space. If you are not in the group of defenders around the ball, you must be aware of the dangerous space that the attack seeks to enter. You are Defense Role 3 (DR3), an assistant helper who aims to prevent any forward penetration either by the ball or by AR3 runs. It is with this role that your team defense tactics become collectively organized and balanced.

To maintain organized defense play, DR3 must learn to cover and control the dangerous space farthest from the ball. Keeping the ball and opponent in your view at all times to deny a penetration pass provides your team a positional advantage to shut off the opponent's most direct route to goal. To execute this position effectively, you must accurately determine your distance from the ball, which is a prerequisite for covering and controlling dangerous space. Organizing capable support for DR2 depends on several factors, including the (a) number of

DR3 assistant helpers, (b) angle of DR3 assistant help, (c) distance of DR3 players, and (d) communication of DR3. DR3 must always concentrate on the next move, readjust to respond quickly to cover AR3 players, and control the dangerous space.

■ *Number of DR3 assistant helpers.* Depth in defense establishes a minimum of one or two DR3 players ahead of the ball and one or two DR3 players behind the ball. The function of DR3 behind the ball is to provide depth in the defense and to do what DR2 is not able to do because of lack of time and space—intercept or tackle the forward ball. Controlling the width space available to the attack forces the opponent to perform attack skills in a narrow area. When two passes away or a distance of 30 yards or more from the ball, Role 3 defenders drop to deeper ball-side and goal-side positions toward the center of the field to restrict space and provide balance. Usually one or more DR3 players provide balance in coverage on each side of the field.

The number of DR3 assistant helpers away from the ball is significant. As a guideline, AR3 players must be marked if they are moving to create dangerous passing options such as *diagonal* and *through* passes. Because your goalkeeper is the last line of defense, a limited number of DR3 players are needed to provide depth and width coverage away from the ball.

■ *Angle of DR3 assistant help.* DR3 players should position themselves to form narrow angles from the DR2 players and the ball, which will allow coverage to intercept long direct passes. Your angle varies according to the position of the opposition and your teammates. The narrower the angle of support, the easier it becomes for the DR3 player to defend the space. If you position directly behind DR2, you are at a disadvantage because the range of dangerous space is greatly enhanced for the opponent, and as the DR3 player, you will have limited vision of the field. If you position directly alongside DR2, there is limited defense effectiveness because of the lack of depth between teammates and the ball. Without depth, AR1 has a greater chance of completing a penetrating pass to AR3. Too much depth by DR3 players allows the opposition to move into the space closer to your goal.

When defending passing lanes in space in front of the ball, it is essential to win the ball-side position in AR3's passing lane. When defending passing lanes in space behind the ball, position on the goal side of AR3 in case DR2 gets beaten. This positioning is especially important close to your own defensive goal because interchanging of Defense Roles can be applied quickly if required, a limited range of passing possibilities is available to the opponent, and AR3's vision of the field is decreased with less time and space. Positioning on correct angles in relationship to the ball, the opponent, and your teammates provides a greater chance to intercept the pass. Maintaining correct angles of width

and depth will also enhance your transition into an Attack Role if possession is gained.

■ *Distance of DR3 assistant help.* As a general rule, there should be no more than 50 to 60 yards between the last field player in behind the ball and the deepest DR3 player in front of the ball. Because the hockey field is 60 yards wide, DR3 players defending width should be 35 to 50 yards from the ball and in line to the near goal post. Because DR3 assistant helpers are positioned two or more passes away from the ball, the actual distance of DR3 is very often determined by where the ball is on the field (see figure 9.4) in relation to your goal, the quality of DR1 pressure, the cover and control of DR2 near the ball, and AR3 positioning away from the ball. Generally when DR2 is applying effective marking, DR3 can take a closer position to AR3 to cover and control the dangerous space. In the defending area of the field, DR3's distance from the ball and AR3 is based on the restriction of space and time. In this area, you must offer immediate help for DR2 in tight defense situations. Opponents must be denied time and space in the shooting circle, especially in the vital scoring zones in the front and center of your goal.

In the midfield area, the distance of DR3 assistant help is from 10 to 15 yards because of the availability of more space to defend. This area of the field is often referred to as the transitional area to organize your Defense Roles. The correct positioning of DR3 players to protect dangerous space in this area will determine organized team defense play.

In the attack area, the DR3's distance can be greater because the main concern of DR3 is covering space. When the ball is in this area, DR3 must cover the passing lanes that would allow a long outlet pass in behind teammates, resulting in a dangerous up-numbered fastbreak.

■ *DR3 communication.* It is a vital responsibility to communicate directives to teammates in front of you, as well as for you to receive directives from your goalkeeper or other DR3 teammates. Through effective communication to deny width and depth space, DR3 can coordinate team play to block areas and discourage the opponent's ball movement. Successful performance of team defense is based on your ability to perform the following DR3 responsibilities in the order listed.

DR3 Protects Dangerous Space

The chief responsibility of all DR3 players is to protect the dangerous space, which in turn helps DR2. It is your assignment to assess the situation while DR1 and DR2 are closing down the point of attack and to protect the depth and width space 30 or more yards from the ball. To be successful, DR3 must drop to the ball-side and goal-side position to cover passing lanes to AR3 in the dangerous space. From here you will be able to read the situation and provide cover for your teammates while reducing space available to AR3 players away from the ball. Recovery to protect the dangerous space provides balance in handling the possible threat against DR2 and DR1. DR3's decisions in how to move to cover dangerous space are based on knowledge of the position of the ball and goal, the quality of DR1 pressure on the ball, where your DR2 teammates are providing help, and where the opponent is positioned.

DR3 Marks and Covers AR3 Runs

Because AR3 is farthest from the ball, she does not pose an immediate threat to the defense. DR3 can therefore support DR2 and DR1 as they attempt to win the ball. But it remains crucial that you position to view and cover AR3 runs while you protect the dangerous space. Ball watching is a frequent mistake that DR3 players make and can prove costly in the defense area (see figure 9.1) of the field. AR3 players make runs for only two reasons—to create space and to use space. DR3 players have to determine quickly what type of run is being made and for what purpose. The most dangerous runs use space such as from the wings to the middle of the field. While keeping AR3 and the ball in view, DR3 must remain on the goal side and ball side of AR3 with awareness of the goal position. The least dangerous AR3 runs create space from the middle out to the wing areas. Should AR3 receive a pass, you have sufficient time to adjust and engage because of the greater distance the ball has to travel. You must attempt to do one of the following if AR3 plays the ball directly from AR1: intercept the pass, prevent AR3 from turning and changing the point of attack, delay the penetration to the center of the field, or tackle.

DR3 Provides Balance

DR3 provides balance to establish cover or defensive depth for DR2. DR3 players away from the ball must be staggered across the field in support and be positioned on a 45-degree angle from their teammates so that sufficient time and space are available to move and play the ball on the forehand side if the ball is passed forward. DR3 players on the side of the field opposite the ball position along an imaginary diagonal line that starts at the ball and travels toward the far goalpost. By keeping the ball and the opponent in view, you can intercept an opponent's pass directed into the space in behind the defense. The farther you are from the ball, the deeper you must be to view the opponent and the ball, which will enable your team to control and protect the dangerous space. From a position along the line of balance, DR3 can accomplish two important objectives: (a) protect the space behind DR2 and (b) keep the ball and AR3 you are marking in view (see figure 9.4).

Only cover attack players for a certain distance. Balance your run coverage between moving away too far and not moving at all so that you have the opportunity to intercept a pass to the outside, close down to the attacker, and protect the central area of the field. A DR3 player who is lured all the way to the outside of the field has opened up the central area. AR1 and AR2 will quickly use this area to execute dangerous attack tactics to goal. The goalkeeper must be prepared to help protect the open space behind DR3 and communicate the need for defensive balance.

DR3 Transitional Play

When DR3's team loses possession of the ball, DR3's responsibility is to immediately protect dangerous space against the fastbreak. A crucial part of DR3's transitional game includes the readiness to move smoothly and effectively into DR2 marking or into the

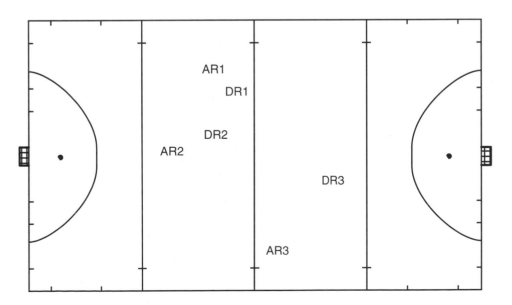

Figure 9.4 Position of DR3 cover.

leader role—DR1! The ability to interchange your Defense Roles as the ball travels is crucial for successful defense team tactics. Organized team defense (see figure 9.5) accompanied by determination, patience, and anticipation will allow your team to deny penetration into dangerous space and eventually win the ball back. The DR3 player who can move from defense to attack to anticipate the opponent's most obvious attacking alternatives will often create the all-important fastbreak opportunity.

FIGURE
9.5

KEYS TO SUCCESS

TEAM DEFENSE

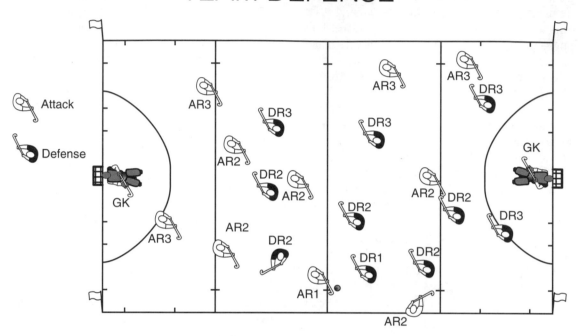

DR1

1. Close distance to AR1 ____
2. Position yourself goal side in ready defensive posture ____
3. Maintain balance and control ____
4. Focus on the ball ____
5. Slow down or force AR1's penetration dribble ____
6. Force AR1 into restricted space ____
7. Force AR1 into DR2 ____
8. Challenge for the ball ____
9. Win the ball ____
10. Start counterattack ____

DR2

1. Protect space near DR1 ____
2. Position at proper angle in relation to DR1 and ball ____
3. Position at proper distance in relation to DR1 and ball ____
4. Mark AR2 near the ball ____
5. Keep the ball and opponent in view ____
6. Intercept ball passed into space behind DR1 ____
7. Assume DR1 if ball is passed to AR2 you are marking ____
8. Assume DR1 when she is beaten on a dribble ____
9. Win the ball ____
10. Start counterattack ____

DR3

1. Protect the space diagonally behind DR2 ____
2. Position yourself along a line of balance extending toward the far goalpost ____
3. Keep the ball and opponents in view ____
4. Alter position along line of balance in response to ball movement and AR3 runs ____
5. Intercept passes into the space behind DR2 ____
6. Win the ball ____
7. Start counterattack ____

ROLES 2 AND 3 DEFENSE SUCCESS STOPPERS

Tactical errors in team defense occur for a variety of reasons but mainly because every field situation involves both technical execution and decision making. Successful defensive pressure, marking, and covering require coordinated help by DR1, DR2, and DR3 players. Each defender must read the situation correctly, anticipate the actions of his teammates, and react accordingly. Poor communication, lack of help or improper positioning of DR2 and DR3, failure of DR1 to effectively pressure the ball, or poor recovery efforts can all result in a breakdown of team defense tactics. Common errors are listed here, along with suggested corrections.

Error	Correction
Role 2 Defense Tactics	
1. AR1 beats DR1 with the dribble, and you fail as the DR2 player to properly position in cover.	1. Communicate to DR1 to delay her tackle and force DR1's dribble in a direction so that you have time to recover and help to restrict space.
2. DR2 near the point of attack does not have enough time to recover to a position goal side of the ball.	2. Communicate or direct DR1 to apply immediate pressure on AR1.
3. DR2 positions directly behind DR1 and fails to prevent AR1's pass through the space beside DR1.	3. Position at a diagonal on an angle from the ball in the space behind and to the side of DR1.
4. DR2 positions too far from DR1 and cannot provide help.	4. When determining the proper distance of DR2, you should consider the ability of DR1, the area of the field, and the location of AR2 you are responsible to mark.
Role 3 Defense Tactics	
1. As the DR3 player, you fail to readjust your position in response to movement of the ball.	1. When playing away from the ball in defense, positioning must be in a state of constant transition. As the ball is played from one area of the field to another, readjust your position to control passing lane options to AR3 in the area away from the ball.
2. AR3 receives through passes to the dangerous space.	2. Protect the dangerous space. Position diagonally behind DR2 along a line of balance extending toward the far goalpost. From here, you will be able to keep the opponent and the ball in view and also intercept a penetrating ball. Remember that the line of balance changes with the movement of the ball.
3. DR3 positions too close to DR2 and as a result is prone to the long cross-field pass into the dangerous space.	3. Avoid positioning too close and directly behind DR2 because your position reduces the number and size of the passing lanes available for AR3. When the ball is played into open space 30 yards or more, you will have sufficient time to recover while the ball is rolling, providing you are not too close to DR2 and you sprint into your recovery.

Error	Correction
4. AR3 beats you to a long diagonal ball.	4. Concentrate on the angle that you position to cover the passing lane to AR3. Position on the ball side of AR3 so you are nearer to the ball than AR3 and can intercept it. Time your move into the line of the passed ball. Keep your stick and body in a ready position.

ROLES 2 AND 3 DEFENSE—DRILLS

1. Organizing Pressure

Organize two teams of two players each. Use cones or markers to outline a rectangular area of 15 yards by 20 yards with a goal 15 yards wide. Start one defender on your goal line. The attack players start with the ball 20 yards from your goal line. The play is started with AR1 passing to AR2. On the first pass, both defenders move into DR1 and DR2 to prevent ball penetration by the attack team. Award one point to the attacking team for each possession that penetrates over your goal line. Award your team one point each time it wins possession or forces the opponents to play outside of the field area. If your team wins the ball, immediately attempt to hit the cones with a pass for a bonus point or return it to the attacking team and continue the game. Play for 10 minutes and keep track of your score.

Success Goal = Score more points than opponents _____

Success Check
- Apply pressure at the point of attack _____
- DR2 organizes pressure/cover _____
- Prevent dribble and pass penetration _____
- Quickly interchange Defense Roles _____

To Increase Difficulty
- Increase size of playing area.
- Add extra attack player.

To Decrease Difficulty
- Reduce size of playing area.
- Decrease goal size.
- Add DR3 cover player.

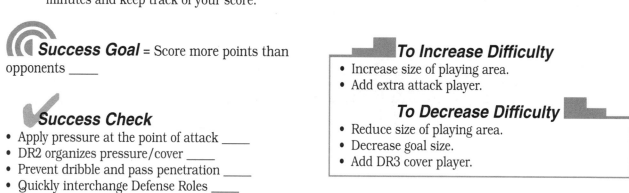
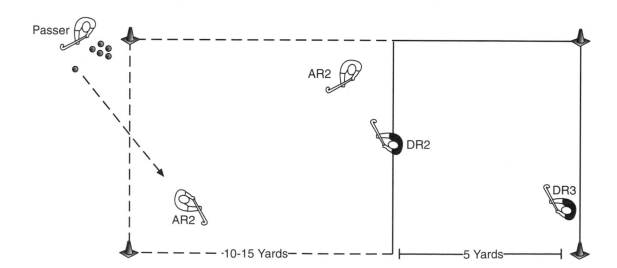

2. Pressure/Cover—Two-on-Two

Organize into two teams of two players each. Use markers to outline a 15-yard-by-25-yard field area and position a goal 4 yards wide at the center of each back line. Each team defends a goal. Begin with a pass from the center of the field. Score goals by hitting or pushing the ball through the opponent's goal from your attack half of the field area. Do not use goalkeepers. Play for 10 minutes.

The main concern in this activity is on defensive pressure and cover. DR1 should apply immediate pressure on AR1 at the point of attack; DR2 should position in cover to help prevent the ball from penetrating past DR1 toward goal. DR2 must be in a ball-side position to challenge for the ball if it is passed to AR2 she is marking.

Success Goal = Score more goals than the opponent _____

Success Check
- DR1 pressures AR1 _____
- DR2 proper distance and angle of cover _____
- DR2 communication to DR1 _____
- DR1 drops to assume DR2 when ball is passed _____
- DR2 positions ball side of AR2's passing lane _____

To Increase Difficulty
- Increase size of field to create more space.
- Require teams to defend 2 small goals on each back line.
- Increase playing time.
- Add a goalkeeper on each team.

To Decrease Difficulty
- Reduce field size.
- Make goals smaller.

3. DR2 Ball-Side Marking—To Goal

Play with three teammates; organize into teams of one player each with two stationary attack passers. Use markers to outline a 15-yard-by-20-yard area with a goal 3 yards wide at the center of the back line. Position the passers on the attack's back line. As the DR2 player, position inside the area and mark the AR2 player. The stationary attack passers start with the ball by passing to each other or attempting to pass to AR2. DR2 readjusts to ball side of AR2 every time the point of attack is changed by the stationary passers. If AR2 receives a pass, DR2 must assume DR1 immediately. Play for five minutes. Award yourself two points for each interception and one point for each successful tackle. Award the attack one point for each completed pass to AR2 and two points for a successful ball penetration through the goal.

Success Goal = Score more points than the opponents _____

Success Check
- Prevent passes to AR2 _____
- Cover the most dangerous attack space _____
- Prevent dribble penetration _____
- Prevent shots from area front and center of goal _____
- Quickly readjust defensive positions in relation to movement of the ball _____

To Increase Difficulty
- Enlarge the playing area.
- Increase goal size.

To Decrease Difficulty
- Reduce size of playing area.
- Make goal smaller.
- Limit attackers to 3 touches to control and play the ball.

4. Down Numbers Grid—Four-on-Two

Use six players. You and one teammate form the defending team while the remaining players form an attacking team. Use cones or markers to outline a 15-yard-by-15 yard grid. Position one attack player at each of the four corners of the grid. The attacking team attempts to keep the ball away from your team by passing, dribbling, or both within the grid. Award the attacking team one point each time it compiles six consecutive passes and two points for each "killer" pass completed that goes between you and your teammate into the dangerous space. Award your team one point each time it wins possession of the ball or forces the opponent to play outside the grid. When your team wins the ball, immediately return it to the attacking team and continue the game. Play for 10 minutes and keep score.

Success Goal = Score more points than opponent _____

Success Check
- DR1 pressure on AR1 _____
- DR1 and DR2 work together to restrict attacker's passing options _____
- DR2 communication to DR1 _____
- Prevent killer pass to dangerous space _____
- DR2 correct distance and angle of cover _____
- Prevent dribble penetration _____

To Increase Difficulty
- Increase size of grid.
- Increase playing time.

To Decrease Difficulty
- Reduce grid size.
- Decrease playing time.
- Limit attackers to 3 or fewer touches to pass and receive the ball.
- Limit attacking team to 3 players.

Drop

5. Sideline Marking Game

Assign 8 to 12 teammates to two equal-size teams. Use markers to outline a field area approximately 30 yards square. Designate the end lines and sidelines of the grid. Position two attackers and two defenders inside the 30-yard grid. Teammates of these players are equally positioned on the outside of both sidelines. Sideline players may not enter the playing area or pressure other opposing sideline players. Permitted to be mobile up and down along the sideline, these players are AR2 and AR3 support players. Each team defends its goal line and attempts to score by dribbling the ball over the opponent's back line. Award one point for each interception. Regulation field hockey rules apply. Play for five minutes before changing from field players to sideline positions. Keep track of the goals scored in a 20-minute period.

Success Goal = Earn more interception points than opponent ____

Success Check
- DR2 players position ball side of AR2 when the ball is on the sideline ____
- While marking, DR2 covers most dangerous space ____
- DR1 applies pressure at the point of attack ____
- DR1 and DR2 play pressure/cover to deny dribble penetration ____

To Increase Difficulty
- Play for 10 minutes nonstop.
- Increase size of playing area.
- Add an extra attacker when the attacking team is in possession.

To Decrease Difficulty
- Shorten playing time.
- Reduce size of field.
- Add cover player on each end line.
- Place a goal 4 yards wide on each back line.

6. Building Cover Defense—Three-on-Three Sideline

Divide 10 to 14 teammates into two equal-size teams. Use markers to outline a field area 35 yards by 35 yards. Designate the end lines and sidelines of the playing area, and station two players and a cover player from each team within the area. The cover player must stay anywhere on her goal line and may only play one step from the line. The remaining team members are equally positioned along the outside of both sidelines. The sideline players may not pressure (tackle or intercept) or move onto the playing area. Only the two-versus-two players may score by controlling the ball over the opposition's back line. Award one point to the attack team for each successful ball penetration into the dangerous space behind the opponent's back line. Regulation hockey rules apply with roll-in substitutions at midfield. Play for 15 minutes and keep track of score.

Success Goal = Allow fewer points than opponents ____

Success Check
- DR3 covers most dangerous attack space ____
- DR1 and DR2 play pressure/cover when ball is in the playing area ____
- Maintain ball-side position when the ball is on the sideline ____
- Position to prevent penetration by attack ____

To Increase Difficulty
- Increase size of playing area.
- Add extra field player for three-on-three plus cover player.
- Replace cover player with a goalkeeper.

To Decrease Difficulty
- Reduce size of playing area.
- Place a goal 4 yards wide on the back lines.

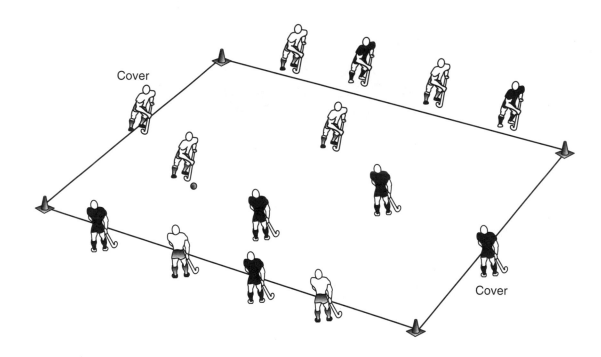

Cover

Cover

7. Pressure/Cover to Goal—Four-on-Three Plus GK

Organize into two teams. You, two teammates, and a goalkeeper form the defending team while four players form an attacking team. Use markers to outline a 20-yard-by-30-yard grid area in front of the shooting circle. Attack players position at each corner of the grid area. Your defensive team positions inside the playing grid. An attack player farthest from the goal starts with the ball by maintaining possession passes to a teammate. When the ball is passed forward to one of the attackers closest to the shooting circle, the passer may join the penetration. Award the attack team one point for a successful penetration pass and one point for a score. Award your team one point each time it wins possession of the ball or forces the attacking team to play the ball outside the grid area. If your team wins the ball, immediately clear it to the outside targets at the farthest corners of the left and right sides of the grid and restart the game. Play for 10 minutes and keep track of your score.

Success Goal = Score more points than opponent ____

Success Check
- Pressure AR1 by DR1 ____
- Cover by DR2 ____
- Cover and balance by DR3 ____
- Deny dangerous space ____
- Quickly readjust Defense Roles in relation to ball movement ____
- Force attackers to take shots from wide angles to goal ____

To Increase Difficulty
- Increase size of grid.
- Do not use goalkeeper.
- Play for 15 minutes nonstop.
- Allow AR3 players to work space in the shooting circle.

To Decrease Difficulty
- Reduce grid size.
- Limit attackers to 2 touches to pass and receive.
- Shorten playing time.

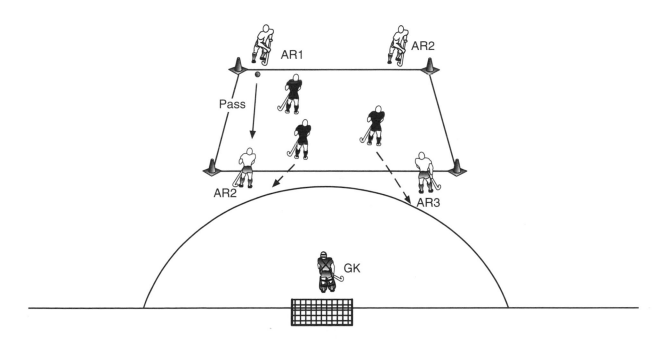

8. Blending Defense Roles—Three-on-Three

Divide into two teams of three players each. Use markers to outline a 30-yard-by-30 yard playing area with a midline dividing the area in half. The entire back line is the goal line at each end. Position both teams within the area. The stationary passer on the outside of the playing area starts play by passing the ball to a member of the attack team. Your defense team must start with DR3 on your goal line and DR2 players marking AR2. When the stationary passer delivers the ball, DR3 may move from the goal line. The attack team tries to maintain possession while achieving penetration over the defense team's goal line. Teams switch from defense to attack and vice versa with each change of possession. After a score, start the game with DR3 positioned on the goal line before the stationary passer puts the ball into play. Regular field hockey rules apply except for the method of scoring. A team wins one point for six consecutive passes without possession loss and two points for each successful penetration over the opponent's goal line. Play for 10 minutes and keep track of points.

Success Goal = Allow fewer attack points _____

Success Check
- Pressure AR1 by DR1 _____
- Cover by DR2 _____
- Cover and balance by DR3 _____
- Adopt Defense Roles to ball and player movement _____
- Deny penetration _____

To Increase Difficulty
- Award point to attack team for 4 consecutive passes instead of 6.
- Increase size of playing area.
- Play for 15 minutes.

To Decrease Difficulty
- Reduce size of playing area.
- Place a goal 4 yards wide on the back lines.

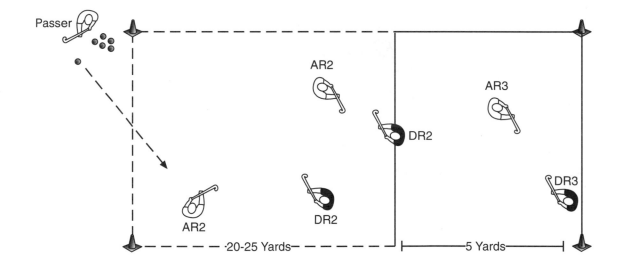

9. Half-Field Defense—Six-on-Four With GK

Designate a four-player defense team with a goalkeeper and a six-player attack team. Use cones or markers to outline a regulation half-field area, 50 yards by 60 yards. Position a regulation goal on the back line and position two 5-yard minigoals on the 50-yard line, one near each sideline. Position the goalkeeper in the regulation goal; do not use goalkeepers in the minigoals. Award the six-player attack team possession of the ball to start the game.

The six-player team tries to score in the regulation goal, defends the minigoals, and earns one point for each goal scored. The four-player defense team earns one point for passing the ball through either of the minigoals. Play for 15 minutes and keep track of your points.

Success Goal = Score more points than the opponent _____

Success Check
- Think safety first in the defense area of the field _____
- Execute all Defense Roles _____

To Increase Difficulty
- Place conditions on 4-player defense team; counterattack can only score with dribble through minigoals.
- Increase playing time.

To Decrease Difficulty
- Decrease playing area.
- Add extra defender to make it 6 against 5.
- Reduce playing time.

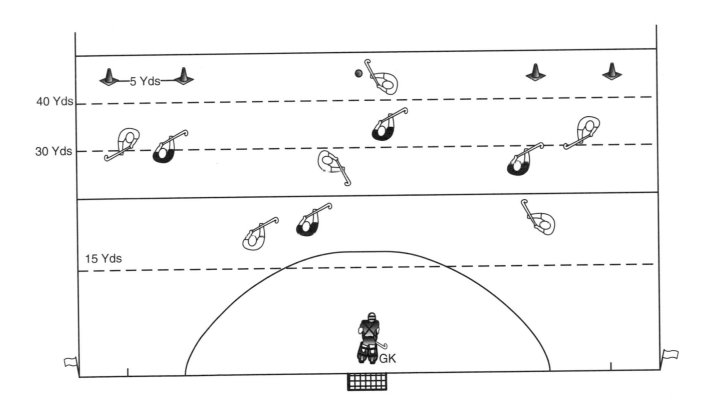

10. Recovery Against Up-Numbers Attack

Play on one half of a field hockey field with a regulation goal centered on the back line and a stationary passer on each long hit mark. Use markers to designate two 5-yard minigoals 50 yards apart on the 50-yard line. Position a goalkeeper in the regulation goal; do not use goalkeepers in the minigoals. Designate a four-player attack team and a four-player defense team. Position two attackers (AR2 or AR3) off the ball near the circle edge, both marked by two DR2 players. From the remaining players, one attacker and one defender position near the minigoals. Play starts with the recovery defender at the right-side minigoal. He passes ball #1 to the attack player 5 yards in front and immediately runs to recover to provide defensive help. Attack players attempt to penetrate to score before defense can organize a three-versus-three counterdefense. If the defense team wins possession, it attempts to pass the ball through one of the minigoals for a point. Award a point to the attack team for a goal. Regulation field hockey rules apply, and play continues until a point is scored or the ball goes out-of-bounds over the end line off the attack team. Continue the sequence: a long hit with ball #2 is crossed into play; after this ball, the recovery defender on the right side plays in ball #3; ball #4 is played from the right long hit mark. Play for 15 minutes and keep track of points.

Success Goal = Score more points than opponents ____

Success Check
- Recover on shortest line to far goalpost ____
- DR2 and DR3 mark and cover ____
- Slow or stop penetration ____
- Prevent shots from area in front and center of goal ____

To Increase Difficulty
- Add a neutral player to the game who plays with the attacking team to create an advantage for the team in possession.
- Increase playing time.

To Decrease Difficulty
- Add a cover defender (DR3) on the 25-yard line.
- Reduce the width of the field.

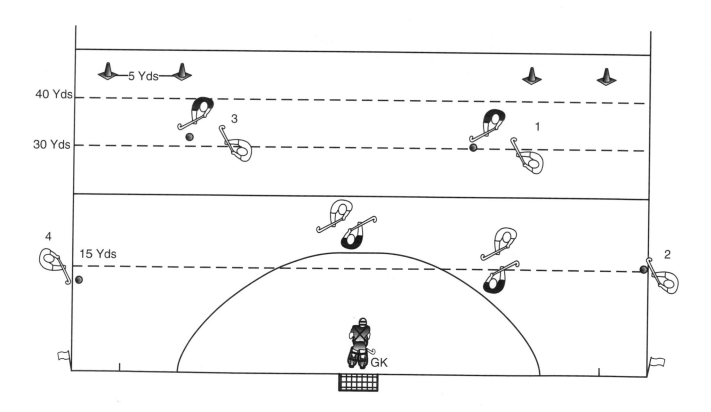

11. Balance—Four-on-Three

Play on one half of a field hockey field with a regulation goal centered on the end line. Place a 5-yard-by-5-yard "distribution square" in the central area of the field approximately 40 yards from the back line. Organize one team of five attack players and one team of three defense players. One of the attack players is the distributor and positions inside the distribution square. The distributor receives a pass from a stationary hitter positioned on the 50-yard line and must pass the ball to either the left- or right-side attackers. The distributor's pass cannot go forward. Your defensive team must quickly drop and slide to the ball side to adjust to the lateral pass, which will keep the ball in front and on that side of the field. Award your defense team two points for each interception resulting from correct cover and balance play and one point for each successful tackle. The attack team scores a point for each goal scored and for a successful point-of-attack change inside 20 yards. Play for 10 minutes and keep track of points.

Success Goal = Score more points than the opponent ____

Success Check

- Apply pressure at the point of attack ____
- Balance on the side of the field opposite the ball ____
- Prevent penetration via pass or dribble ____

To Increase Difficulty

- Allow the distributor to join attack and add a goalkeeper for the defense.
- Increase playing time.

To Decrease Difficulty

- Make the field narrower.
- Restrict the 5-player attack team to 3 or fewer touches.
- Reduce playing time.

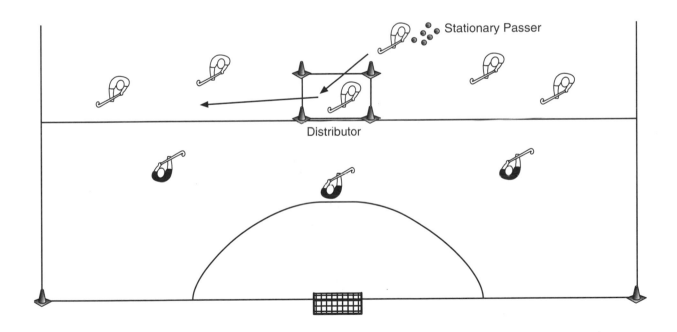

Stationary Passer

Distributor

12. Marking in the Circle

Play on the regulation hockey field from the 25 yard-line to the goal. Position three passers 10 yards outside the shooting circle on the left, center, and right areas. Organize into two teams of two players and one goalkeeper and position them inside the circle. The passer (P1) on the outside left starts play by serving a pass to one of the AR2 players. Defenders are marking ball side in an attempt to intercept. Passer (P2) in the center area serves the next ball, followed by passer (P3) on the right. The passers do not serve a ball until the previous ball has been scored, lost out-of-bounds, or cleared out of the circle by the defense team. Award one point to your defense team for each interception or tackle that allows you to clear the ball to outside the circle and away from the passers. Award the attack team one point for each goal scored. Play for nine serves and keep track of points.

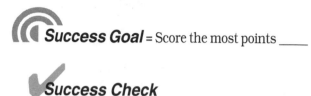 **Success Goal** = Score the most points _____

✔ **Success Check**
- DR2 view ball and opponent _____
- Communication of Defense Roles and goalkeeper _____
- Ball-side marking distance and angle of cover _____

To Increase Difficulty
- Add a third attack player who is unmarked. Permit only the unmarked attacker to shoot.
- Increase number of serves or playing time.
- Passer can serve or shoot by joining attack play with penetration dribble.
- Play without a goalkeeper.

To Decrease Difficulty
- Add cover player.
- Reduce number of serves or playing time.

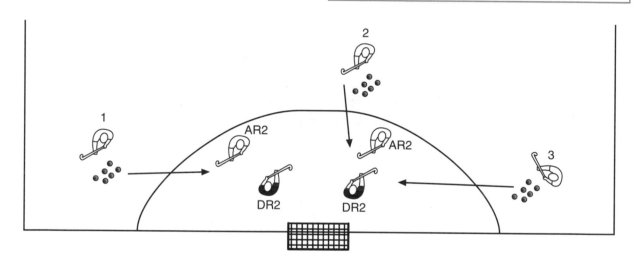

DEFENSE ROLES 2 AND 3 SUCCESS SUMMARY

Successful defense is a team effort. Outstanding defense requires good individual defending, quick and thorough organizational abilities, and the physical ability to outnumber the opponent between the ball and the goal. Although DR1 skills are the foundation of good defense, defenders who are covering players in space away from the ball also must not be beaten. Based on the assessment of the opponent's attack threat, the organization of team defense profits from the tactical and technical efforts of DR1 discussed in Step 4 and Step 5.

Your defensive strategy will influence the organization of all three Defense Roles. As DR1 pressures the ball, DR2 players support DR1 and cover the nearest AR2 players. DR3 players cover less threatening AR3 players and then try to protect the space behind the defense to provide balance. By denying space, your defense achieves the objectives of preventing goals and regaining possession of the ball.

Ask someone who is knowledgeable about field hockey defense tactics to analyze execution of your Defense Roles 2 and 3. Helpful advice from an observer will improve your team defense play and provide input to whether you are coordinating your responsibilities within all the Defense Roles.

STEP 10

TEAM PLAY: ORGANIZING ATTACK AND DEFENSE

The final phase of field hockey tactics is the unified organization of all 11 players on the field. Commonly referred to as a system of play, team organization is based on the style of play that your team is capable of performing. The tactics of Attack and Defense Roles that you have learned thus far are universal to all systems, differing only in individual and team abilities and the tactical objective of the opponent. The system of play is only a frame that offers your team unlimited possibilities to apply a variety of tactical ideas.

Several distinct systems of play have been used on all levels and within various entities of field hockey competition. Many teams play with three forwards; others play with four or five forwards. Occasionally, one or two forwards spearhead the attack. On defense most teams engage a full-time cover defender commonly called a *sweeper*. But some teams play without a true sweeper in a three- or four-back alignment. Some teams select to play a man-to-man defense, while others play a zone system or a combination of both. None of these systems are better than the others, and all are effective if played correctly with the fundamental understanding of the Attack and Defense Roles while incorporating positional responsibilities based on player abilities. Teams use different systems partly because of their field hockey philosophy, style of capable play during certain playing conditions, and the opponent's personnel and style, but the choice of the system depends primarily on the unique talents and abilities of their players.

Why Is a Team System Important?

The system of play defines each player's positional responsibility within the team. For example, four players may be aligned as backs but have significantly separate expectations. One might be strictly a defensive back whose sole task is marking the opposing team's dangerous and speedy wing forward, whereas the other might be an attacking back who creates scoring chances for her teammates. To accomplish the teamwork necessary for successful team performance, each player must understand his positional responsibility within the structure of the team.

How Systems Are Organized

A system of play is implemented as a plan to give your team an advantage. Advantages allow your team to exploit an opposing team's weakness, capitalize on your own strength, counter the opponent's strength, or cover a weakness in your team. Before adopting a system of play, you should understand your team's style of play and your positional responsibilities. Remember, all that the team formation or system of play can do is give a general collective direction for your team based totally on you and your teammates' abilities to execute the Attack and Defense Roles.

Style of Play

Two teams competing against each other may use essentially identical systems. Yet there are major differences in the game played in respect to the style in which the teams perform their tactics. Tactics performed from team to team and in different stages of the game can be translated in very different manners or styles. Teams develop different styles of play shaped on the mental and physical abilities of the players, tradition of the team, the coach's philosophy, and the environments in which some games are played. For example, the Canadians have played a hit-and-rush style; the Germans have played a structured and methodical style; the British have played a highly aggressive style with one-on-one toughness and elevated tempo consisting of competitive energy; the Americans work hard for physical dominance; the Australians and Koreans have played a fast, wide-open attacking style using direct passes across wide spaces; and Dutch individuals have played an aggressive but controlled game full of varied tempo and rhythm changes and cleverly designed tactics. Many South American teams, notably those from Argentina, are characterized by their short passes and dazzling stickhandling.

As with India and Pakistan, their style is rich in techniques and full of magical ballhandling abilities that last long in a defender's memory. Common factors that influence style of play are listed here.

■ *Mental and physical abilities.* Your mental and physical abilities will shape the style of hockey that you perform and are vital to the team's style and system of play.

The importance of a team's mental attitude to the game and its surroundings is well represented by the fact that a team can play with the same players and operate the same system in home and away games, yet achieve vastly different results. Mental abilities consist of responses such as courage, will power, confidence, perseverance, and discipline—essentially those emotions that drive or motivate performance. Strong and determined mental tools are necessary to acquire and drive into action competitive hockey skills.

To have an opportunity for success, your level of physical ability must meet the demands that the game presents. Physical factors that you and your teammates possess will also influence style of play. Players who possess a great deal of speed, skill, and fitness will obviously show a different style from players who are slow but skilled. As inadequate physical preparation will always remain a limiting factor in acquiring hockey skill, it also will be a determining factor in the manner in which your team is organized.

■ *Tradition.* The duplication of certain hockey skills from player to player or from last year's team roster to this year's often leads to the handing down of a tradition of play. Because tradition helps expose specific traits and provides constant inspiration and wisdom, you and your teammates can work toward common goals. Teams that exhibit strong traditions demonstrate a strong interest and commitment to field hockey, a desire to reach a high level of attainment in field hockey, and a willingness to put in great amounts of time and effort to achieve success. Tradition of a team is built on the expectations of success. Often your expectations of success determine the effort you and your team place on preparation of the mental and physical skills. If you expect to be skillful and dangerous on attack, then most likely you will be. If you expect not to recover when your teammate loses possession of the ball, then most likely you will not do so. Your team's tradition of play is another factor that influences the style and subsequently the system of play.

■ *Coach's philosophy.* Two teams can be arranged in the same way in number of players in the back positions, midfield positions, and forward positions but play different styles of games. The reason for this difference, apart from the players' abilities, is the schooling given by the coach. Based on a philosophy, the coach's instructions to her players are designed to get a reaction or performance. Instructions that produce desired responses are based on "how" the coach gives instructions, not so much on what she says. To speak of philosophy is to reveal your beliefs and how you stand for these beliefs. The philosophy of a coach provides guidance and direction and helps to interpret the events that surround the team; it also helps to formulate training rules, discipline and conduct, a competitive outlook, and team goals and objectives. The style that you and your teammates play will certainly reflect the coach's philosophy and the chosen system of play.

■ *Environment.* All formations of team play should be flexible so they can adjust to environmental factors, such as weather and field conditions, the opposition, and the type of competition. On a cold, hard, icy surface, small players can keep their footing better than taller players because of a lower center of gravity; players not physically fit could struggle on a humid afternoon; and on muddy grass fields, strength is required. On watered artificial surfaces, technical skill and speed is a requirement. While good coaches prepare to use specific tactics to counter the strengths and weaknesses of the opposition, knowing the type of competition is also an important factor. A tie may be good enough in a scrimmage but not in a tournament semi-final where only the winner advances.

Positional Characteristics and Responsibilities

When field hockey players learn to retreat to defend and advance to attack, they are ready for game positions that carry overlapping Attack and Defense Roles. Team systems or team formations are developed from the players' characteristics and from requirements of game positions. General descriptions of player positions can provide the player with an overall understanding of where the responsibilities lie within the Attack and Defense Roles. Regardless of the game position, all players take on their Attack Roles when their team is in possession of the ball and perform their Defense Roles when the opponent has the ball. Use the following list of positional characteristics and responsibilities to better understand a chosen system of play.

1. *The goalkeeper.* The goalkeeper prevents goals from being scored, clears the ball out of the circle to a safe space or to a teammate, directs team defense in the circle, covers and clears balls that penetrate behind her teammates, tackles breakaway forwards, coordinates with directives the positioning and play of the backs and sweeper, defends penalty strokes, and organizes defense of all defensive penalty corners. Goalies must have good concentration and the ability to quickly spot the angle of the shot. Courage, confidence, quick reflexes, mental toughness, excellent vision, excellent eye-to-hand and foot coordination, gymnastic ability, strength and agility, the ability to read the game, and

willingness for leadership are all properties needed by the goalkeeper.

2. *The backs.* The backs marks opposing forwards or midfielders in their area of the field, set up attack play by distributing balls to midfield and forwards, co-ordinate with nearby teammates to defend against the opponent's attack tactics, provide depth support to change the point of attack, assist with or take free hits in the defensive area of the field, use tackling and positioning skills for marking and covering, communicate Attack and Defense Roles, and assist in set pieces of the attack and defense penalty corners.

• *Sweeper,* or *fullback.* These players must read the game as well as anyone else on the playing field because it is essential for the sweeper to spot the main danger area of an opponent's attack. Sweepers need to be skillful in winning the ball in one-on-one situations, mark and/or cover in all defensive situations, coordinate all Defense Roles, take 16-yard defense hits, demonstrate agile footwork with composure, and have a high level of leadership ability. All sweepers must have the ability to pass the ball hard and accurately over long distances.

• *The right side back.* This player provides balance and cover when the ball is on the opposite side of the field, takes most sideline hits on the right side and assists or takes deep defensive hits, and prevents shots on goal. These players need good speed and mobility to mark the opposing left outside forward and be in position to counterattack by supporting the midfielders and forwards. The right back must demonstrate composure and be very skilled in intercepting and passing, particularly hitting the through pass that runs parallel to the right sideline and hitting the long centering pass from the right to the left side of the field.

• *The center back.* The center back's main responsibility is to tightly mark the opposing center forward and demonstrate good tackling skills. To stay close to a particular opponent throughout a 70-minute match, a center back must have a high level of fitness. Center backs need to be physically strong and mentally tough to cope with the blows sometimes generated with marking tightly. Other skills needed to effectively play center back include the ability to pass and to intercept the opponent's passes, assist in free hits out of the defense area, and take or assist free hits in the midfield and attack areas.

• *The left back.* The left back provides balance and cover when the ball is on the opposite side of the field, takes most left sideline hits and assists or takes deep defensive hits, and communicates Attack and Defense Roles with left midfielder, center back, left wing, and sweeper. It is important that the left back have good foot speed because her main assignment is to mark the opposing right outside forward who is usually a very fast sprinter. The left back must be able to mark tightly and to tackle the ball with strength to prevent right-side attacks. When the left back wins the ball, she must exercise her ability to pass the ball and especially hit passes accurately from the left to the center and to the right side of the field.

3. *The midfielders.* The midfielders provide a link between backs and forwards, mark opposing midfielders in attack, midfield, and defense regions of the field, position to control space in the midfield region to limit passing options to the opponent, help teammates with marking assignments, take midfield free hits and assist on free hits out of the defense zone, have tackling and positioning skills for marking and covering, have attacking and finishing skills, communicate Attack and Defense Roles with nearby teammates, and assist in set pieces of the attack and defense penalty corners. To effectively play any midfield position, players must be able to execute transitional play in all the Attack and Defense Roles.

• *The outside midfielders.* These players must have quickness and speed with endurance because they cover and control the most space (between the 25-yard lines). They must have excellent wide vision and be very skilled with good, close ball control when building the attack play. In addition to being good combination-style passers with the ability to think quickly to locate the best pass to give, outside midfielders must possess the instincts to score. They usually set up successful attacks by threading intelligent passes through the opponent's defense. Equally important is their ability to demonstrate the responsibilities of all three Defense Roles, particularly marking.

• *The center midfielder.* The center midfielder marks opposing center midfielder in the attack and midfield region of the field, assists in marking the inside forwards in defense region, provides an AR2 link between backs and forwards, assists center back with controlling midfield space, supports forwards and provides depth in attack to allow the point of attack to change quickly or to allow dangerous penetration, and provides a pass option for the ball out of the defense. The center midfielder is a total field hockey player who possesses creative and imaginative attack play and determined defense skills that keep the opponent's attacks to one side of the field. This player needs to see all options and possess the ability to choose the best option under pressure and with composure. These players must be tactically sound with great leadership abilities to demonstrate all the same abilities of the outside midfielders. A good center midfielder has the exceptional ability to receive and control passes from all sides of her body and pass accurately to teammates in AR2 and AR3. It is the "busiest" position in terms of visual information.

4. *Forwards.* Forwards create and finish goal-scoring opportunities, combine with nearby teammates to build attack tactics, create depth and width spaces for ball penetration and to stretch the opponent's defenses, use space created by others, position in front of midfielders, play Defense Roles in all three regions of the field, and assist in set pieces of the attack and defense penalty corners.

- *The center forward.* Players in this position need physical and mental strength (risk taker) to play in a tight or crowded space so that they can get to the ball first. It is vital that the center forward possess goal-scoring skills with a quick release and cleverly anticipate centering passes. Swiftness, good close-ball control, and one-on-one skills with and without the ball are requirements that enable center forwards to find space to the goal. The Defense Roles of the center forward find her covering the attack moves of the opponent's center back.

- *The wing forwards.* The left and right outside forwards must have speed and quickness to use the one-on-one dribble to spot and play the space in behind the opponent. Also, wing forwards need the ability to hit hard, accurate centering passes and be a threat to score goals. In addition to the execution of all Attack Roles, they must execute all three Defense Roles while covering and marking the opponent's corresponding side backs.

Other Factors Influencing Systems

When selecting a system of play, a coach must consider which kind of team attack and defense tactics his team is capable of performing. Again, this decision is derived from the team's style of play. Environmental factors such as field conditions and climate may also influence your style performance, but it remains important to learn how to play effectively in various environments that allow you to use your strengths. Team defense tactics such as man-to-man marking, zone marking, and a combination of both may influence the selection of a system of play.

Team Defense Tactics

- *Man-to-man marking.* In *man-to-man marking*, one defender takes on the specific responsibility for one opponent. Although the opponent may have difficulty escaping and using space, man-to-man marking requires a huge amount of discipline from every player on the team. If one player fails to perform her defensive assign-

ment soon enough, there is an immediate chance that the team defense will become weak and disorganized.

- *Zone marking.* With *zone marking*, each defender takes responsibility for an opponent entering her zone of defense. The zone concentrates on the region of greatest danger but also ensures that cover is provided around the zone should the point of attack be changed to another area on the field. The ability to maintain discipline and organization is critical to zone marking. Zone tactics within a system have many benefits: the ball can be kept in an area of the field using intelligent positioning, DR2 and DR3 interceptions can lead to counterattacks, defenders learn to play against an extra attacker, and the zone defense is less physically demanding. The weakness of a zone occurs when a zone is overloaded, which allows the opponent to execute two-on-one attacks.

- *Combination of zone and man-to-man marking.* The *combination* of both zone and man-to-man marking is the most effective of defense team tactics. The combination defends zones of the field and marks man-to-man when opponents enter the areas of greatest danger. In actuality, the Defense Roles and the combination defense tactic are the same. Both provide efficient marking of the attack players around the ball and cover for balance in distance spaces away from the ball. Good combination defense will force the opponent to play the ball square or back because you have denied the opponent the opportunity to penetrate.

Team Attack Tactics

Team attack tactics include the fastbreak and the possession attack.

- *Fastbreak attack.* Although field hockey is a highly technical game with various unpredictable situations, it also has certain recurrent patterns. For example, one team may play possession hockey, controlling the ball for long periods, while the opponent occasionally initiates quick counterattacks, or *fastbreaks*. Despite the possession team's apparent dominance, the score may be close or the fastbreaking team may win. Rapid fastbreaks into the dangerous space behind the opponent usually start from a turnover in midfield or a poorly placed clear to the center of the field by the goalkeeper. The space behind the defense is used with through passes or fast dribbling if there is no opponent between the ball and the goal. Speed of execution is the key to fastbreak success against retreating defenses or pressure defenses.

- *Possession attack.* Possession attack uses frequent square and back passes to execute the buildup of the team attack. To play this style within a system, your team must have excellent support help, movement, communication, and one- and two-touch passing skills. An effective means of attack, the possession style can be used to protect a scoring lead or draw out a team that retreats and sets up its defense near the defensive 25-yard area.

Common System Alignments

In hockey today, coaches gravitate toward two fundamental alignments—based on either a defensive scheme or an attacking scheme. If based on defense, the choice is to play with a designated cover player or sweeper or play an alignment without a designated cover. Playing without a designated cover requires players in the back positions to assume cover responsibilities along with their marking when the situation warrants. If the system of play is based on an attacking scheme, the choice remains with how many forwards and midfielders are used to spearhead the attack so that the Attack and Defense Roles can be successfully interchanged and executed. The team personnel and abilities of the personnel allow the coach to determine which system or alignment will best use the strengths of the team.

In describing a system of hockey play, the first number refers to the forwards, the second to the midfielders, the third to the backs, and if necessary, the last to the sweeper. The goalkeeper is not included in the numbering of players. The following systems are just two of the alignments used in modern field hockey.

The 3-3-3-1 System

One of the most widely used alignments in field hockey today is the 3-3-3-1 system (figure 10.1). Derived from European hockey (primarily the Dutch), the 3-3-3-1 system employs a sweeper back who is generally designated as the "free" cover defender. Strong and fast AR1 skills are especially needed by the forwards in the 3-3-3-1 sys-

tem. The three forwards are organized with two outside players, or wings, and the inside center forward. The forwards are free to run anywhere to create width and depth that can produce disorder in defenses that play zone, man-to-man, or a combination. In a three-player forward line, the diagonal run is the most effective attack run. Many one-on-one breakaways can occur when an opponent fails to effectively interchange Defense Roles, resulting in the drawing of penalty corners and scoring goals. On defense, the three forwards look to mark or cover the passing lanes to the opposing backs and sweeper and back tackle for double-teaming defense.

The three midfielders must possess a great deal of fitness along with the ability to execute tactical and technical skills. Close man-to-man marking is generally employed by the two outside midfielders, making it extremely difficult for the opposition's corresponding forwards and midfielders to receive the ball and break away into open space. The side midfielders support the forwards on attack and provide a line of defense in front of the backs. The center midfielder has the freedom to move laterally or even overlap on attack, which can create more space for a possession-type attack. The defensive marking assignment is generally a zone or a combination. It is crucial for all midfielders to possess exceptional transition abilities in both attack and defense.

The backs usually mark closely in the midfield and defense regions of the field to prevent the opposition's forwards from receiving the ball and penetrating to goal. The center back is more effective in a man-to-man marking of the opposition's most dangerous inside forward but can be effective using a combination in the attack half of the field. Backs must be very disciplined with strong tackling skills.

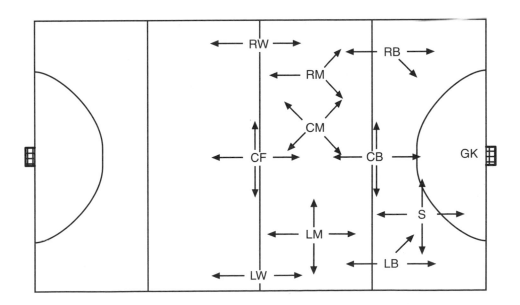

Figure 10.1 3-3-3-1 system

The sweeper is a fast evaluator of the play and often receives the ball with space and time to set up attack play. Because the sweeper is not assigned to mark a specific opponent, a good sweeper can make the 3-3-3-1 system a very effective formation as she provides leadership and cover for the other three backs. The sweeper position is a very vital position for any system employing a designated cover player(s). The ability to field loose balls, make the final one-on-one tackle before circle penetration is achieved, join the attack when coverage is assumed by a teammate, and be a willing participant in all special situations makes the responsibility of the sweeper highly important in the 3-3-3-1 system. The 3-3-3-1 system or any system using a sweeper back(s) such as a 4-2-3-1 or 5-3-2 requires an agile, explosive goalkeeper who can support the sweeper and read the play. It is essential for the goalkeeper to be an excellent defender against the penalty corner.

The 3-3-4 System

In the 3-3-4 system, players are spread out over the field to provide balance between attack and defense. This system is usually suited for teams with young and inexperienced tactical players or for the team that does not possess the talents of a "bona fide" sweeper. The forwards, midfielders, and backs are in place to play the ball to the outside of the field. Although this system of balance may initially lose some of its flexibility to vary the game tactics, it is possible to develop into a more adaptable formation as the team develops into improved tactical understanding and technical skill.

The three forwards occupy the front of the attack and play their positions with similar responsibilities to the 3-3-3-1 forwards. Speed is an asset for the wing forwards, and finishing skills are a must for the inside center forward.

The center midfielder is an important player in the 3-3-4 system and must be a total player. He must be able to read the game of hockey so that creative play making is swift and effective. Good passing and dribbling skills are requirements, along with the ability to penetrate and finish. On defense, the center midfielder must be a strong tackler of the ball as the outside midfielders cover and position off the center midfielder's movement.

The four backs are aligned to mark the opposing team's forwards and the most dangerous attack-oriented midfielder. The inside backs establish similar responsibilities of the sweeper and center back of the 3-3-3-1 system, working together to mark the center forward while the other is providing cover. The outside backs usually match up against the opponent's outside forwards or side midfielders and provide cover and balance. The 3-3-4 system requires that the backs and midfielders contribute to their team's attack using overlapping runs from behind.

Alignments such as a 2-4-4 or a 4-2-4 are created from the 3-3-4 (see figure 10.2) to provide a greater emphasis on player mobility and interchanging of positions. The trend in modern-day field hockey is to load the midfield area to establish improved space coverage and pressing tactics.

Organizing the Penalty Corner

Every field hockey game contains a number of stoppages that are an integral part of organized team play. The penalty corner is an important situation in which

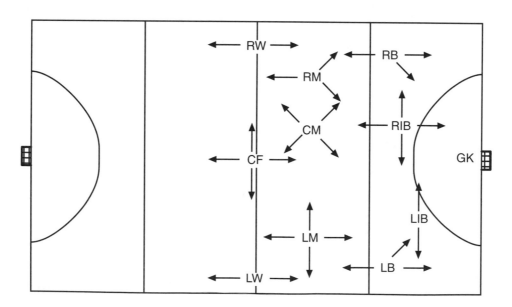

Figure 10.2 3-3-4

the attacking team will seek to maximize its goal-scoring opportunities while the opponent organizes a defense to deny a scoring chance. The selection of penalty corner organization for your team, both attack and defense, is based on players' abilities.

Attack Penalty Corner

In principle, with only five defenders to beat, every penalty corner should produce a quality shot at goal. Because the rules place no restrictions on how many attackers can take part in the penalty corner, it is important to exploit those areas of the shooting circle (see figure 10.3), which the defenders find difficult to protect. Numerous organized attack plays may be devised for the attack penalty corner. But the most organized team attack will only be as successful as your team's ability to execute with speed and accuracy three fundamental attack techniques—the push pass, receiving, and the hit.

The Penalty Corner Defense

The penalty corner defense team consists of five players, each having critical and disciplined assignments. As the leader of the penalty corner defense, the *goalkeeper* must assume important responsibilities of her teammates. Although positional play is of fundamental importance in goalkeeping, penalty corner positioning is based on the individual ability that must be carried out with consistency. The goalkeeper is expected to organize her defense and concentrate on the ball the moment the penalty corner is awarded. Always alert for a quick push out from the opponent, the goalkeeper moves quickly from the goal line to a position to block the path of the shot. As the goalkeeper, you should avoid being screened or blocked out from the sight of the ball by focusing your eyes on the ball during the pass from the back line, the trap or stick stop, and the shot. Because most penalty corner shots at goal are taken from a distance of 13 to 14 yards, it is important for the goalkeeper to develop and master a style of defending

and have an organized penalty corner defense system that can be practiced.

Three styles of goalkeeping are used in defense of the penalty corner: the upright style, the lying position, and the running slide. The *upright style* is the most effective position that reinforces goalkeeping techniques previously learned and should be practiced before other styles. The standing goalkeeper in the ready position requires the ultimate in skill and reaction, and this style is used as basic training on all playing surfaces and with players of varying abilities.

To execute the upright position, advance quickly from the goal line to a three- to five-yard distance. The distance will vary for each goalkeeper because of individual size and reaction time. It is important to coordinate your reaction time with your position off the goal line. Use breakdown footwork to settle into a stationary line of the ball before the ball is shot at goal. You must concentrate and be balanced in your ready position at the time of the shot. Your eyes are focused on the ball the entire time so that you can clearly respond to the speed and direction of the shot. Your team's decision to use one or two post players will depend on your abilities as a goalkeeper. If using two post players who defend the shot near to the goalpost, you defend the shot between the post players. When using only one post player (see figure 10.4), the goalkeeper is responsible for three-fourths of the goal away from the post player. The assignments of the remaining defenders include a flyer—the first runner off the goal line who lines up on the left of the goalkeeper when the ball is taken on the right side of the circle. The flyer's assignment is to pressure the initial shot. The right cover player takes a position outside the left post and runs from the goal line even with the goalpost to cover the flyer. The right cover's assignment is to cover the flyer's right side and pick up any rebounds or lay-off passes to the right. When one post player is used, a left cover player covers the flyer's left side and breaks up play behind the flyer.

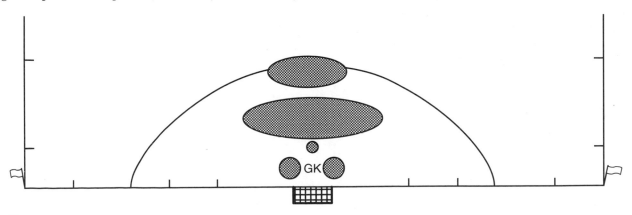

Figure 10.3 Areas of the shooting circle that are difficult to defend.

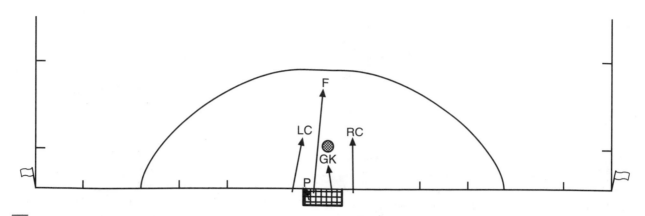

Figure 10.4 Positioning when defending goal with one post player.

The *lying position* is sometimes referred to as logging and can be a dangerous style if the goalkeeper is not fully protected. The lying style is effective if the goalkeeper's abilities include poor reaction time and skill in defending the initial shot in an upright position. The objective is to block horizontal space along the ground because the initial shot, if struck with a backswing, can only score if the ball is hit 18 inches or lower over the goal line.

To execute lying down, move two or three yards from the goal line and position your body weight on the right foot and on the inside of the left foot. Lean to your right. Drop on your right side as the ball is struck to create a wide barrier with your body. Bend at the waist and support your weight on your right hand/stick or elbow with the left glove hand raised. Use your left glove hand in front of your body to save as much as possible for your teammate on your left side to clear. Keep your head behind the line of the ball. Shots to your right are saved with both the glove and stick together. Shots to your legs are saved with the feet, but your glove and head move to the ball. In the lying position, you will have more difficulty handling shots over your waist, legs, and extended stick.

Except for the flyer, your teammates' penalty corner assignments (see figure 10.5) during your lying style change from the upright position. The left post player comes out level or slightly behind your feet to clear balls off your pads or hand. She must also cover the space in front and to the left in the shooting circle. The right post player comes out and covers area to the goalkeeper's right. She clears your saves to the extreme right and defends attackers who run into the penalty spot area. To complete the organization of a lying goalkeeper, the fifth defender is a runner who covers the flyer's left or right side.

The *running slide* style (see figure 10.6) is used occasionally as a variation or element of surprise on the most advanced levels of play. This method is the least used because it leaves your right and left sides vulnerable to passes. To execute the running slide, you run from the goal line as far and as fast as possible to slide down and smother the ball as it is hit. The double-leg slide (stack) is your skill objective as you create a large barrier with your body between the goal line and the ball. It is crucial to keep your eyes on the ball to time your slide because the slide tackle requires perfect timing. The defense assignments for your teammates are similar in principle to the lying goalkeeper. Because the goalkeeper becomes the flyer, a right cover player defends space to the goalkeeper's right side and a left cover player positions to cover the goalkeeper's left side. Usually two post players remain near the goal line to protect the space in front of the goal.

When a goalkeeper learns to master an effective style in the defense of the penalty corner, your team will enjoy organizing the challenges to protect your goal.

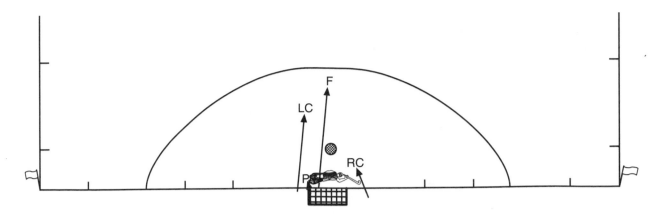

Figure 10.5 Positioning when defending goal with the goalkeeper in the lying position.

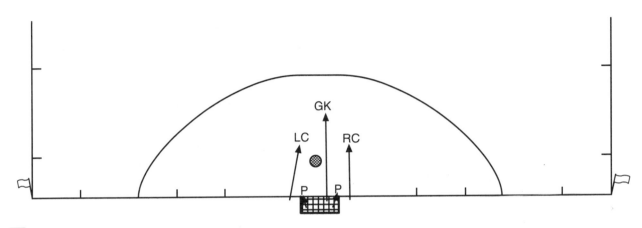

Figure 10.6 Positioning when defending goal with the goalkeeper using the running slide style.

TEAM PLAY—DRILLS

1. Skeleton Drill for Team Attack

Play on a regulation-size field with goals. Select the system to be used and position your teammates accordingly in one half of the field. Position your goalkeeper in the goal with a supply of field hockey balls. A back begins the exercise by taking a 16-yard defense hit. From that point you and your teammates collectively one- or two-touch pass the ball down the field and shoot it into the opposing goal. Do not involve any opponents in this exercise. Emphasize proper attacking movement of all positional players in relation to the movement of the ball as you pass it down the field toward the goal. After each score, players should return to their original positions. Repeat the exercise 10 times at half speed and 15 times at game speed or until all players feel comfortable with their positions in the system.

Success Goal = 20 repetitions at game speed ____

Success Check
• Provide width and depth in attack ____
• Provide support for AR1 ____
• Readjust positioning in relation to movement of the ball ____

To Increase Difficulty
• Limit players to 2 or fewer touches to pass, receive, or shoot the ball.
• Add 6 opponents who try to prevent your team from moving the ball the length of the field.

To Decrease Difficulty
• Slow speed of repetition.

2. Skeleton Drill for Team Defense

Use same setup as the previous drill and add opposing team to the exercise. Position your team to defend a goal while the opponents position in the opposite half of the field. The opponent's back has the ball to begin the drill with a 16-yard defense hit. The opponent attempts to move the ball down the field to shoot at your goal. You and your teammates work together using all three Defense Roles to prevent shots, gain possession of the ball, or both. The attacking team wins one point for each shot on your goal. After a shot on goal or if your team tackles the ball or intercepts a pass, immediately return the ball to the opposing sweeper or back for a 16-yard defense hit. Repeat 20 times at game speed.

Success Goal = Yield 5 or fewer points to opponents ____

Success Check
• Pressure, mark/cover, and balance on defense ____
• Protect the center of the field ____

To Increase Difficulty
• Use cones to enlarge the defending team's goal.
• Require defending team to play with only 8 field players.

To Decrease Difficulty
• Limit attacking team to 3 or fewer touches to pass, receive, and shoot the ball.

TEAM PLAY SUCCESS SUMMARY

Each system of play is characterized by acquired strengths and weaknesses both in team style and positional responsibilities. It is the coach's responsibility to evaluate her players and select a system that best satisfies the team. No system will overcome inaccurate passing or shooting, improve ball control, allow for players who will not help each other, or allow for players who cannot or will not run. A team can play as many forwards as it wishes, but if it does not have the capacity to gain and maintain possession of the ball, the system employed will amount to nonsense. Furthermore, a team can place as many players as it wishes behind the ball to defend, but if they lack the ability as individuals or as a team to interchange the Defense Roles, the system will again amount to nonsense.

It is your responsibility as a team member to become familiar with the system of play, understand your positional responsibilities within the system, and execute the Attack and Defense Roles. Acceptance of your position will enhance your technical, tactical, physical, and psychological success in the exciting game of field hockey.

RATING YOUR TOTAL PROGRESS

Rate your overall progress to this point by writing the appropriate number in the space to the right of each field hockey technique or tactic listed. After rating your performance, assess your strengths and weaknesses, set new goals and objectives, and continue to improve your hockey.

Rating Points: **4** = excellent   **3** = good   **2** = fair   **1** = poor

Field Hockey Techniques

Your first success goal in field hockey is to develop the techniques needed to play the game. Rate yourself on the following techniques.

Moving with Your Stick—Improving Quickness Techniques

Attack stance _____
Defense stance _____
Shake hands grip _____
Reverse grip _____
Control box _____
Breakdown steps _____
Change of pace—stutter step _____
Change of direction—stop and turn _____
Engage and give _____
Slide/shuffle _____
Drop step _____
Backward run _____

Passing Techniques

Forehand push pass _____
Reverse push pass _____
The hit _____
The flick _____

Receiving Techniques

Forehand along the ground _____
Reverse along the ground _____
Forehand aerial _____
Reverse aerial _____

Ball Control Techniques

Ball check _____
Drop step _____

Dribble Techniques

Speed dribble _____

Power dribble _____
Indian dribble _____
Spin dribble _____

Tackling Techniques

Jab tackle _____
Forehand block _____
Reverse block _____

Shooting Techniques

Quick hit _____
Deflection shot _____
Dive shot _____
Edge shot _____
Chip shot _____

Goalkeeping Techniques

Goalkeeper stance _____
Goalkeeper positioning—covering angles _____
Goalkeeper zones of the circle _____
Block save _____
Double-leg stack save _____
Lunge save _____
Split save _____
Right-side stick dive _____
Reverse stick dive _____
Glove saves _____
Jab kick clear _____
Cross-over jab kick clear _____
Punch clear _____
Dropkick clear _____
Punt clear _____

Field Hockey Tactics

To improve your level of performance in field hockey, you must also understand and be able to execute the tactics in all three Roles of Attack and Defense. Rate your ability to use the following tactics in a game situation. *Note:* Systems of play are not listed since an evaluation of team alignments depends on the entire team.

Role 1 Attack Tactics

Maintain ball possession ____
Cut the ball to free space ____
Go one-on-one ____
Penetrate shortest line to goal ____
Shooting areas of circle ____
Shooting targets ____

Role 2 Attack Tactics

Support movement ____
Combination play—give and go
  • Wall pass ____
  • Double pass ____
Transition play ____

Role 3 Attack Tactics

Width and depth support movement ____
Runs
  • Overlap ____
  • Blind-side ____
  • Diagonal ____
  • Split diagonal ____
  • Checking or leading ____
Transition play ____

Role 1 Defense Tactics

Position to block dangerous space ____
Engaging distance to ball ____
Defensive stance ____
Playing distance ____
Forcing or channeling ____
Tackle the ball ____

Role 2 Defense Tactics

Controlling immediate space ____
Marking and covering ____
Transition play ____

Role 3 Defense Tactics

Protects dangerous space ____
Marking and covering AR3 runs ____
Balance ____
Transition play ____

Overall Field Hockey Progress

How would you rate your overall progress of the previously listed field hockey techniques and tactics?

____ Excellent
____ Very good
____ Fair
____ Needs improvement
____ Should consider another sport

GLOSSARY

Advantage Pass—A forward pass in which ball possession is maintained.

Advantage Space—Space forward toward the goal but not really behind the opponent that gains an advantage. Usually a diagonal pass.

Angle (Narrowing the)—Applied to goalkeeper moving nearer to the ball in order to reduce passing or shooting space to goal.

Assistant Helper—Another term for Role 3 players.

Attacker—A player whose team is in possession of the ball.

Attack Stance—An attack player's balanced ready position which prepares the body for skill. Also referred to as the goalkeeper's basic stance when the ball is within shooting distance.

Backhand—Maneuvering the stick to execute skills on the left side of the body.

Balance in Defense—Defensive position that provides depth and support. Defenders nearest the ball mark opponents while teammates on the side of the field opposite the ball cover dangerous space behind the defense.

Ball Check—A ball-control technique used to momentarily stop the ball or to control the ball so that a change of direction and speed may occur.

Ball Control—Keeping the ball within good contact distance and being able to prevent it from rolling beyond a balanced reach.

Ball-Side Positioning—Refers to a defender who positions on the side of the opponent who is closest to the ball.

Blind Side Run—A method of off-ball running that is made outside of the opponent's vision and in behind a defender to utilize space or create space. Usually a blind side run is behind Role 1 defender and sometimes a Role 2 defender.

Blocking Space—Defender(s) who position to intercept or take away the forward pass or dribble by the opponent.

Block Save—A goalkeeper technique used to stop the ball before clearing.

Block Tackle (Open Stick Tackle)—A defensive skill used to dispossess the ball from AR1 by extending both arms out in front of the body and placing the stick on the ground in the path of the ball.

Box (GK)—The GK's save area (area which goalkeepers train to make 100% save) of the goal cage referred to during the penalty stroke.

Breakdown Steps—Shorter intense running footwork intended to bring the body into a balanced position after longer sprint strides were used.

Bully—A situation in which each team fouls simultaneously or ball gets lodged in GK's equipment. One player from each team stands square to each other facing the sidelines w/ball on the ground between them. At the same moment both must tap first the ground beside the ball and then each other's stick over the ball 3×'s alternately after which they may make an attempt to play the ball.

Center Back—A defensive position usually in the back 3 or 4 that forms the center of the defense.

Center Forward—A striker who leads the attack. Usually one of the primary goal scorers on the team.

Centering—The act of passing a "cross" ball from the wing into the middle of the field of play.

Center Line (Halfway Line)—Refers to the line in the center of the field that is 50 yards or equal distance from each end line.

Channeling—A defensive act used to force the AR1 player in a direction organized by the defensive team.

Checking Run—Movement used by attackers to create a greater distance between the defender and the ball. Attack player runs toward the goalside defender then suddenly stops and cuts back toward the ball.

Chip Shot—Aerial hit of the ball often used to project the ball over an advancing goalkeeper by bringing stick in a very low arc with the wrists open and hitting under the ball.

Circle (Striking or Shooting Circle)—Refers to the (16-yard radius) semi-circle out in front of each goal. To count as a goal, a shot must be made within this circle.

Clip Hit—The act of hitting the ball quickly from power dribble by allowing left hand to slide down to join right hand (choke up grip).

Close Down—When a player reduces the space between herself and the opponent or opponent with ball.

Controlling Space—The act of positioning by defender(s) to restrict space that forces opponents to slow their attack to a predetermined area.

Control Box—Distance of area established in front of player's feet by hand reach from squat position and shoulder-width distance where ball control and other AR1 skills can best be executed.

Corner (Long Hit)—A boundary hit awarded by an umpire when the ball passes over the end line (back line) after having been last touched or deflected accidentally off the stick of a defender. Ball is put into play 5 yards from the corner flag on the nearest sideline where the ball crossed the end line.

Cover—Defensive support; as a defender challenges an opponent, she should be supported from behind by a teammate in the event that the challenging defender is beaten.

Cut the Ball—Running diagonally forward while dribbling the ball.

Decoy Run—A cut movement mainly used by attack players to draw the attention of the opponent away from the ball or another teammate.

Defender, (Committing the)—While with or without the ball, the act of attracting the exclusive attention of a defender by moving him or her from occupied space.

Defenders—Term used for players positioned nearer to the goalkeeper who have the role to prevent the opposition from penetrating their half of the field and goal.

Defense Hit (16-Yard Hit)—A free hit awarded to the defending side after the ball has been hit over the end line by the attacking side.

Defense Stance—A balanced ready position assumed by a defender which finds the stick head close to the ground and a lead foot so that a skill or a change of direction is possible.

Deflection Shot—A shot where the path of the passed ball is altered without the shooter actually stopping or trapping the ball. See *Wall Pass*.

Diagonal Run—Run made from wings into the middle of the field (to utilize space) and from the middle of the field out to the wings (to create space).

Dive (Sliding) Shot—Deflection shooting while sliding your body along the ground.

Double-Leg Stack—An advanced goalkeeping technique used at a close distance from the ball to slide and smother a shot on goal.

Double Pass—Passing combination in which the ball travels back and then forward.

Dribble—The act of running with the ball while keeping the stick close to the ball. See *Indian Dribble*, *Open Field Dribble*, and *Power Dribble*.

Dropkick Clear—A half volley kicking technique used by the goalkeeper after successfully blocking an aerial shot with the glove hand.

Drop Step (Attack and Defense)—An individual ball-control technique for AR1 which creates space away from DR1 from a forward to back direction. A defense player uses a drop step when he or she is beaten on the lead foot side.

Edge Shot—Shooting the ball with the edge of your horizontal stick.

End Line—The line at the end of a grid or game field.

Flick—A push stroke that raises the ball off the ground at various heights and speeds.

Forehand—The maneuvering of stick skills on the right side of the body.

Forwards—Players who occupy the front attacking positions closest to the opponent's goal; sometimes known as *strikers* or *wing players*.

Foul—An infringement of the rules when a player has been adjudged by the umpire to have kicked the ball, tripped, pushed, or obstructed an opponent.

Free Hit—A possession hit or push stroke awarded to one team to restart play when an opposing team player disregards the rules.

Full Volley—A GK kicking technique used to kick clear the ball directly out of the air with the instep of the foot. See *Punt Clear.*

Goal—This is achieved when the whole ball crosses the goal line either on or above the ground and between the two goalposts and the cross bar. The construction of the posts and net is also known as the goal.

Goalkeeper—A specialty player who defends the goal with his or her body and stick. The GK must wear the required protective equipment—helmet w/face mask, chest protector and throat guard, gloves, leg guards, and foot kickers/boots. GK privileges—use of body to save shots and to kick clear—is only permitted inside the shooting circle.

Goal Line—The portion of the back line which runs from the goal post to goal post across each end of the field of play. The goal cage is situated behind the outside edge of the goal line.

Goal-Side Position—Nearer to the goal; position between the goal being defended and opposing player being marked.

Green Card—Triangular-shaped card awarded by the umpire as a final warning for persistent misconduct or breaches of the rules.

Half Volley—A GK technique used to kick the ball which is dropped from above the instant it contacts the ground. See *Drop Kick.*

Hit (Drive)—When a backswing and hitting action is used to strike the ball with the head of the stick to propel it long distances or when shooting at goal.

Indian Dribble—An advanced dribbling technique used to tap the ball to the left or right direction by rolling the left wrist and turning the stick over the ball.

Inside Foot Kick—Most controlled kicking style used by GK. The flat area between the inner ankle bone, heel, and big toe of boot is used to execute accurate low kicks.

Instep Kick—A GK technique where the area of the foot (shoe laces) in a line along the big toe towards the ankle is used to kick the ball.

Jab Tackle—A defense technique providing a greater reach with the left hand and an easier shift into other tackles; utilizes a "pan handle" grip with left hand. Execution resembles a push or poke action with the stick driven by legs in a balanced stride position.

Line of Recovery—The path the defender takes when running back towards his or her goal to establish a position on the goal side of the ball.

Low Tackle—Defensive skill used to dispossess the ball by placing the stick parallel and on the ground in front of defender's feet and in path of the ball.

Lunge Save—A GK block save technique using the foot to block the ball when it is shot outside jab kicking range but inside split save range. The lunge save is performed with hips opened to side of body where ball is shot, head and shoulders over bent saving leg, and saving foot and toes on a straight perpendicular line from trail leg.

Man-to-Man Defense—Defensive system in which each player is responsible for marking a particular opponent.

Marking— Tight defensive coverage of an opponent that blocks the direct passing lanes to the AR2 players.

Midfield—The position played by creative members of the team whose role is to link attack and defense.

Obstruction (Block Out, Shepherding, Shadow Obstruction)—Body or stick interference that prevents the opponent's attempt to play the ball.

Open Field Dribble—The act of tapping the ball ahead when in possession of the ball in the open and to move at speed or break away over a short distance so the player can scan.

Overlap Run—A supporting teammate runs from behind and on the outside to a position forward of the player with the ball. The overlap is often used to move defenders into attacking position.

Pass Back—Method of starting the game from the center line at the beginning of the halves and after a goal has been scored.

Penalty Corner (Short Corner)—Awarded by umpire for a breach by a defender within the striking circle or for a deliberate foul outside the goal circle but within the 25-yard line. No more than five defenders must start behind goal line and the attackers who start outside striking circle must stop the ball with the stick before a shot for goal is taken.

Penalty Stroke—Awarded by an umpire when a breach of rules stops a certain goal from being scored or deliberate foul within the striking circle. Any stroke but a hit may be used for this free shot taken at a spot 7 yards from the goal. The goalkeeper must defend the penalty stroke.

Point of Attack—The center of attack where the ball is located.

Possession Pass—A low-risk pass to maintain control of ball.

Possession Space—Space further from goal where ball control is maintained in order to make dangerous space more vulnerable (lateral or back pass).

Power Dribble—Dribbling technique used to maintain possession of the ball in tight crowded space. The ball is kept in close contact with the stick at all times.

Power Points—The balls of the feet located under the front portion of the foot.

Punch Clear—A goalkeeping technique used to play a loose ball by executing a one-leg slide tackle into the ball with sole of lead leg foot punching the ball away from pursuing attacker.

Punt Clear—A GK kicking skill used to full volley kick an aerial glove save up high and over the heads of all players.

Push-In/Hit-In—A hit or push along the ground that is used to restart game after ball has been put out of play over the side line. Opposing players must be 5 yards.

Push Pass—A stroke that moves the ball along the ground by starting with the stick close to the ball and pushing the ball with the stick.

Rebound Clear—A GK kicking technique in which a shot is saved and cleared with one touch of the foot.

Receiving Box—A visualized area or space where attack player traps the ball using proper breakdown footwork to achieve body balance and ball control.

Red Card—A circular-shaped card awarded by the umpire to indicate that a player has been dismissed from the field of play permanently for the duration of the game.

Red Zone(s)—The areas on the field to include inside the 25-yard lines to the goals both near and in the attack and defense circles.

Scanning—The ability to observe the immediate area while in possession of the ball so that decisions of when to pass, move, or change direction can be made. Types of scanning include distance, peripheral, and photo.

Scoop (Lob)—A stroke technique (shoveling action) used to lift the ball in a high trajectory by rapidly bringing the lower hand upwards.

Shaft—The surface area of the hockey stick located between the handle and the stick head.

Shake Hands Grip—The basic hockey grip from which all other grips originate. The forefinger and thumb of both hands form a "V" so that a straight line from the tip of the "V" would run down and bisect the middle line of the handle and toe. Sometimes called the *Split Grip* or *Receiving Grip*.

Skeleton Play—A method of coaching which allows players to execute skills/movement without opposition.

Slide/ Shuffle—Defensive footwork used to maintain a balanced defensive stance while moving in a side direction.

Speed Dribble—Dribbling technique used to advance the ball into open spaces on a straight or diagonal line.

Spin Dribble—The act of dribbling or moving the ball away from the defender by turning body and immediately dribbling into free space.

Split Angles—Term used to describe GK positioning—positioned in the center of the space from the ball and the goal.

Split Save—GK save technique used to block a shot along the ground beyond the reach of a lunge save. Executed with the extended leg/foot nearest to the ball path while dropping the body to the ground in a hurdle seat position.

Split Diagonal Run—An effective result of diagonal running in which two attacking players move in opposite directions from the middle of the field to the wings to create space between opposition in the center of the field that can then be "split" by other attacking players moving forward from deep positions.

Square Pass—A pass made laterally across the field.

Square up—Term used for the goalkeeper to position into attack stance or *ready position* by facing both hips to the ball.

Step Up—A defensive communication used to encourage a teammate to move closer to the ball and opponent while positioning in the passing lane.

Sticks—Raising of the shaft or the heel of the stick above shoulder height that leads to dangerous play. "Sticks" does not apply to the GK position.

Stop and Turn—Change of direction footwork used by attack players to misfoot defenders and win races to open space.

Stutter Step—Hesitation or change-of-pace footwork used to fool the opponent into a slow run or stop.

Systems of Play—The positional organization and responsibility of player personnel based on ability, style, tactics, game conditions. Player formations in field positions represent a balance of attack and defense (i.e., 5-3-2; 3-3-3-1; 2-4-3-1; 4-2-3-1, etc.).

Sweeper—The last field defender used by teams to play behind the defensive backs. The sweeper provides cover for marking defenders and support for attacking play.

Tackle—A defense technique used to challenge an opponent (AR1) who is in possession of the ball.

Take Ball—Defensive communication used to direct a teammate in a ready position to apply pressure keeping the attacker with the ball in front.

Thirds (1/3's) of the Field—Areas roughly 35 yards in length signifying the defending, the middle, and the attack third of the field.

Third-Party Obstruction—A foul caused by a player off the ball interposing herself between an opponent and the ball that permits a teammate to gain an unfair advantage.

Through Pass—A penetrating pass which retains possession while eliminating at least one defender. Usually involves two attackers against two defenders.

Toe—The curved or hooked portion of the stick.

Trapping—The action of controlling, stopping, or receiving the ball.

Triangular Pass—Means of passing the ball between two players to eliminate a defender by passing square followed by an angled pass behind the defender. See *Double Pass* and *Wall Pass*.

Triple Threat—AR1 ball position where ball is on the stick and to the right side of body near the right foot ready to (1) shoot, (2) pass, and (3) dribble.

Turn and Shoot—The act of receiving the ball when facing own goal and turning with the ball under control to face opponent's goal to shoot.

Two-Touch Passing—Type of interpassing in which the receiving player (AR1) controls the ball with her first touch and passes to a teammate on her second touch.

Wall Pass—Combination passing with a teammate where one player's stick serves as a wall to block and redirect the path of the ball. A player usually runs forward to receive return wall pass around opponent.

Width in Attack—Tactic of using the width of the field to attempt to draw defending players away from central positions. The objective is to create space for scoring opportunities in the most dangerous space (attacking zones).

Wing Backs (Side Backs)—Defenders positioned near the sideline areas who usually mark the opposing wing forwards.

Winger—A front-running forward positioned near the sideline areas.

Yellow Card—Square-shaped card awarded by umpire to indicate that a player has been temporarily suspended from the game (5 minutes or more).

Zone 1—Center area in the defensive circle from the goal out to the 25-yard line.

Zone 2—Diagonal areas both on the right and left of Zone 1.

Zone 3—Five-yard area from the back line on both sides of the goal cage.

Zone Defense—System of play in which each player is responsible for defending a certain area of the field when the ball or the opponent, or both, enter that area.

APPENDIX

The following organizations administer field hockey competition internationally and in the United States:

Federation of International Hockey (FIH)
Avenue des Arts 1, Box 5
1210 Brussels, Belgium
Phone: (32)-219-45-37   Fax: (32)-219-27-61

United States Field Hockey Association (USFHA)
One Olympic Plaza
Colorado Springs, CO 80909
Phone: 719-578-4567   Fax: 719-578-4539

National Field Hockey Coaches Association (NFHCA)
NCAA
Nall Avenue at 63rd Street
P.O. Box 1906
Mission, KS 66201
Phone: 918-494-8828

The following English-language periodicals give detailed information on current competition:

Hockey Digest
29 Romily Street
London W1V 6HP
England
Phone: (44)-171-437-6437   Fax: (44)-171-434-1214

World Hockey
The Harrow Press Unit E6
Aladdin Workspace 426 Long Drive, Greenford
Middlesex, UB6 8UH, England
Phone: (44)-181-575-3121   Fax: (44)-181-575-1320

Hockey Circle
P.O. Box 127
Glen Iris, Victoria 3146
Australia
Phone: (61)-9-885-7235   Fax: (61)-9-885-9949

ABOUT THE AUTHOR

Elizabeth Anders is a dominant figure in U.S. field hockey. Her impressive list of accomplishments includes being the winningest coach in college field hockey, leading her teams to seven NCAA National Championships, and serving as coach of the USA National Field Hockey Team from 1990 to 1993. During her 35 years as a field hockey player, Anders twice earned a spot on the U.S. women's Olympic field hockey team and is the current Olympic Games scoring record holder. She was also inducted into the United States Field Hockey Association Hall of Fame in 1989.

Anders has coached and taught field hockey for 24 years. She is currently the head field hockey coach at Old Dominion University. A frequent writer on the sport, Anders is the author of *Lessons in Field Hockey, Fitness Training for Field Hockey, Summer Training for Field Hockey,* and *On the Rebound: The Hit.* She resides in Virginia Beach, VA.